Inventing Palestine: A Journey

Douglas L. Hildreth

DEDICATION

To all those who have played a part, however big or small, in the completion of this work, please accept my heartfelt gratitude.

Abstract

The notion of Palestine, though intangible in the natural world, thrives within the realm of human consciousness. We find ourselves identifying with this place because it bears a name, which holds the key to our connection with it. Unnamed locations, mere coordinates on a map, lack the essence that sparks our emotional ties. However, naming alone does not suffice; we must be immersed in the tales of a place, weaving narratives of famines, wars, conquests, tribes, and multifaceted histories. Through the lenses of geography, economy, archaeology, and myriad other topics, these engaging stories foster our identification with Palestine.

Moreover, our bond with Palestine is reinforced by the creation of maps that chart its geographical contours. As we continuously map this land, the roots of our affiliation grow deeper. Gradually, we set Palestine apart from other places, elevating its splendor and allure, and fervently declaring our special relationship with it.

This book delves into the captivating chronicle of how this collective identification with Palestine came to be. It examines the precise moments, methods, and motivations behind its inception, unraveling the intricate fabric of human consciousness that gave rise to this powerful connection. By exploring the interplay between names, narratives, and maps, this work unravels the enigma of how a place that seemingly exists only in our minds can profoundly shape our identities and societies.

© 2023 by Douglas L. Hildreth

TABLE OF CONTENTS

Abstract..iii

Table of Contents...iv

Acknowledgments...v

Tables and Figures..xvi

Introduction...1

Chapter 1: Who Cares about Palestine?...................................7

Chapter 2: The Origins of Palestine.......................................45

Chapter 3: The Pre-Modern World..87

Chapter 4: The Modern World...141

Conclusion...204

Bibliography..209

Appendix 1..257

TABLES AND FIGURES

Table 1. Contents of the 13th century
Ashrafiya Library in Damascus...132

Figure 1. Palestine Coin, minted in 1927..13

Figure 2. Palestine Stamps, 1920s-1940s. 14

Figure 3. United Airlines Security Question:
"What is your favorite sea animal?" 48

Figure 4. Neanderthal Geometric Pattern..57

Figure 5. Map of "Southern Syria,
or Palestine and the Arab East"..82

Figure 6. Padiiset's Statue..91

Figure 7. Section of Byzantine floor mosaic map at
St. George Church Madaba depicting "οροι Αιγυπτου
και Παλαιστινης" (the border of Egypt and Palestine)..........................105

Figure 8. A 7th Century coin minted in Jerusalem
by the Caliph with the word *Filastin*...129

Figure 9. A map of Palestine, or *Filastin*, used in
American missionary schools in the mid-19th century..........................155

Figure 10. "A Natural Map of Modern Palestine,"
in an atlas likely used in missionary schools...162

Figure 11. The first Ottoman printed map of Palestine (1804)...............167

Figure 12. Ottoman map of "Anatolia
Administrative Divisions" 168

Figure 13. Published in *The Palestine Handbook*, 1915.......................169

Figure 14. Photo from inside the Jaffa Gate in
Jerusalem's old city with Duetchse Palastina Bank
sign visible (circa early 1900s)...182

Figure 15. "A Map of Palestine for Cars"..192

Figure 16. "Map of Palestine" 195

Figure 17. Map of "Palestine" 196

INTRODUCTION

Palestine exists in our minds, not in nature. If Palestine doesn't exist, why do we identify with it? We identify with Palestine, first, because it has a name. In fact, we *only* identify with places we've named. Unnamed places, such as 22°29′05″N 22.48 to 53°46′19″E 53.77, have no identities based on them. But we don't identify with every place we've named. We need to hear stories about a place if we are going to identify with it, stories about famines and wars, conquests and tribes, history, geography, economy, archeology and millions more topics. The more engaging the stories, the more likely we are to identify with places like Palestine. We also make maps of places like Palestine. The more maps we make, the more likely we are to identify with places like Palestine as well. Finally, we distinguish Palestine from other places. We exaggerate its glory and beauty and claim we have a special relationship to it. This dissertation explains when, how and why it all happened.

* * *

Style. Some writers pay rent by selling what they write. They appeal to emotion, insight and humor. They paint colorful characters, describe exotic scenes and tell great jokes. They strike at our nerves, hearts and minds to boost their email subscriber counts. They earn a living as writers for late night television shows, multinational corporations, media conglomerates and youtube channels. More people earn money as writers today than at any previous time in history.

Other writers, however, do not pay rent by selling what they write. They are called academics, and do not need clicks, sales or reads. Instead, publishers sell what they write to libraries, and academics pay their bills with grants, fellowships and jobs. They are paid to write with rigor, truth and novelty in mind rather than emotion, contagion or punchlines. Much like writers, more of them exist today than at any other time in history.

History lies at the meeting point of the writer's craft—art, and the academic's craft—science. Writers set scenes, embellish characters and exaggerate sexual tension while academics are loyal to facts, evidence and nuance. Writers arrange data points for emotion, suspense and laughter, while academics arrange facts to absolve themselves of accusations of naiveté.

Historians are uniquely well-suited to do both. We take the dyes, clothes and metals of the past and paint pictures, weave quilts and construct edifices. We cannot invent raw materials *ex nihilo*, but we can turn raw materials into very different histories. We can amuse and entertain but also explain and edify. "History is the only science enjoying the ambiguous fortune of being required to be at the same time an art," said the 19th century Prussian, Johann Gustav Droysen. But its appeal "is in the last analysis poetic." Few have said it better than the 20th century historian Garrett Mattingly. "History is the most difficult of the belles-lettres, for it must be true."[1]

* * *

---

[1] These quotes can be found in James Axtell, "History as Imagination," *The Historian* 49(4)(1987): 453.

My Argument. My aim is to understand when, how and why people identified as Palestinian in history. The identity is based on a few critical biological abilities that we probably developed hundreds of thousands of years ago. Standing on one foot, we invented infinitely complex language, grasped abstract thought, learned to describe space with complexity, make maps and distinguish things. That led us to name places like Palestine, map them on walls and floors, tell stories about them with language and distinguish those places with words and images, all of which led us to identify with them.

Identities like "Palestinian" are not modern, pre-modern or early modern, nor do they date to antiquity or the ancient Near East. They've probably been around for tens of thousands of years, and evolutionary psychologists, biologists, anthropologists, primatologists, linguists and archeologists are better equipped than historians to understand their origins. This helps explain some of the scholarly disagreement over the origins of nations, to the extent that nations tend to identify with places.

But what led identities like Palestinian to proliferate? The first major factor was sedentary life, which long pre-dated history as it's commonly understood. We became settled when we learned to fish, hunt migratory birds and subsist in wetlands environments. As a result, we developed identities based around our places of settlement. This probably happened first many tens of thousands of years ago. But permanent settlement did not become the principle lifestyle choice of our species until after the Agricultural Revolution about 10,000 years ago when farming replaced hunting and gathering as the dominant human form of subsistence. As farmers, the places we inhabited became even more important to us, which made us more likely to develop identities around on them, identities such as Palestinian.

Second, identities like Palestinian also came about as a result of states. States, polities, republics, chiefdoms, regimes, countries or governments refer to groups of people who monopolize the use of force in a given area. To do that effectively, they have to develop a chain of command. In order to facilitate communication between members within the chain of command, place names were essential. They were essential to ensure command and control, tax collection, conscription and loyalty in their subjects. It would have been too wordy for states to record on slabs of stone or papyrus that the people of "the fourteen-mile expanse of land due east from the southern-most hilltop of the rugged terrain south of Hebron to the land extending north for eighteen miles until the narrow valley past the third river" had paid their taxes. It was much more concise to say that the people of Palestine had paid their taxes. So names were very useful. Names made governance easier. Nameless places were a mess to govern. This had a trickle-down effect. That's why identities based on Palestine were strongest (holding all else equal) when Palestine was either a state or an administrative unit within one—i.e. during the 8th, 9th and 10th centuries, and from 1920-1948. As states came to control more and more of the world in the past couple of thousand years, and as they became more powerful, identities based around places proliferated.

Third, identities like Palestinian also proliferated as a result of agricultural surplus. People could earn a living as bureaucrats, teachers, historians, geographers, cartographers and journalists. The agricultural surplus enabled more people to manage the affairs of the state, write eloquent stories, make beautiful maps, conduct geographical surveys and organize scholarly associations. These folks gave places like Palestine purpose, coherence and beauty, a distinct geography and marvelous history, and made it more likely people would identify as Palestinian.

Fourth, a Palestinian identity came into existence for incidental reasons that are not generalizable to other parts of the world. In the case of Palestine, followers of many successful religions believed the Bible was sacred. This had a ripple effect on the survival of its geographical lexicon, including *Pleshet* (Philistine) and *Plishtim* (the Philistines). Muslims believed their earliest traditions were sacred as well, and they were written in the 8th, 9th and 10th centuries when Palestine was an administrative district. Those traditions also survived long after Palestine fell from administrative use, keeping Palestine alive. Another incidental factor was that Renaissance Europeans grew fascinated by classical Greek and Latin texts and adopted their geographical nomenclature—including Palestine. This led to its gradual re-popularization in Europe in the 16th and 17th centuries, and thus its re-popularization in the 19th century Middle East when Europeans and Americans descended on it as consular officials, missionaries and tourists. Those folks taught the geography and history of Palestine in missionary schools, conducted archeological surveys of Palestine and toured it with their Palestine guidebooks. By the late 19th century, Zionists were moving to Palestine and speaking openly of Jewish independence in it, making Palestine even more important than it had been. These were all incidental events, not part of predictable patterns, that led people to identify as Palestinian.

* * *

History. But why read a book of history in the first place when you can read Adam Grant's *Originals* and become an original thinker or Aziz Ansari's *Modern Romance* and boost your reply rates on Tinder? You probably shouldn't. But once you finish those books—consider reading some history, because knowing history is really empowering. Take a banal example of the history of lawns. They first became popular in medieval Europe because they produced nothing of value despite requiring lots of maintenance. They represented a class of society whose excess, wealth and privilege was made possible only by the suffering of others. Knowing that, you might feel empowered to talk smack about lawns. Or look at the rise in popularity of engagement rings in the mid-20th century United States, a result of De Beers marketing campaigns linking diamonds to eternal love: "a diamond is forever." Knowing that engagement rings became popular to enrich American corporate executives at the cost of great human suffering, you might also choose not to spend three months of salary and plunge your household into decades of debt on a shiny symbolic pebble. So, if knowing the history of lawns affects your decision to maintain a lawn, or if knowing the history of diamond engagement rings affects your desire to buy one, knowing the history of "Palestine" might affect how you chose to identify with it. It might even affect what you are willing to die for.[2]

---

[2] On lawns, see Yuval Noah Harari, *Homo Deus: A Brief History of Tomorrow* (New York: Harper, 2017), 59-65.

CHAPTER ONE

Who Cares about Palestine?

Palestine is a figment of our imagination, but so is every other place and country in the world. Why write a whole book just about Palestine? I don't have a good answer, other than so many people are obsessed with it. Judaism, Christianity and Islam each claim a history in the land, and so Palestine has been at the center of the Jewish, Christian and Muslim world's attention for millennia. Dozens of public figures, including American presidential candidates like Ted Cruz, Mike Huckabee and Newt Gingrich, have claimed to know something about the historical usage of the words "Palestine" and the "Palestinians." So have media companies like Arutz Sheva, Haaretz, Fox News, AJ+, the Guardian and the Washington Post. Regrettably, historians have often served as warriors in the propaganda battles, and so myths continue to persist about the history of these two words. This chapter explains what those myths are, how they have evolved over the past century and why they persist today.

* * *

"Welcome to Israel-Palestine." So said an AirFrance pilot upon landing in Tel Aviv's Ben Gurion airport in 2002. The state-run Israeli telephone company, Bezeq Israel Telecom, went berserk, mandating its employees to boycott Air France unless the pilot was fired. A year later, an Alitalia pilot touched down in TLV airport and welcomed passengers to "Palestine." Israeli passengers were furious, as was Alitalia. "One thing is certain," declared a spokesperson for the company. "This captain will not fly to Israel again." The Spaniards were never too far behind the French and Italians. Twelve years, in this case, when in 2015 a Spanish pilot also announced to his Tel Aviv bound travelers they had touched down in Palestine. That was his last trip to Tel Aviv too. What was so infuriating about the word Palestine?[3]

* * *

On 9 August 2016, the media company AJ+ posted a video called "Some people are slamming Google for removing Palestine from its maps." Of all the videos I had watched on mute in my Facebook News Feed, this was the first that dealt directly with my dissertation. Naturally, I clicked the volume icon to listen, which did exactly what Facebook wanted it to do: expand the video to full screen.

Watching the video, I remembered I had written about a change.org petition to add Palestine to Google Maps for an article earlier that year. It didn't make sense that "some people" would be slamming Google for removing Palestine from its maps. Palestine was not on Google Maps. Realizing the AJ+ story was false, I started getting the goosebumps. I would finally get retweeted more than 3 times and my twitter follower count would almost certainly soar into the high-290s. It was going to be glorious.

---

[3] BBC, "Palestine Destination Angers Jewish Passengers," *BBC.co.uk* 5 July 2002 (https://goo.gl/4ChQz4); Zohar Blumenkrantz, "Alitalia Pilot Stuns Passengers landing in Tel Aviv," *Haaretz.com* 6 May 2003 (https://goo.gl/ET71oc); Cynthia Blank, "Iberia Pilot Welcomes Passengers to 'Palestine'" *Arutz Sheva* 28 October 2015 (https://goo.gl/aY18fj)

As I sat down to craft 140 characters of glory, I quickly checked how many change.org users signed the older petition. My heart sank before Google had even finished finding me results. It was the same feeling of irreversible loss felt by a child who learned that mom bought mint instead of chocolate chip cookie dough ice cream for dessert. Someone else had already written a story and exposed AJ+'s fabrication.[4]

The whole affair must have felt like déjà vu for Google. In May 2013, they changed the '.ps' homepage tagline from *the Palestinian Territories* to *Palestine*. This made no difference to most people, but Israeli authorities were furious. "Google is in essence recognizing the existence of a Palestinian state," wrote Deputy Foreign Minister of Israel to Google CEO Larry Page. "Any formal use of the word Palestine" was "pre-judging the outcome of currently stalled peace talks." Little did they know, but, by using the word "Palestine" on landing pages, Google was recklessly shattering the imminent prospects of a historic resolution to the Israeli-Palestinian conflict. Recall that this was 2013—and a coalition had recently formed that had finally promised hope for peace in the Middle East: a union of Likud and Yisrael Beiteinu.

Google saw things differently. "We're changing the name *Palestinian Territories* to *Palestine* across our products." In its defense, Google confessed it was following the lead of obscure organizations like the so-called "United Nations" and what they ambiguously referred to "other

---

[4] AJ+'s decision to publish before fact checking was not all in vein, though. A new petition to add Palestine to Google Maps soon gained traction, and now has hundreds of thousands of supporters. Nada Elsayed, "Add Palestine to Google Maps," *change.org* 2013 (goo.gl/I99ZcK); on my reference to it, see Zachary J. Foster, "What's a Palestinian?" *Foreign Affairs* 12 March 2015 (https://goo.gl/f5dlnV); then see AJ+, "Some People are Slamming Google for Removing Palestine from its Maps," *twitter.com* 9 August 2016 (goo.gl/kaMw3x).

international organizations." As of 17 August 2017, Google continues to bear the brunt of the responsibility for the continuation of occupation and conflict.[5]

* * *

What was wrong with calling it Palestine? Donald Trump probably would have liked to know before he uttered that word three times during his March 2016 AIPAC Policy Conference speech. (As far as I know, he hasn't said it since). "Let me say at the outset," pronounced his gleeful opponent Ted Cruz in his opening remarks shortly after Trump in front of a stadium full of AIPAC supporters. "Perhaps to the surprise of a previous speaker, Palestine has not existed since 1948." The audience roared with applause. They agreed that Palestine hadn't existed for more than half a century. Cruz chuckled and nodded to a campaign advisor, winning that battle (even though he lost the war). Cruz knew what to say to the one of largest annual gatherings of Israel enthusiasts. It wasn't Palestine.[6]

* * *

The controversy over Palestine has played out in politics, on planes and on the internet, as we've just seen. People also talk about it at Shabbat lunch and dinners tables. Here, I have to get anthropological. In January 2014, a hospitable American-born Jewish woman invited me to her

---

[5] Tovah Lazaroff, "Elkin Asks Google to Rethink 'Palestine,'" *Jerusalem Post* 6 May 2013 (goo.gl/FwL0mK)
[6] For Trump's speech, see "Donald Trump AIPAC Full Speech," *youtube.com*, Published on Mar 21, 2016 (goo.gl/t7NQQI); for Ted Cruz's speech, see "Ted Cruz AIPAC Full Speech, Washington DC March 21, 2016 [HD]," *youtube.com*, streamed live on Mar 21, 2016 (goo.gl/V2wBpf); for a nice review of Cruz's speech, see Jennifer Rubin "Ted Cruz at AIPAC: Eight Takeaways," *The Washington Post* 22 Mach 2016 (goo.gl/lqQkne).

Old City Jerusalem loft for Shabbat lunch. At the time, I was renting an apartment in the Muslim quarter of the Old City of Jerusalem. The fastest route to reach her house that Shabbat afternoon was a walk from Bab al-Zahra Street, turning right at Via Dolorosa, then left onto Al Wad Street, the same path Jesus took to his crucifixion. I was hoping my afternoon would end differently.

Five minutes separated my flat from her loft, but life proceeds at different intervals in the Muslim and Jewish Quarters. They speak Arabic in the Muslim quarter, not Hebrew. Most residents carry Jordanian passports, not Israeli ones. The lights go up on Ramadan, not Hanukah. The street kids support Hamas, not Likud. In the Jewish quarter, the tourists are religious Jews, not Christian Zionists. The beggars wear kippot, not head scarfs. There are also probably fewer Hamas aficionados.

We blessed wine and broke bread. I explained that dissertation research brought me to the city. "Your dissertation is about Palestine?" the hostess retorted in disbelief. "That must be a very short dissertation." Palestine had not existed since Roman times, she thought. How could I possibly be writing an entire dissertation about it?

A few months later in June 2014, a Turkish friend of mine visited Jerusalem on pilgrimage. She was one of many thousands of Muslim Turks who travel to the Holy Land every year. Groups of them passed by my front door every week on their way to the al-Aqsa Mosque. As the third holiest site in Islam, Jerusalem has attracted visitors from around the Muslim world for more than a millennium, many Turks among them.

I tagged along with her to a Shabbat dinner invitation in Ma'alei Adumim, a settlement built on land occupied by Israel after the 1967 War. It's the largest of Jerusalem's satellite neighborhoods, considered an inseparable part of the city by Israelis and an illegal settlement by the rest of the world, including Israel's three strongest allies—the United States, the Marshall Islands and the Federated States of Micronesia. "You said your dissertation was about the history of the word Palestine?" the host asked, somewhat perplexed. This is usually where I'm given a brief history lesson on the topic I've spent the better part of a decade researching. "You know that the Arabs used to call the place Southern Syria, not Palestine, right?"

The conversation went from cordial to heated. As I was about to dive into some details of my dissertation, a freshly baked platter of *shnitzel* glided onto the table, landing in front of me. My mouth began to water, and it seemed like the right moment to change topics to something we could all agree on: the cultural degeneration brought to the country by French Jewish immigrants.

After dinner, we gazed onto the naked hilltops in the heart of the occupied Palestinian Territories—what our hosts called the Judean desert, of course, in one of the most contested cities in the world in the place the Arabs apparently used to call Southern Syria, debating the history of the land and its peoples in the languages of every group to have ruled it over the past five centuries.

* * *

These are only the most recent manifestations of a controversy that dates to at least the 1920s. After the First World War, the British Empire gained approval from the League of Nations to administer what became known as a Mandate for Palestine, which the British decided to call the Government of Palestine. From the 1920s onwards, Zionist leaders protested the Government of Palestine's decision to print the word *Palestine* in Hebrew as *Palestina* on coins, bills and stamps. Zionists preferred the Land of Israel, or *Erets Yisrael* in Hebrew.

Figure 1. Palestine Coin, minted in 1927.

The British struck a compromise, printing the word *Palestina* in Hebrew, but also the Hebrew initials *aleph yud* for the Land of Israel (see figure 1), which could be presented as *Erets Ishmael*, or the land of Ishmael, to the Arabs. It was just enough to placate the Zionists but not enough to anger the Palestinian Arabs, at least not too many of them. It was classically British.[7]

---

[7] I was not able to track down the original statement, but it is mentioned by Habib Ibrahim Katbah, "al-Haraka al-Sahyuniyya: Ma-la-ha wa-ma-'alayha," cited in John S. Salah, *Filastin wa-Tajdid Hayatuhu* (New York: The Syrian American Press, 1919), 157; on the stamp controversy, see Meir Persoff, *The Running Stag: The Stamps and Postal*

Figure 2. Palestine Stamps, 1920s-1940s.

* * *

Occupation (Egypt). In the late 1970s and early 1980s, Israeli delegations traveled to Alexandria to negotiate the 1979 peace accord between Israel and Egypt. The Israeli Interior Minister Yosef Burg, refused to stay at the best hotel in the city—The Palestine Hotel, opting instead for the San Stefano Hotel, named after Saint Stephen. San Stephen (d.34) is often venerated as the first martyr of Christianity. He proclaimed that Jesus stood side by side God in heaven, considered at the time an act of heresy by the Jews of Jerusalem. According to the New Testament, the Jews of the city orchestrated his gruesome execution by stoning. Since then, many thousands of Jews have been slaughtered in Saint Stephen's name, an irony presumably lost on the Israelis officials, although not the journalist Danny Rubenstein, who pointed this out at the time.[8]

History of Israel (London: R. Lowe, 1973), 16-17; on *Erets Ishmael*, see Bernard Lewis, "The Palestinians and the PLO," *Commentary Magazine* 1 January 1975; on the Arab response, see Katbah, "al-Haraka al-Sahyuniyya," 152; 'Umar Abu al-Nasr, Ibrahim Najm and Amin 'Aql, *Jihad Filastin al-'Arabiyya* (Beirut: n.p., 1936), 83; Yurghaki Bishara Mansur, *al-Dima' al-Zakiyya aw Arwah al-Shuhada'* (Jerusalem?: Dar al-Tiba'a al-Ittihad al-Sharqi, 1929?), 8; Aziz Shihadeh, *A.B.C. of the Arab Case in Palestine* (Jaffa: The Modern Library, 1936), 7; al-Nafir, *Majmu'a Shahadat 'Arab Filastin amam al-Lajna al-Milkiyya al-Britaniyya* (Haifa: al-Nafir, 1937?), 16-17; Wadi' Talhuq, *Filastin al-'Arabiyya: Fi Madiha wa-Hadiruha wa-Mustaqbaluha* (Beirut: Majallat al-'Alman, 1945), 46. Arab students also protested when British authorities included the phrase *Erets Yisrael* (the Land of Israel) instead of *Palestina* (Palestine) on Hebrew diplomas given to Jewish law school graduates. See Assaf Likhovski, *Law and Identity in Mandate Palestine* (Chapel Hill: University of North Carolina Press, 2006), 112.

[8] Danny Rubenstein first pointed this out in *Davar*, cited in William Claiborne, "Israel Loses New Round in Effort to Prohibit the Use of 'Palestine,'" *The Washington Post*, 11 March 1981.

(Jordan). The conflict over the name Palestine spilled over into Jordan when hundreds of thousands of Palestinian refugees fled there after the 1948 War. After King Abdullah I of Jordan annexed the West Bank in 1948, he issued a decree prohibiting the use of the term. As a young child of Palestinian refugees, Dina Matar spent her early childhood in the Jalazone Refugee Camp near Ramallah, annexed by Jordan in 1948. "One incident remains vivid in my mind," Matar wrote in her recently published memoir, *What it Means to be Palestinian*. In the 5th grade, her teacher asked where she was from. Matar responded innocently, "Palestine." Then Matar described the incident in detail: "He beat me with a cane and asked me to stand facing the wall. Then he asked me the question again and, each time I answered that I was from Palestine, he beat me ever harder." Matar, today a professor in Arab Media and Political Communication at SOAS, in London, was too young to know that Abdullah I had issued a decree prohibiting the use of the term, Palestine, out of fear that Palestinians would overthrow his government. I suspect she was also too young to realize the insurrection would be led by law-abiding 11-year old school girls.[9]

(Gaza). A few decades later when Israel captured the Gaza Strip in 1967, they froze the assets of the Bank of Palestine, Gaza. In 1980, the bank was permitted to reopen, but only if it removed the word Palestine from its name. "It was felt that the term would incite nationalistic feelings among Arabs in the occupied territories and endanger Israel's security," claimed an Israeli military spokesperson at the time.

---

[9] Dina Matar, *What It Means to be Palestinian: Stories of Palestinian Peoplehood* (London: I.B. Tauris, 2011), 81-2.

The bank petitioned Israel's Highest Court, arguing that use of the word Palestine was not itself an incitement to violence. "Our bank has always been called the Bank of Palestine," said Hatem Abu Ghazaleh, one of the bank's directors. "What is going to be achieved by erasing the name Palestine from a few signs and letterheads? The problem here is larger than just a name," he told the *Washington Post* in 1981. Abu Ghazaleh had a good point: Palestine. Palestine. Palestine. Not much harm done. The court forced the military to demonstrate how the word Palestine would endanger Israelis. The bank prevailed, since the word Palestine is obviously not dangerous. But the victory was only partial. The Bank could keep its name since it was "grandfathered in," so to speak. But Gabriel Levi, Israeli Justice Ministry spokesman, claimed *new* Arab businesses could not be named Palestine.

(Jerusalem). Israeli military censors also tried to shut down the Jerusalem-based Arabic language daily newspaper, *al-Fair*, in the 1980s over its subtitle, "Palestinian Weekly." But the military soon realized that Jewish-owned businesses might then be forced to change their names as well. The *Jerusalem Post*, for instance, at that time listed on its master head, "owned by the Palestine Post Ltd." Since Palestine was the name of the country only a few decades earlier between 1920 and 1948—Jewish and Palestinian Arab owned businesses both used the word Palestine. In the end, the military censors gave up, and *al-Fair* prevailed. The Israeli government's attempts to forbid use of the word Palestine had the exact opposite effect as intended. It brought international attention to Palestine at a time when that was not the term of choice used outside the Arab or Muslim worlds to describe it.

* * *

Southern Syria. We've already mentioned Southern Syria above twice. Both my Shabbat hosts in the Jewish Quarter of the Old City and Ma'alei Adumim thought the Arabs called the place Southern Syria. Why did they think that? Perhaps the first Zionist scholar to popularize this theory was Mikha'el Asaf. He argued in the 1930s in his widely translated *The Arab Movement in Palestine* that Palestine had never existed in Arab history as a unit in and of itself, whatever he meant by "unit." Instead, the Arabs apparently considered it part of the land of Sham. He claimed that they emphasized the name Southern Syria, rather than Palestine, to show that the land was indistinguishable from Syria.[10]

The idea that the Arabs called the place Southern Syria surfaced again in 1973 when an American journalist asked the then-Prime Minister of Israel, Golda Meir, if there was "any legitimacy in talking about an Arab Palestinian Homeland?" "No, I think not," Meir replied sedately, as if she was giving a eulogy. Then Meir went straight to history. "There were no independent Arab countries before World War I. This area, Israel today, and up to the Jordan, was considered the southern part of Syria," Meir said with a glimmer in her eyes. This was a mirror image of what Asaf said decades earlier and what my Shabbat hosts in Jerusalem and Ma'alei Adumim claimed four decades later.

So what's the deal with Southern Syria, and why do Zionists and Israelis seem to bring it up all the time? Was is true that Arabs considered what is today Israel "the southern part of Syria"? I'd

---

[10] Mikha'el Asaf, *The Arab Movement in Palestine* (Masada, Youth Zionist Organization of America, 1937); Mikha'el Asaf, *Ha-Tenu'ah ha-'Aravit be-Erets Yisrael u-Mekoroteha* (Tel Aviv: Hotsa'at ha-Mishmeret ha-Tse'irah le-Mifleget Po'alei Erets Yisrael, 1947), 32-3.

like to briefly address the history of this phrase, before continuing on with the history of the controversy over Palestine, since it's so widely known by Israel's propagandists and yet so poorly understood. The Arabs described "the area that became Israel," as Meir put it, in at least ten different ways in the decades prior to World War I, roughly in this order of frequency: Palestine; Syria; Sham; the Holy Land; the Land of Jerusalem; the District of Jerusalem + the District of Balqa + the District of Acre; southern Sham; the southern part of Sham; the Land of Jerusalem + the land of Gaza + the land of Ramla + the land of Nablus + the land of Haifa + the land of Hebron (i.e. cities were used, not regions); "the southern part of Syria, Palestine"; and southern Syria. The Arabic term "southern Syria" so rarely appeared in Arabic sources before 1918 that I've included every reference to the phrase I've ever come across in the footnote at the end of this paragraph (it did appear more often in Western languages). Golda Meir, Mikha'el Asaf and my Shabbat hosts were right about Southern Syria, but by focusing only on the facts that supported their arguments and ignoring all the others, they got the story completely wrong. They used facts to obscure the history.[11]

If the term rarely appeared in Arabic before World War I, how do propagandists even know it existed? Before World War I, they don't. It took me nearly a decade to find a handful of references, and I can assure you few if any propagandists are familiar with its Arabic usage before 1918. But that changed dramatically in 1918, when the term gained traction for a couple of years until 1920. That's because the Hijazi nobleman Faysal revolted against the Ottoman

---

[11] On "the southern part of Syria, Palestine," see Yusuf Dibs, *Kitab Tarikh Suriya* (Beirut: al-Matba'a al-'Umumiyya, 1893), 6; on "southern Syria", see Salim Jibra'il al-Khuri and Salim Mikha'il Shihada, *Kitab Athar al-Adhar: al-Qism al-Jughrafi* (Beirut: al-Matba'a al-Suriyya, 1875), 500; "Naql al-'Ayn," *al-Muqtataf* 11 (1887): 704; on northern Syria and southern Syria, see *Filastin* 30 November 1912; on "the southern part of Sham" see "Suriya," *al-Mashriq* (1903): 127; As'ad Ya'qub Khayyat, *A Voice from Lebanon: With the Life and Travels of Assaad Y. Kayat* (London: Madden & Co., 1847), 160; on European sources, see Daniel Pipes, *Greater Syria: The History of an Ambition* (Oxford: Oxford University Press, 1992), 14.

Empire in 1916 during the First World War (alongside "Lawrence of Arabia"), and established an Arab Kingdom in Damascus in 1918 which he ruled until the French violently overthrew him in 1920. During his period of rule, many Arabs in Palestine thought naively that if they could convince Palestine's British conquerors the land had always been part of Syria—indeed, that it was even called "southern Syria"—then Britain might withdraw its troops from the region and hand Palestine over to Faysal. This led some folks to start calling the place southern Syria. The decision was born out of the preference of some of Palestine's Arabs to live under Arab rule from Damascus rather than under British rule from Jerusalem—the same British who, only a few months earlier, in 1917, had declared in the Balfour Declaration their intention to make a national home for the Jews in Palestine.[12]

But even during its period of ascendency, southern Syria was an aspiration, not the term people unconsciously used to describe the land. During the heyday of southern Syria in 1919, John Salah published a wonderful collection of essays in Arabic titled *Palestine: The Renewal of its Life*. The Jaffan doctor Fu'ad Shattarah contributed an essay to the volume titled "Health Reform in Palestine." "I will use the word 'Syria' in this study," he claimed, "to refer to the piece of land stretching from the Taurus Mountains to al-'Arish, Egypt, because I believe Palestine is

---

[12] On this point, see Foster, "What's a Palestinian?"; Most famously, in January 1919, shortly after King Faysal took power, urban notables from Jerusalem, Haifa, Jaffa, Nablus, Jenin, Acre, Gaza and elsewhere met at a series of meetings dubbed "the First Palestinian National Congress." The delegates supported a statement of principles that described Palestine as 'Southern Syria' and declared that we "should not be separated from the Independent Arab Syrian Government." See Yehoshua Porath, *The Emergence of the Palestinian National Movement 1918-1929* (London: Cass, 1974), I, 82. Around the same time 'Arif al-'Arif and Muhammad Hassan al-Budayri founded a newspaper called Southern Syria, which was soon shut down by the British for its harsh anti-Zionist rhetoric. Meanwhile, Jamal Husayni requested that the initials "S.J.," for *Suriya al-Janubiyya* (Southern Syria), be added after the word *Filastin* on stamps. See Persoff, *The Running Stag*, 16. During the Nebi Musa riots of 1920, protestors filled the streets of Jerusalem chanting slogans such as, "you, Syria, are my country!" Interview with Khader Salameh in Jerusalem (17 May 2014). Salameh explained that his father told him this story, and recalled from memory the chant: *"Anta Suriya Biladi; Anta 'Unwan al-Fakhkhama; Kul Man Ya'tika Yawm'an Tami'a Yalqa Hamama."* The exact same song appeared in n.a., *Anashid al-'Arabiyya* (Jerusalem: Matba'at al-'Arab, 1933), 3.

'southern Syria.'" He admitted candidly that the term southern Syria was an aspiration, not a description. No one today says, "I believe this country is called Germany or France." It's not a belief, it's a fact. And, indeed, Shattarah unconsciously called the place Palestine, rather southern Syria, throughout the remainder of his essay. Najib Ibrahim Katbah also contributed an essay to the volume and similarly paid lip service to "southern Syria." Yet whenever he used the phrase, he nearly always added "i.e., Palestine." Why, again, the need to specify what southern Syria was if it was so self-evident? Of course, it was not evident, something we already knew from its infrequent usage in Arabic before 1918. A third contributor, Rashid Taqi al-Din, also insisted on calling Palestine southern Syria. "Palestine is a part of Syria, and Syria is a part of Palestine," he wrote. "Palestine is the southern part of Syria, and therefore it is necessary to call it southern Syria." Here, again, Taqi al-Din is making the case it *should* be called southern Syria rather than unconsciously describing it as southern Syria. "Palestine or Southern Syria was never independent at any period in history, and like its sister, Syria, but the two countries are one, geographically and historically, intellectually and politically." No surprise that he, as well, usually included Palestine in parenthesis after mentioning southern Syria, or wrote "also known as Palestine," or "i.e., Palestine."[13]

Since 1920, Southern Syria was remembered sporadically for political purposes, as we have seen. The term was embraced by Arabs who believed that an Arab state in greater Syria was the best way to stem Zionist immigration and land purchases, while Zionists such as Asaf, Meir and

---

[13] See Fu'ad Shattarah, "al-Islah al-Sihhi fi Filastin," cited in John S. Salah, *Filastin wa-Tajdid Hayatuhu* (New York: The Syrian American Press, 1919), 117; Najib Ibrahim Katbah, "al-Mawqif al-Siyyasi: Nahnu wa-l-Sahyuniyyun," cited in John S. Salah, *Filastin wa-Tajdid Hayatuhu* (New York: The Syrian American Press, 1919), 140; Rashid Taqi al-Din, "Bayn Suriya wa-Filastin," cited in John S. Salah, *Filastin wa-Tajdid Hayatuhu* (New York: The Syrian American Press, 1919), 167-8.

my Shabbat hosts revived it to show that the Arabs never cared much for Palestine. Of course, it was concern for Palestine that gave prominence to the idea of southern Syria in the first place.[14]

That's why many Arabs proclaimed there was no Palestine, only Syria, well into the 1930s and 1940s. They continued to believe the best chance of stopping Zionist immigration was to insist that the object of Zionist desire—Palestine—didn't even exist. Consider what the central political institution of the Arabs of Palestine—The Arab Higher Committee—wrote as late as 1948:

> Palestine never had a special status [during the Ottoman period]. Some of it was a part of the District of Beirut and some of it was known as the District of Jerusalem. Its name [i.e. Palestine] was not in widespread circulation at that time, neither was it known to people. Instead, it was considered a part the Shami Land or Syria. There is no natural border between it and Syria, nor between it and Lebanon. The Syrians, Lebanese and Palestinians are one people in terms of the property, genealogy, trade, agriculture and industry, not to mention their close linguistic ties, shared customs, traditions, religion, blood and interests.[15]

To emphasize the ironies of history, some Zionists and Arabs agreed in the 1930s and 1940s that there was no Palestine. To some Zionists, no Palestine meant the Arabs living in it would apparently be happy moving to Lebanon or Syria. To some Arabs, no Palestine meant the British might hand over the country to Arabs in Damascus, Amman, Beirut or Cairo rather than Zionists

---

[14] For a sampling of folks who used the term southern Syria after 1920, see Mahmud al-Charkis, *al-Dalil al-Musawwar lil-Bilad al-'Arabiyya* (Damascus: Matba'at Babil Ikhwan, 1930), 11; Ihsan al-Nimr, *Tarikh Jabal Nablus wa-l-Balqa* (Damascus: Matba'at Zaydun, 1938), I, 34, 67; n.a., *Rihla Bayn al-Jibal fi Ma'aqil al-Tha'irin* (Jafa: al-Matba'a al-Jami'a al-Islamiyya, 1936), 13, 17; Sahil al-Sayyid, *Al-Murshid al-'Arabi, Filastin* (Jerusalem: al-Matba'a al-'Asriyya, 1936), 11; George Haddad, *Filastin al-'Arabiyya* (Damascus: Matba'at al-Mufid, 1954), 15; Maktabat Bayt al-Maqdis, *Tarikh Filastin min Aqdam al-Azmana ila Ayyamina hadhihi* (Jerusalem: Maktabat Bayt al-Maqdis, 1934), 7; Muhammad Libada al-Nabulusi, *Thawrat Filastin al-Kubra* (Damascus: Matba'at al-Fayha', 1936), 9, 39, 77, 79, 83, 87; Nuri al-Sa'id, *Istiqlal al-'Arab wa-Wihdatuhum: Mudhakkira fi al-Qadiyya al-'Arabiyya* (Baghdad: Matba'at al-Hukuma, 1943), 9; Ghayrath Pitrus, Suriya al-Jadida (trans.), *Filastin, Shahidat al-Isti'mar al-Sahyuni* (San Paolo: Dar al-Tiba'a wa-l-Nashr al-'Arabiyya, 1940), 7; for further examples, see Zachary Foster, "Arabness, Turkey and the Palestinian National Imagination in the Eyes of Mir'at al-Sharq (1919-1926)," *Jerusalem Quarterly* 42 (2010): 69; Weldon C. Matthews, *Constructing a Nation: Arab Nationalists and Popular Politics in Mandate Palestine* (I. B. Tauris, 2006), 138; Daniel Pipes, *Greater Syria*.

[15] al-Hay'a al-'Arabiyya al-'Ulya, *Qadiyyat Filastin al-'Arabiyya* (Cairo: Matba'at al-Sa'ada, 1948?), 4.

in Jerusalem. Few people used the phrase to unconsciously describe any place at all. To this day, the phrase southern Syria continues to be used to score political victories, and not much else.

* * *

Scholars. Now let's return to the history of the controversy over Palestine. In the early 1970s, the Egyptian diplomat Tahseen Bashir persuaded his friend, Bernard Lewis, that the Egyptian President Anwar Sadat was ready for an interim peace settlement with Israel, a message Lewis was asked to convey to the then Prime Minister of Israel, Golda Meir. The British Jewish historial apparently had a direct line of communication with the sitting Israeli head of state. Lewis complied, convinced that Sadat wanted peace.[16]

Reportedly, Lewis and Meir met in the early 1970s. Meir seems to have rebuffed Lewis. In response, Lewis published a magnum opus on the history of the conflict for *Commentary Magazine* in 1975. 15,000 words, 33 footnotes and two appendices later, Lewis aimed to reassure Meir that his sympathies lied with Israel, not the Arabs. This is how he began his essay:

> The name "Palestine" is first attested in the history of Herodotus, and appears in the works of later Greek and Latin writers […] From the end of the Jewish state in antiquity to the beginning of British rule, the area now designated by the name Palestine was not a country and had no frontiers, only administrative boundaries; it was a group of provincial subdivisions, by no means always the same, within a larger entity.[17]

Strangely enough, despite his expertise in Islamic rather than Greek and Roman history, Lewis had virtually nothing to say about the history of "Palestine" during the early Caliphate,

---

[16] On the meeting between Lewis and Bashir, see Itamar Rabinovich, "Can One be Simultaneously a Zionist and a Great Historian of Islam?" *Mosaic* 14 June 2016 (goo.gl/hmZxVp).
[17] Lewis, "The Palestinians and the PLO."

Umayyad, Abbasid, Fatimid, Crusader, Mamluk or Ottoman periods. [The above ellipses included a few more sentences about the ancient Greek and Roman world.] Lewis continued:

> With the British conquest in 1917-18 and the subsequent establishment of a mandated territory in the conquered areas, Palestine became the official name of a definite territory for the first time since the Middle Ages...From the outset, Jews living under the Mandate refused to use this name in Hebrew but instead used what had become the common Jewish designation of the county—Eretz Yisrael, the land of Israel... For Arabs, too, the term Palestine was unacceptable, though for other reasons. For Muslims, it was alien and irrelevant but not abhorrent in the same way as it was to Jews. The main objection for them was that it seemed to assert a separate entity which politically conscious Arabs in Palestine and elsewhere denied. For them there was no such thing as a country called Palestine. The region which the British called Palestine was merely a separated part of a larger whole. For a long time organized and articulate Arab political opinion was virtually unanimous on this point.

Jews did indeed use the term *Erets Yisrael* in Hebrew rather than *Palestina*, as Lewis claimed. Zionist officials even lobbied the British to exchange the Hebrew term *Palestina* for *Erets Yisrael* (the Land of Israel) on stamps, bills and coins. But such efforts were not based on an "abhorrence" of the word Palestine, as Lewis claimed. In fact, by the last decades of the 19th century, Palestine was the word of choice for most Zionists in their own native languages—e.g. Yiddish, Russian, Polish, Ukrainian, Ladino, French, German, Hungarian, English, Arabic and Italian. That's why Zionists established the Palestine Post, the Palestine Office, the Palestine Zionist Executive, later renamed The Jewish Agency for Palestine and the Anglo-Palestine Bank, the financial front of the Zionist enterprise. Zionists didn't have problems with the word Palestine. Quite the contrary, using a word *other* than Palestine in English, German or Russian would have sounded odd.

So why was the word Palestine never embraced in Hebrew? Did Jews "abhor" the word, as Lewis suggested? No. For more than two millennia, Hebrew survived as a written, not a spoken language. It was therefore not subject to the same influences as its living counterparts and was thus slow to embrace the word Palestine when it rose dramatically in popularity in the 17th and

18th centuries in Europe and in the 19th century Middle East. Instead, the Zionist objection to the word Palestine on coins and stamps was a political act. The enemies of the Zionists decided their homeland was called Palestine, and so a few Zionists thought it politically useful to declare war on the word itself. Mikha'el Asaf, discussed above, may have been the first historian-casualty of that war. Lewis might have been the second.

Lewis also suggested that from the rise of Islam in the 7th century up until World War I, Arabs considered the word Palestine "alien and irrelevant." It's strange that Lewis wrote that, since his dissertation covered a period of history when Palestine was an administrative district, which we'll discuss in greater depth in chapter 3. (Perhaps the problem was that Lewis had written his dissertation 40 years earlier and had completely forgotten about it!). Lewis repeated his misunderstanding of this history, if watered down slightly, in his memoir of a lifetime, published at 96 years young, claiming not that the Arabs and Muslims abhorred the word Palestine, but that they simply forgot about it. I'll deal with this question directly in chapters three and four.[18]

Edward Said is a household name to anyone who has pursued a degree in the humanities. The book that made him famous was *Orientalism*, followed by *The Question of Palestine* in 1979. In

---

[18] Lewis wrote that "the name Palestina was retained for the remaining centuries of Roman and then Byzantine rule, and, for a while, by the Arab conquerors. Before long however it was forgotten, and the country had no separate name, being seen simply as part of some larger entity. In Christian Europe, where the country was usually known by the name of "The Holy Land," the Roman name Palestina reappeared with the classical Renaissance, and became a common term to designate the country. From Europe it was brought again to the Middle East, but was used almost exclusively by Europeans and other Westerners, and not by Jews or Arabs. The former preferred to use the biblical names; the latter had no need for a special name for what was simply part of a larger whole of the Arab world, or at least of Syria. With one brief interlude, that of the Crusader states in the Middle Ages, this remained the situation of the country for almost two millennia, from the triumph of Rome to the fall of the Ottomans." Bernard Lewis with Buntzie Ellis Churchill, *Notes on a Century: Reflections of a Middle East Historian* (New York: Viking, 2012), 213; see also Bernard Lewis, "Palestine: On the History and Geography of a Name," *The International History Review* 2(1) (1980): 6.

the later, Said wrote that Zionists [read: Bernard Lewis] asserted dubiously that "Palestine was used only as an administrative designation in the Roman Empire, and never since—except […] during the British Mandate period after 1922." But the truth, Said insisted, was that "if one were to read geographers, historians, philosophers and poets who wrote in Arabic from the eighth century on, one would find references to Palestine." Said was correct, as we shall discover in chapter three, although he failed to italicize the word *if*, since it seems he did not read many geographers, historians, philosophers or poets who wrote in Arabic from the 8th century onwards. Instead, he cited a single passage about Palestine from the 10th century Arab geographer al-Maqdisi (a.k.a. al-Muqaddasi) (d.991) which mentioned the term Palestine. Ironically, the passage was translated by Guy Le Strange—the same Guy Le Strange Said had accused only a year earlier in *Orientalism* of being an Orientalist—one who also apparently offered a rebuke to Zionist mythology. Anyways, the point is that Said didn't bother to cite any other Arabs who apparently wrote so much about Palestine. The mystery over Palestine persisted.[19]

The prominent historian Rashid Khalid rejected the Lewis thesis outright in his 1997 *Palestinian Identity*. The book won the Albert Hourani book award, the closest thing Middle East scholars have to a Pulitzer Prize. It also helped Khalidi land the poignantly named Edward Said Chair of Arab Studies at Columbia University, arguably the most coveted job in Middle East Studies today. The book's contribution to the history of the name Palestine was based significantly on a

---

[19] Edward Said, *The Question of Palestine* (New York: Times Books, 1979), 10-11; for Said on Guy Le Strange, see Edward Said, *Orientalism* (New York: Vintage Books, 1979), 15, 224. The historian Beshara Doumani [*Rediscovering Palestine: Merchants and Peasants in Jabal Nablus, 1700-1900* (Berkeley: University of California Press, 1995), ch. 1, note 1] added that "it is doubtful whether the name Palestine was commonly used by the native population to refer to a specific territory or nation before the late nineteenth century," although he acknowledged that the issue still awaited a more systematic investigation.

1701 petition of Jerusalemite notables and a 1726 document also from Jerusalem, both found in the Khalidiyya Library. (Khalidi did not provide the full text of the two sources, and neither are accessible to the public). Khalidi argued that both documents showed that Palestine was thought of as a special and sacred place, with Jerusalem as its focus. According to Khalidi, a group of Jerusalemite notables signed the 1701 petition demanding that the Ottoman governor revoke permission for a visit to Jerusalem of a French consul based in Sidon. In Khalidi's words, the petition showed "Palestine as a special and sacred space" and recapitulated "the idea of Palestine as a special and sacred land with Jerusalem as its focus." As for the 1726 document, Khalidi quoted one line from it: "The transfer of *waqf* [religious endowment] property to foreigners in Jerusalem constituted a threat to the future of the city, which must be built up and populated if Jerusalem were to be defended against the covetousness of these external enemies." The document, for Khalidi, showed that "modern nationalism was rooted in long-standing attitudes of concern for the city of Jerusalem and for Palestine as a sacred entity."[20]

But neither the 1701 petition nor the 1726 document, nor any other documents Khalidi cited before 1899, mentioned the word Palestine. A careful reader of Khalidi's book might conclude (incorrectly, as we shall discover in chapters three and four) that the word Palestine was not known to anyone in the Arab world before 1899. And yet Khalidi's *Palestinian Identity* remains *the* book on the origins of a Palestinian identity even though it had preciously little to say about Palestine before the 20th century. The mystery over the history of the name Palestine continued.[21]

---

[20] On the lack of public accessibility to the documents in the library, see my acknowledgments section.
[21] Rashid Khalidi, *Palestinian Identity: The Construction of Modern National Consciousness* (New York: Columbia University Press, 1997), 29-30. Khalidi repeated his own misinterpretation of these documents throughout the text (ibid, 29, 32, 46, 232 and 254). [Note that Jerusalemite notables had on several other occasions presented similar

A year later, in 1998, the historian Haim Gerber broke new ground. He argued that the inhabitants of the region had known about Palestine from the 16th century onwards in senses that went "far beyond mere objective geography" and they had a "social awareness" of living in it. "There are sufficient indications," he wrote, "that on the eve of the Great War [1914] the concept and idea of Palestine was well entrenched in the minds of the Arabs of Palestine." Gerber dispelled the myth that Palestine had been completely forgotten in the 16th, 17th and 18th centuries. But he based this claim on seven sources, even though Arabs and Ottomans left behind many hundreds during that period. What did everyone else have to say about Palestine?[22]

In the past few years, the English professor Nabil Matar has also joined the front lines in the battle over Palestine. "The view of the land by the peoples from the Ottoman Empire and beyond (from Morocco to India)," he claimed, was that "*ard Filastin* [the Land of Palestine] was part of

---

petitions to the Ottoman authorities. See K. J. Asali (ed.) *Jerusalem in History* (New York: Olive Branch Press, 2000), 209; Henry Maundrell, *A Journey from Aleppo to Jerusalem at Easter, A.D. 1697* (London: C.V. Rivington, 1823), 39]. The 1899 reference to Palestine, the first reference to that word cited in the book, appeared in Yusuf Diya al-Khalidi's letter to Theodor Herzl, in which he tells Herzl to "leave Palestine in peace." See Khalidi, *Palestinian Identity*, 75.

[22] He included anecdotes from Mujir al-Din al-'Ulaymi's (d.1522) *al-Uns al-Jalil*, al-Tamartashi's (d. 1644-5) *al-Khabar al-Tamm*, Khayr al-Din al-Ramli's (d.1671) *al-Fatawa al-Khayriyya*, Ebussuud Efendi's (d.1574) fatwa, Evliya Çelebi's (d.1682) *Seyahatname*, and a few other sources which mention the word Palestine during the Ottoman period. See Haim Gerber, "'Palestine' and Other Territorial Concepts in the 17th Century," *International Journal of Middle East Studies* 30 (1998): 567. He argued elsewhere that "two very important legal scholars of eighteenth and early nineteenth century Damascus refer to Khayr al-Din al-Ramli as the 'great scholar of Palestine.'" Haim Gerber, "Zionism, Orientalism and the Palestinians" *Journal of Palestine Studies* 33(1) (2003): 27. His source is his very own "Palestine and Other Territorial Concepts," in which he found one (not two) scholars who described Khayr al-Din al-Ramli as a scholar of Palestine (the other described him as from *al-Diyar al-Qudsiyya*, or the Jerusalem region). See ibid, 569. Gerber also used the words "Palestine" and "Palestinian" uncritically in his studies on the history of the use of those words: "in the seventeenth century all of Palestine was divided into three such autonomous districts (sanjaqs), which developed symbiotic, even friendly, relations with each other, together resisting Lebanese forces that tried to encroach on Palestinian territory from the North [...] Amazingly, a recent study found that by the end of the century the three dynasties had intermarried, so here in effect was a rudimentary Palestinian state, in territory more or less coterminous with the area of western Palestine." See Haim Gerber, *Remembering and Imagining Palestine: Identity and Nationalism from the Crusades to the Present* (New York: Palgrave, 2008), 45.

their traveling and living experience." For the Muslim, Christian and Jewish populations of the Ottoman Empire, "*ard Filastin* [the Land of Palestine] was part of the *lebensraum* [habitat] in which their personal history took shape." Matar found two sources to support the claim—the same 17th century Ottoman traveler Evliya Çelebi that Gerber had found two decades earlier, and a 17th century Aleppan Orthodox Priest, Makariyus III ibn Zaʿim. But, much like Lewis, Said, Khalidi and Gerber, Matar drew sweeping conclusions over the course of four centuries and among three religious traditions spanning three continents based on only a handful of sources.[23]

The UK-based scholar Nur Masalha recently published a lengthy study of "The Concept of Palestine" from its origins in the late Bronze Age to the modern period. His argument was that "the concept of Palestine is deeply rooted in the collective consciousness of the indigenous people of Palestine." He wrote that "Palestine is the collective watan (homeland) of the Palestinian people—the indigenous people of historic Palestine," a sentence that feels more fitting for a political rally than a peer-reviewed paper. He also made sweeping conclusions based on a small number of sources, especially from the 13th through early 19th centuries.[24]

* * *

---

[23] Nabil Matar, *Through the Eyes of the Beholder: The Holy Land, 1517-1713* (Leiden: Brill, 2013), 226.
[24] Nur Masalha, "The Concept of Palestine: The Conception Of Palestine from the Late Bronze Age to the Modern Period," *Journal of Holy Land and Palestine Studies* 15(2) (2016): 143-202. He also used the adjective Palestinian to describe people without any apparent recourse to a source when it is precisely their Palestinian-ness he is trying to explain.

The Palestinians. We've discussed the history of the controversy over Palestine. Now let's move to the second part of this chapter, the history of the controversy over the Palestinians. When did people first start to deny their existence? In this section, I'm interested not in the actual origins and development of a Palestinian identity—dealt with in chapter three and four—but rather the controversies that have surrounded it over the past century.

In 2019, we will reach the centennial of the first American news correspondent in history to have reportedly declared the Palestinian race "a creature of allusion." The point was reported second hand by Habib Ibrahim Katbah, and little else is known about the identity of the American journalist who penned to paper the claim. But, if true, it would place the slogan that "there is no such thing as a Palestinian" nearly as old as the first people in modern history to use that term to describe themselves. The Palestinians were burdened by controversy almost from the time they first came into the existence.[25]

We take for granted that the term Palestinian means something to us, but that was not always the case. In 1922, U.S. lawmakers discussed a resolution to support "the re-creation of Palestine as the national home of the Jewish Race" in what appears to be the oldest recorded debate over the meaning of the term, *Palestinians*, in English. This was only a few years after the 1917 Balfour Declaration, when Britain declared its intention to turn Palestine into the National Home of the Jews, and around the same time the League of Nations ratified the British Mandate of Palestine, giving the British international legitimacy to rule over people it denied the right to self-determination.

---

[25] See Katbah, "al-Haraka al-Sahyuniyya" in Salah, *Filastin wa-Tajdid*, 157.

In one session, Congressman James Reed and Congressman Bourke Cockran quarreled over the idea of establishing a Jewish legion in Palestine (Ze'ev Jabotinsky tried to establish an organized Jewish defense force in the country after World War I). Mr. Reed realized this would not go over well and that "people," as he called them, would be unhappy and discontented.

"Which people?" asked Congressman Cockran.

"The Palestinians," said Mr. Reed.

"[Did you mean] the Syrians?" Mr. Cockran retorted.

"I mean the non-Zionist population of Palestine."

Was Congressman Cockran a troll, or did he think the people who would have opposed a Jewish legion in Palestine called themselves Syrians? It seems he was neither a troll nor a Zionist propagandist. As an Irish immigrant, he opposed British imperialism in Ireland and apartheid in South Africa. He also lobbied against the American conquest of the Philippines in 1899 and supported organized labor and immigrants. Although he was racist and supported the disenfranchisement of black voters in the United States, he was progressive on foreign policy. It appears he thought these people who opposed a Jewish legion in Palestine called themselves Syrians, and he was not entirely wrong for thinking that: self-identified Syrians outnumbered self-identified Palestinians in the United States by an order of magnitude in the years leading up to 1922.[26]

---

[26] Most Ottoman immigrants to the New World at the time came from Mount Lebanon, smaller numbers came from Homs, Bethlehem, Ramallah and elsewhere. Most of them called themselves Syrian in the New World—and would have been annoyed had you called them something else, such as Turks, a term that sounded more like a curse word in English than a self-appellation. Khalil Totah—from Ramallah—spent time in the US in the early 20th century and described himself as from Syria in his diary. (See Thomas Ricks, *Turbulent Times in Palestine: The Diaries of Khalil Totah* (Beirut: Institute for Palestine Studies, 2009), 194). The strongest evidence for the preference of Syrian comes from U.S. immigration records. Until 1899, all immigrants from the Ottoman Empire were called Turks. The first year the immigrants were given the option Syrian or Turk, 99.3% of them chose Syrian. See Asher Kaufman, *Reviving Phoenicia: The Search for Identity in Lebanon* (London: I.B. Tauris, 2014), 100-101, note 65. Most

Still, by 1922, very few of the people Mr. Cockran thought were Syrians called themselves Syrian. (Most would have called themselves Arabs, the Arabs of Palestine, the Muslims and Christians of Palestine, the Palestinians or the people of Jaffa, the people of Jerusalem and the people of Nablus, etc.). Two exceptions were folks from the northern areas of the British Mandate for Palestine—i.e. Haifa or Acre—some of whom may have thought they were from Syria, not Palestine (in the early 1920s), and others who used the term out of aspiration to be Syrian rather than a self-evident appellation.[27]

Confusion over the term persisted later in the hearing. "I know the Palestinians, I have talked with them. They are sensible," insisted Mr. Reed. "How would you feel if the German troops were holding you down until enough Frenchmen came in to take possession of the State?" Mr. Reed understood that whatever these people were called, they were not happy about Zionist immigration. They would "make a ban to immigration for 10 years," Mr. Reed added.

"Who would?" Mr. Cockran responded, now appearing to troll Mr. Reed.

"The Palestinians," shouted another Congressman in defense of Mr. Reed.

Ottoman immigrants in Brazil also preferred the term *Sirios* to *Turcos* so as not to be mistakenly confused for Muslims. See Akram Fouad Khater, "Becoming "Syrian" in America: A Global Geography of Ethnicity and Nation" *Diaspora: A Journal of Transnational Studies* 14(2/3) (2005): 304. The American traveler, Adela E. Orpen [*The Chronicles of the Sid: Or, the Life and Travels of Adelia Gates* (New York: Fleming H. Revell Co, 1897), 301-2] also conflated the terms Palestinian and Syrian in her 1897 travelogue, writing that "I like the name Shechem best, though Palestinians, whether Christian, Jew, Syrian or Arab, now say Nablus." For a similar example, see "Durr al-Malh 'ala al-Jarh," *Filastin* 25 October 1911; the term "Syrian" was occasionally used instead of Palestinian well into the Mandate period (1920-1948). Sa'id al-Sabbagh [*al-Madaniyyat al-Qadima wa-Tarikh Suriya wa-Filastin* (2nd ed.) (Jaffa and Haifa: al-Maktaba al-'Asriyya, 1944), 187-8], for instance, described Yusuf Diya Pasha al-Khalidi (from Jerusalem) as Syrian.

[27] Some people might have thought places like Haifa or the Galilee were part of Syria, not Palestine. The newspaper *al-Nafir* (28 July 1909 and 10 May 1910) described Haifa as a city in Syria and in Palestine (10 May 1910). In 1923, the geographer 'Abd al-Hadi may have thought Nazareth, Haifa and the Galilee were part of Syria, not Palestine. See Zachary J. Foster, "Arab Historiography in Mandatory Palestine, 1920-1948" (MA Thesis, Georgetown University, 2011), 39-40.

Mr. Reed jumped in to correct Mr. Cooper. "No, the non-Zionists," he said. They out to be called "non-Jewish Palestinians." In the end, he decided that Palestinian ought to be qualified as not Jewish *by definition* to avoid confusion.[28]

* * *

Palestinian Civic Identity. Congressman Reed was not the only one to insist Jews were not Palestinians. "The Palestinian people consisted of two races, the Christians and Muslims," claimed one Palestinian Arab writer in 1929, Bishara Mansur. "The Palestinian Arabs are no doubt made up of two races, not three," he added for emphasis. Other Palestinian Arab writers like Grigorios al-Hajjar and Rashid Ibrahim agreed with Mansur that Jews were not Palestinians.[29]

Some writers insisted Jews were not Palestinians, in part, because legally they *were* Palestinians. The British specified in a 1920 interim report that all Christian, Muslim and Jewish government officials were *Palestinians*. The interim decision was expanded in 1925 with the Palestinian Law of Nationality, which granted "Palestinian nationality" to all subjects of the Government of Palestine. The British High Commissioner, Herbert Samuel emphasized that "Palestinian citizenship is enjoyed by all the residents of Palestine, whether Jewish or not Jewish." This is why you'll often hear propagandists claim that Jews, not Arabs, called themselves Palestinians

---

[28] United States Congress, House Committee on Foreign Affairs, *Establishment of a National Home in Palestine, H. Con. Res. 52* (Washington: Government Printing Office, 1922), 31, 35.
[29] Mansur, *al-Dima' al-Zakiyya*, 16; Rashid al-Hajj Ibrahim, *al-Qadiyya al-Filastiniyya Amam al-Wafd al-Parlamani al-'Iraqi* (Haifa: Matba'at al-Nafir, 1936), 5; Grigorios al-Hajjar (a.k.a Garigoriyus al-Hajjar), *Britanya al-'Udhma: al-Shahadat al-Siyasiyya amam al-Lajna al-Milkiyya al-Britaniyya* (Damascus: Matba'at al-Sha'b, 1937), 53; for a similar point, see al-Nafir, *Majmu'a Shahadat 'Arab Filastin*, 31.

from the 1920s-1940s. Such propagandists are absolutely correct: legally, Jews were as Palestinian as Arabs were Palestinian.[30]

In fact, the British legal system in Palestine was designed to give Jewish Palestinians advantages over non-Jewish Palestinians in matters of travel, immigration, diplomatic protection, repatriation, and the regulation of the franchise. That's why many Muslim and Christian Palestinian students, migrants, merchants or travelers who had traveled abroad Palestine prior to the codification of the nationality laws in the early 1920s had trouble returning. After all, the purpose of the Mandate was to facilitate the establishment of a national home for the Jews in Palestine. Arabs were hostile to the idea that Jews could be Palestinians as a way of registering their disapproval with the Law of Palestinian Nationality, which they saw discriminating against the very people it was named after.[31]

Having said that, Arabs still used the term "Palestinian" in the British sense of the word even if they rejected the moral foundations of the Mandate. Since the government defined citizenship as

---

[30] For the most comprehensive treatment of this subject, see Lauren Banko, *The Invention of Palestinian Citizenship, 1918–47* (Edinburgh University Press, 2016); on the interim report, see Likhovski, *Law and Identity in Mandate Palestine*, 25; for the order itself, see Government of Palestine, *Palestinian Citizenship Order* (n.p: n.p., 1925); the order was translated immediately into Arabic, as Government of Palestine, *Filastin: Taqrir al-Mandub al-Sami,1920-1925* (Jerusalem: Matba'at al-Dar al-Rum al-Urthudhuks, 1925?), 14; on Samuel's definition of a Palestinians citizen, see ibid, 26-27; see also Najib Sadaqa, *Qadiyyat Filastin* (Beirut: Dar al-Kutub, 1946), 70; this usage made its way into Arabic. See, for instance, Muhammad Rif'at, *Qadiyyat Filastin* (Cairo: Dar al-Ma'arif, 1947), 59; Lester Hopkins, "al-Sukkan," in Sa'id Himadeh (ed.), *al-Nizam al-Iqtisadi fi Filastin* (Beirut: al-Matba'a al-Amrikiyya fi Beirut, 1939), 48-9. Strictly speaking, Jews rarely if ever called themselves *the* Palestinians, but rather "Palestinian subjects" or "Palestinian Jews." Shimria Yellin, for instance, defined herself as a "Palestinian subject" in an inquiry to British officials. See Tel Aviv School of English, Central Zionist Archive (CZA) A580/22. I would like to thank Liora Halperin for this reference. Hannah Arendt [Jerome Kohn; Ron H Feldman (eds.) *The Jewish Writings* (New York: Schocken Books, 2007), 397] wrote in 1944 that, if current trends were to continue, "the Palestinian Jews would degenerate into one of those small warrior tribes about whose possibilities and importance history has amply informed us since the days of Sparta." For further references to Palestinian Jews, see "Palestinian Jews in England," *The Zionist Review* 1(10) (1918): 185; for Palestinian Jewry, see, for instance, "The Zionist Commission and Palestine," *The Zionist Review* 1(11) (1918): 203; see also R. Gottheil, "The History of Zionism," pp. 117-137 in *Zionism and the Jewish Future* H. Sacher (ed.) (London: John Murray, 1917), 130.
[31] Banko, *Palestinian Citizenship*, 24-5.

"Palestinian citizenship," Arabs also referred to it as "Palestinian citizenship." As we shall discover in the next few chapters, states often played an important role how we refer to places, peoples and even how we describe ourselves.[32]

A small number of optimists hoped that the label Palestinian could include everyone who lived in Palestine. The Polish Jewish American Orientalist Morris Jastrow wrote in 1919 that there were too many "nationalities in Palestine" for the state to serve the interests of just one nationality. What followed in his prescient comments was a fascinating discussion of the difference between a civic and ethnic state. "A Jewish State, wrote Jastrow, "necessarily involves of the older conception of a nation based on a single nationality. In Palestine, the conditions preclude a State of a single nationality, except by the forcible submission of other nationalities already represented, it is an injustice to give preference to any single group." He proposed a simple solution: "anyone can become a Palestinian, as any person can become an American or an Englishman, by obtaining nationalization papers and swearing allegiance to the principles of the country."[33]

Jastrow was not the only one who believed that the term Palestinian ought to be inclusive. The prominent activist Najib Sadaqa wrote in 1936 that the Mandate should have established neither a Jewish nor Arab state in Palestine, but rather a "Palestinian state." In 1946, Muhammad

---

[32] The newspaper *Filastin* (6 July 1921) described two Jews in 1921 as "Palestinian Jews"; the Palestine Workers Union [Ittihad 'Ummal Filastin, *Kashf al-Qina': Majmu'a Mushahadat wa-Haqa'iq 'an Ahwal al-Idhtirabat al-Akhira fi Filastin* (Haifa: Matba'at Zaytuni, 1937), 25] claimed the *Histadrut* called all Jewish and Arab workers "Palestinian workers" without distinguishing between them; Rashid al-Barrawi [*Mashru' Suriyya al-Kubra* (Cairo: Maktabat al-Nahda al-Misriyya, 1947), 48] added a state called "United Syria" would facilitate economic cooperation with the "Palestinian citizens of Jewish decent." For similar usage, see Jabir Shibli, *Asra' am Ta'awwun fi Filastin?* (Jerusalem: Sharika Matba'at al-Umma, 1940), 52.
[33] Morris Jastrow, *Zionism and the Future of Palestine: The Fallacies* (New York: Macmillan, 1919), 108-110.

Bayhum described a long tradition of Arab tolerance towards Jews, including after the Spanish expulsion. Arabs sought cooperation with Zionists from beginning, he claimed, on condition that they become Palestinian citizens. But Bayhum believed the Jews had no interest in becoming Palestinian citizens. "Their only aim was to establish a state of Israel." Hasan Siddiqi al-Dajjani argued similarly that the Jews had desired to live in the country as Jews rather than as Palestinians living in an Arab country, alongside the Arabs. Likewise, Kunstantin Thuyuduri hoped that the Muslims, Christians and Jews would abandon the terms Muslim, Christian and Jews and replace them with "brothers" or "Palestinians." A small minority of optimistic thinkers, Jewish and Arab alike, thought that the term Palestinian could or should have been embraced by all people who lived in Palestine.[34]

In short, the word Palestinian from 1920 to 1948 meant all subjects of the government, no matter their ethnic or religious background. It also meant only Muslim and Christian Arabs, not Jews. It also meant Muslims, Christians and some Jews. It was also used an appellation of aspiration rather than description. Today, many propagandists recall with great ignorance only part of the history of the term.

Golda Meir. The controversy over the Palestinians picked up again in the late 60s when the newly elected Israeli Prime Minister, Golda Meir, famously explained that "there were no such thing as Palestinians":

---

[34] First see Najib Sadaqa, *Qadiyyat Filastin*, 245; then see Muhammad Bayhum, *Filastin: Andalus al-Sharq* (Beirut: Matabi' Sadir, 1946), 39; then see Hasan Siddiqi al-Dajjani, cited in al-Nafir, *Majmu'a Shahadat 'Arab Filastin amam al-Lajna al-Milkiyya al-Britaniyya* (Haifa: al-Nafir, 1937?), 35; then see Kunstantin (a.k.a. Constantine) Thuyuduri, *Filastin wa-Mustaqbaluha* (Jerusalem: al-Matba'a al-Tijariyya, 1930), 12. On Thuyuduri's background, see Ya'qub al-'Awdat, *Min A'lam al-Fikr wa-l-Adab fi Filastin* (3rd ed.) (Jerusalem: Dar al-Isra', 1992), 82.

> When was there an independent Palestinian people with a Palestinian state? It was either southern Syria before the First World War, and then it was a Palestine including Jordan. It was not as though there was a Palestinian people in Palestine considering itself as a Palestinian people and we came and threw them out and took their country away from them. They did not exist.[35]

So adamant about the point, Meir once displayed her British-issued Government of Palestine identity card during a media appearance and pointed to the word *Palestinian* in English. As we just saw, Meir was correct, emphasizing the usage of term according to Palestine's British colonizers, the usage that guaranteed Jews legal privileges over Muslims, Christians and others.

Former Prime Minister of Israel, Menachem Begin, followed in her footsteps. He insisted that the Hebrew translation of the 1978 Camp David Accords—the Israeli-Egyptian peace treaty—use the term the "Arabs of the Land of Israel" instead of "Palestinian Arabs." The same thing happened during the Oslo process in 1993, when the Israeli delegation insisted that the unofficial Hebrew translation of the agreement use the phrase "the Arabs of the land of Israel" rather than the Palestinians. The very existence of people called the Palestinians was a problem for Israel.[36]

The belief that there are no Palestinians is still quite popular today. Yehezkel bin Nun's 2001 article, "The Myth of the Palestinian People," still performs well in Google searches more than 15 years later. "Who are the Palestinians?" he asked. "Who are these people who claim the Holy Land as their own? What is their history? Where did they come from? How did they arrive in the country they call Palestine?" Bin Nun narrated textbook Zionist mythology about the land on the eve of the Zionist movement. It was "practically empty," he wrote, populated by Arab

---

[35] The interview with Meir first appeared in *The Sunday Times* (London) 15 June 1969 and was re-printed in the "Golda Meir Scorns Soviets: Israeli Premier Explains Stand On Big-4," *The Washington Post* 16 June 1969.
[36] On Begin, see Dan Horowitz and Moshe Lissak, *Trouble in Utopia: The Overburdened Polity of Israel* (Albany: State University of New York Press, 1989), 36-7; on the Oslo process, see Kenneth Levin, "What Gold Meir Said About the Palestinians," *New York Times*, 12 October 1993 (https://goo.gl/oQ2my8).

"immigrants" from the surrounding countries interested in work opportunities created by Zionists. "If the Palestinians are indeed a myth," bin Nun concluded, "why invent a fictitious people?" His answer was the myth of the Palestinian people justified "the Arab occupation of the Land of Israel."[37]

* * *

Scholars. From the 1970s onwards, scholars joined the race to determine when Palestinians first started to call themselves Palestinians. Expectedly, Bernard Lewis played a key role in propagating myths about their origins:

> In Ottoman times, that is, immediately before the coming of the British, Palestine had indeed been a part of a larger Syrian whole from which it was in no way distinguished whether by language, culture, education, administration, political allegiance, or any other significant respect [...] For the rest of the period of the British Mandate, and for many years after that, their organizations described themselves as Arab and expressed their national identity in Arab rather than in Palestinian or even in Syrian terms. The emergence of a distinctive Palestinian entity is thus a product of the last decades and may be seen as the joint creation of Israel and the Arab states.[38]

Bernard Lewis believed a Palestinian "entity" —whatever that is supposed to mean—emerged only in the 1950s and 1960s. This should immediately seem odd to readers, since we just explained that the controversy in and of itself over the Palestinians dates to some 40 years earlier.

---

[37] Yehezkel Bin-Nun, "The Myth of The Palestinian People," *Arutz Sheva*, 26 December 2001 (https://goo.gl/0lsbbl). His belief that the very existence of the Palestinians was itself an act of violence persists today. The billionaire casino mogul and chief financial supporter of the Israeli settler movement, Sheldon Adelson thought the Palestinians were "southern Syrians" or Egyptians until Yasir Arafat, then leader of the Palestine Liberation Organization, "came along with a pitcher of Kool-Aid and gave it to everybody to drink and sold them the idea of Palestinians." See Jodi Rudoren, "A Mogul Comes to Lunch, and He Doesn't Hold His Tongue," *New York Times* 28 May 2013 (https://goo.gl/rDpxRW).

[38] Lewis, "The Palestinians and the PLO."

The historian Meir Litvak told me in 2009 that Muslims did not identify as Palestinian in the late Ottoman period. He has argued in print that Arabic sources from the inter-war period used phrases such as "the Arabs of Palestine," "the Arab nation in Palestine" and "the Arab youth of Palestine" rather than the terms "Palestinians" or "Palestinian people."[39]

In response, historians sympathetic to the Palestinians pushed back. Haim Gerber, discussed above, argued in a classic essay on the subject that a "local Palestinian identity existed in the country before both the British [1917] and Zionist presence [1882]," even though he did not find any sources mentioning Palestinians before the Zionist movement in the 1880s. Gerber insisted, nevertheless, that "their most basic identity was simply Palestinian, with which they identified with all their soul." Even if we excuse the momentary lapse in scholarly pedigree ("with all their soul"), Gerber didn't find anyone who called him or herself Palestinian before the 20th century, let alone before the Zionist presence, and he never explained what it was that existed before Zionism.[40]

Other experts on Palestinian history have chimed in as well. "What can be seen in the press, as in few other sources," wrote Rashid Khalidi, "is the increasing use of the terms 'Palestine' and 'Palestinians' [from 1908-1914].'" Khalidi was certainly right about that, as we shall discover in chapter four, but he found only a handful of references to the term Palestinian before 1914. How widespread was the identity before 1914? I will try to answer that question in chapter four.

---

[39] Meir Litvak, "Constructing A National Past: The Palestinian Case," in Meir Litvak (ed.) *Palestinian Collective Memory and National Identity* (New York: Palgrave, 2009), 125, n. 7.
[40] See Gerber, "Zionism, Orientalism and the Palestinians," 28 and Gerber, *Remembering and Imagining Palestine*, 75-6, respectively.

The director of the Center for Contemporary Arab Studies at Georgetown University, professor Rochelle Davis, went even further. She argued that a "large portion" of Arabs, Jews, Armenians, Greeks and Ethiopians from Jerusalem "would have called themselves Palestinians" in late Ottoman Jerusalem, even though she did not make mention of any Jerusalemite Arabs, Jews, Armenians, Greeks or Ethiopians who used the term Palestinian. Discerning readers should wonder why the world's leading experts of the history of the Palestinians have made such sweeping statements based on little or in some cases no evidence at all.[41]

This has generally been the tenor of the public debate surrounding the origins of the Palestinians: sweeping conclusions with little to no evidence. The same can be said for the prominent journalist, David Remnick, who wrote in the *New Yorker* that "in the late nineteenth and early twentieth centuries, the Palestinian Arabs identified themselves not as a unified people but as subjects of the Ottoman Empire and of the greater community of Islam; their local identities were tied to their villages, clans, and families." First of all, it's notable that David Remnick had something to say about the topic. But he, too, didn't cite any sources to support his claim. The origins of the Palestinians remained elusive.[42]

* * *

---

[41] See Khalidi, *Palestinian Identity*, 58-9, 155; then see Rochelle Davis, "Ottoman Jerusalem," pp. 10-29 in Salim Tamari (ed.) *Jerusalem 1948: The Arab Neighborhoods and their Fate in the War* (2nd ed.) (Jerusalem: The Institute for Jerusalem Studies, 2002), 10-11.
[42] David Remnick, "Blood and Sand: A Revisionist Israeli Historian Revisits his Country's Origins," *The New Yorker* 5 May 2008 (https://goo.gl/d4GrgQ).

U.S. Presidential Candidates. During the 2012 U.S. Republican primary campaign, Newt Gingrich reminded the *Jewish Channel* that "there was no Palestine as a state. It was part of the Ottoman Empire. I think that we've had an invented Palestinian people who are in fact Arabs and who were historically part of the Arab community. And they had a chance to go many places, and for a variety of political reasons we have sustained this war against Israel now since the 1940s, and it's tragic." To paraphrase, the identity *Palestinian* is not genetically determined. And Palestinians should have left Palestine when the Zionists decided it belonged to them.[43]

Gingrich's remarks seemed mildly insensitive to the mainstream media. The Washington Post, the Guardian, Fox News and the AP all went looking for clues to the mysterious origins of the Palestinians. The Guardian claimed, "most historians mark the start of Palestinian Arab nationalist sentiment as 1834, when Arab residents of the Palestinian region revolted against Ottoman rule." The revolt was of course not against Ottoman rule. It was against Muhammad Ali's Egyptian occupation. The Guardian did not cite any sources, but as far as I can tell, only two scholars have ever claimed the 1834 revolt marked the beginning of a Palestinian national identity: the late Israeli sociologist Baruch Kimmerling and the American political scientist Joel Migdal. Neither were historians and neither cited any sources from the 1830s in the book where they claim 1834 was so important.[44]

---

[43] For the full transcript, see The Washington Post, "Newt Gingrich Interview with Jewish Channel (Transcript)," *The Washington Post* 9 December 2011(https://goo.gl/xAcGNt)

[44] The revolt stemmed from the conscription policies of the region's new Egyptian occupiers, who naively thought they could conscript the boys of Nablus, Hebron and Jerusalem without raising the ire of local leaders. The countryside peasants revolted against military service and high taxes, not identity crises. For Gingrich's statements, see The Associated Press, "Palestinians are an invented people, says Newt Gingrich," *Associated Press*, 9 December 2011 (https://goo.gl/oFHVbQ); then see Baruch Kimmerling and Joel Migdal, *Palestinians: The Making of a People* (Cambridge, Mass: Harvard University Press, 2003), 6-13.

The Washington Post turned to a darling of the Zionist right, Dr. Daniel Pipes. "Everyone from the PLO to a Mitt Romney spokesman jumped on Gingrich for this assertion, but he happens to be absolutely correct," Pipes reportedly said. The term Palestine before 1920 "embodied a purely Jewish and Christian concept, one utterly foreign to Moslems, even repugnant to them." He added "no Arabic-speaking Muslims identified themselves as 'Palestinian' until 1920, when, in rapid order, this appellation and identity was adopted by the Muslim Arabs living in the British Mandate of Palestine." To paraphrase Dr. Pipes: Palestine was repugnant to hundreds of thousands of people in 1919 and embraced by them in 1920.[45]

Fox News was the least inaccurate, ironically. "Palestinians never had their own state," they wrote correctly. The Palestinians were instead "ruled by the Ottoman Empire for hundreds of years, like most of the Arab world." This was also accurate. "When the Ottoman Empire collapsed in the aftermath of World War I," Fox News added, "the British, then a global colonial power, took control of the area, then known as British Mandate Palestine [sic]. During that time [1920-1948], Jews, Muslims and Christians living on the land were identified as 'Palestinian.'" This was also correct, if missing some critical information. Fox News, much like Golda Meir, only recalled the colonial usage of the term Palestinian, forgetting that many Arabs rejected the colonial definition of Palestinian since it was designed to discriminate against them.[46]

On his return from a tour of the Holy Land in early 2015, former Governor of Arkansas and then Republican presidential hopeful Mike Huckabee borrowed from Newt Gingrich's playbook four

---

[45] See Daniel Pipes, "The Year the Arabs Discovered Palestine," *The Jerusalem Post* 13 September 2000 (https://goo.gl/eQZjA6).
[46] Fox News, "Gingrich Describes Palestinian People as Invented," *Fox News*, 10 December 2011 (goo.gl/WLwgC8).

years earlier. He told the Washington Post "there's really no such thing as the Palestinians." "The idea that they have a long history, dating back hundreds or thousands of years, is not true," Huckabee continued, citing one of the tour's speakers, Zionist Organization of America president Morton Klein.

There's hardly a news cycle that passes without "Palestine" or the "Palestinians" making headlines. In February 2016, An Israeli lawmaker claimed there was no such thing as the Palestinian people because the Arabic language lacks the consonant "P." After the President of Uganda kept calling Israel 'Palestine' during Netanyahu's visit to the country in July 2016, some Israeli radio stations reportedly cut off broadcast of the Ugandan President's speech. In March 2017, Likud MK Oren Hazan repeated that "there is no Palestinian people. And there has never been a Palestinian people." However, "there is a Palestinian moron."[47]

* * *

Conclusion. What connected the Jewish and Israeli passengers on European airlines in the 2000s to the Israeli military authorities in the 1980s? And what did my Jewish American-Israeli Sabbath hosts in Jerusalem in 2014 have to do with Ted Cruz's AIPAC supporters in 2016? Ever since states came into existence, our species has struggled with the question: who has the legitimate right to rule? This question plagues the people of Israel and Palestine today. Many of the propagandists of our story—Israelis, Jews, Ted Cruz and AIPAC enthusiasts—believe that

---

[47] Siobhán O'Grady, "The President of Uganda Kept Calling Israel 'Palestine' During Netanyahu's Visit," *Foreign Policy* 5 July 2016 (goo.gl/aVxceX); Jonathan Lis, "Israeli Lawmaker Says Palestinian Nation Doesn't Exist, Because Arabic Doesn't Have 'P' read more," *Haaretz* 10 February 2016 (goo.gl/MjNGnt); on Oren Hazan, see Bradley Burston, "Five ways Israel Will Make you Hate Israel this Week," *Haaretz* 7 March 2017 (goo.gl/kO0jje).

Jews should have the right to independence in Israel for the Jewish people. Many others, including most Palestinians, believe that the Palestinians should have such rights in Palestine for the Palestinians. These claims rest on the belief that peoples or nations have collective rights as peoples or nations. "Two states for two peoples." We've all heard that before.[48]

The problem is that although Israel and Palestine occupy the same piece of real estate, the Jews and the Palestinians are not the same people. This has led many propagandists around the world to seek to erase traces of Palestine and the Palestinians in history to bolster Israel's claims to self-determination for Jews in Israel and undermine Palestinian's claims of self-determination in Palestine. (Of course, Palestinians did the same thing to Israel and Jews, seeking to delegitimize their claims as well). That is why the history of "Palestine" and "the Palestinians" has been so toxic.

Historians were not exempt from the madness, as we saw. They joined the frontlines as soldiers in the propaganda war, eager to prove or disprove the people did or did not use the words "Palestine" and "Palestinians." Those sympathetic to the Palestinians traced their history as far back as possible—the 1880s, 1830s or 1701—while those hostile to the Palestinians claimed the Palestinians were a recent and artificial invention whose very *raison d'être* was to undermine the millennia long struggle for Jewish freedom from tyranny.

Today, most leaders around the world still think nations or peoples should have collective rights. The controversy over "Palestine" and the "Palestinians" seems likely to continue so long as both

---

[48] There is a lovely Wikipedia article called, "Lists of active separatist movements," that surveys dozens of such movements around the globe.

groups continue to believe that peoples or nations should have collective rights. But what will happen once people stop believing that nations or peoples should have collective rights to statehood?

CHAPTER TWO

The Origins of Palestine

Now that we've covered the controversy over Palestine and the Palestinians, let's go back in time to when these ideas came into existence. It is critical to go back to their origins since, had we began our story in the modern world, pre-modern world, the iron age, the Neolithic or even the Late Upper Pleistocene, we might have come away with the false impression that identities like "Palestinian" came into existence only when we started looking for them. I think a sounder approach to understanding the origins of identities like "Palestinian" requires leaving history altogether to a time before we had any socially constructed identities at all.

This approach will no doubt make most historians uncomfortable—myself included—because it means leaving behind the primary source of history: texts. But it was during the formative period of our evolutionary history, long before any texts existed, when we developed identities like "Palestinian." It was during this era of pre-history when we learned to name things, describe space with complexity, tell stories, make maps and believe in beauty. These are things that enabled us to identify with places like Palestine, call ourselves "Palestinian," and care deeply about it. The first part of this chapter explains when, why and how each of these things happened.[49]

---

[49] Yuval N Harari [*Sapiens: A Brief History of Humankind* (London: Harvill Secker, 2014), 61] agreed that the danger of dismissing 70,000 or 80,000 years of human history is that we might come to the false conclusion that our ancestors did nothing of importance.

The second part of this chapter looks at how identities like "Palestinian" evolved since we started to domesticate plants and animals, build cities, states and civilizations. Domesticating plants and animals forced us into permanent settlements. Places like Palestine scored big victories as result, since settled peoples often identify themselves and others with their respective places of settlement. Settled peoples also produced agricultural surpluses, incentivizing conquest. Conquers and governors found places like Palestine useful for conquest and governance because named places were a lot easier to conquer and govern than unnamed places. States thus played an important role in the rise and fall of places like Palestine and the identities that sprung forth from them. States also brought cities into the world, which we associated with bigger places that surrounded them. This made identities based on lands and cities very fluid, one often bleeding into the other.

The main argument of this chapter is that identities based on places—including Palestinian—have been around for tens, if not hundreds of thousands of years. Once we strip the idea of a nation down to its bare bones—an identity based on a place—it becomes clear that nations are just as old. No surprise that scholars are now finding evidence of nations whenever and wherever we became sedentary, adopted agriculture, built states and left behind records. In short, nations have been around long before we have any records attesting to their existence.

* * *

Names. Palestine is a name, and names have a long evolutionary history. If we define a name as something that enables us to distinguish between and among other members of our own species, then dogs, birds and fish can do that through facial or odor recognition. A prurient male Herring Gull, for instance, can identify a specific female he wants to mate with from 30 yards away. Although the skill probably evolved after we diverged from the Herring Gull tens of millions of years ago, it nevertheless suggests we've been fine-tuning our mastery of facial recognition for millions of years. No wonder we can remember thousands of faces over the course of a lifetime.[50]

Symbols. We may remember faces, but we forget names in an instant. That's because names are not merely about facial recognition. We only developed a talent for names in the last few million years at most, probably more like a couple hundred thousand years or even less. Names are a lot more difficult to remember than faces because they are arbitrary. We invent them out of nothing, and they rarely have anything to do with what they represent. This was very difficult to do, but it gave us tremendous flexibility with naming. (The only two other species that use names in the wild are bottlenose dolphins and spectacled parrotlets, and they do it with one another only, not other things like patches of seaweed, bays of water, or forests). Names forced us to make a leap of faith in our minds, associating arbitrary sounds with individuals, things or places. Since names are arbitrary, they are easy to forget, just like lock combinations, phone numbers and security questions. In 2016, United Airlines found the perfect solution to this conundrum: don't ask something arbitrary, ask something deep and immutable, like your favorite sea animal (see figure 3).

---

[50] On herrings, see Niko Tinbergen, *The Herring Gull's World: A Study of the Social Behavior of Birds* (New York: Basic Books, 1960), 80-81, 99-100.

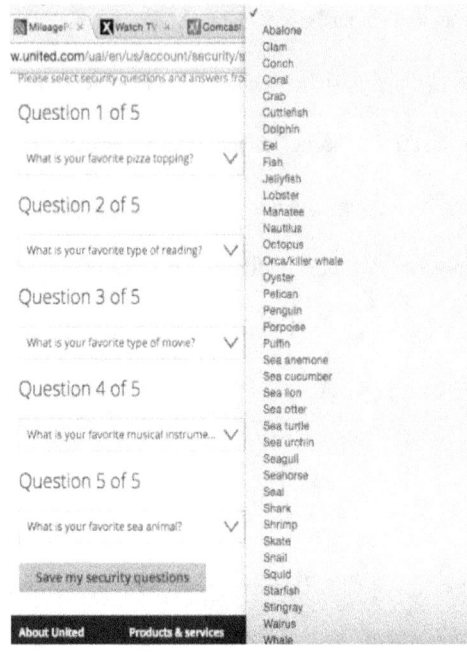

Figure 3. United Airlines Security Question: "What is your favorite sea animal?"

I am only joking, of course. I forgot what I selected as my favorite Sea Animal because it was an arbitrary choice, and arbitrary things are very difficult to remember. That's why most species, including the great apes, struggle with remembering arbitrary things. Gorillas, orangutans, chimpanzees and bonobos recognize each other not by something arbitrary like a name but by voice, size, facial features, habits and behavior. In the wild, they gesture in pairs, and respond to one another's gestures, but they don't commit to completely arbitrary symbols to refer to one another—much less places in the world. We mastered the ability to name things, and went about naming everything.[51]

---

[51] Bottlenose dolphins address their relatives with unique whistles that function as names. In one case, two dolphins had been separated for 20 years and still remembered their unique whistles for each other. See Stephanie L. King and Vincent M. Janik, "Bottlenose Dolphins can use Learned Vocal Labels to Address Each Other," *Prec Nat Acad Sci* 110 (32) (2013): 13216-13221; spectacled parrotlets also make unique calls to their siblings, mating partners and others. If two parrotlets separate in what scientists have dubbed "a divorce," the parrotlets often try to re-establish

Our talent for associating arbitrary sound with meaning turned out to be an evolutionary miracle. Once we learned to associate arbitrary symbols and ideas, we could apply the logic to all kinds of things—including places like Palestine. The symbol "Palestine" differs from dolphin and parrot naming practices and vervet monkey warning calls for predators in that "Palestine" lacks cells, membranes, proteins or ligaments. It doesn't even have a nervous system or spinal cord! Actually, Palestine has no physical manifestation of any kind. Palestine exists only in our minds, not in nature.

Some might struggle with this idea, because Palestine seems very real. But even if we ignore epistemological problems associated with its varying spellings, pronunciations, and connotations in different languages—Prst, Filastin, Pasita, PeLeSeT, Plst, Paelestina, Pleshet, Philistine, Palestine, etc.—the term has meant many things in history. To the ancient Hebrews, it referred to five cities and perhaps the areas connecting them—Gaza, Ashkelon, Ashdod, Ekron, and Gath. To the ancient Greeks, it referred to an area "from Egypt to Phoenicia"—for Herodotus, or from "Syria to Arabian Petraea"—for Ptolemy and other ill-defined areas as well. Many Muslims thought it was an area bound by Rafah and Lajjun in the north and south, and by Jaffa and Jericho in the east and west. Others thought it was merely the town of Ramla and its surroundings. Some early modern Europeans thought it referred to the coastal plain until the mountainous interior. Others thought it was defined as the whole of the Holy Land, i.e.,

---

relationships with their siblings to compensate for the social loss. They do that with names. See Ralf Wanker, Jasmin Apcin, Bert Jennerjahn, Birte Waibel, "Discrimination of Different Social Companions in Spectacled Parrotlets (Forpus Conspicillatus): Evidence for Individual Vocal Recognition," *Behavioral Ecology and Sociobiology* 43(3)(1998): 197-202; on the importance of symbols in language evolution, see Terrence W Deacon, *The Symbolic Species: The Co-evolution of Language and the Brain* (New York: W.W. Norton, 1997)

"Jerusalem and its Mountains." From the 1870s-1910s, lots of people thought Palestine extended as far north as the northern boundary of the District of Jerusalem, between Ramallah and Nablus. By the 1920s-1940s, Palestine was now believed to have extremely precise borders extending as far north as Ras al-Naqura. Today, as we learned in the previous chapter, there are small armies of people claiming it doesn't even exist. Palestine has referred to lots of different places in history—as well as nothing at all. It's a concept we completely made up.[52]

All humans name places. The Yaghan people, for instance, hunter-gatherers who inhabited the channels and islands of the southernmost part of Tierra del Fuego (Argentina-Chile), name bays or beaches stretching several kilometers in length, including *Canagush Yamana*, *Putroaya Yamana*, *Wullaia Yamana* and *Lashuf Yamana*. The Solega people of the southern Indian state of Karnataka, who subsisted as hunter-gatherers until the 1970s, "can name with ease every single mountain peak, hill, watercourse, patch of flat land, and rocky area that is visible from that settlement, as well as much smaller landscape features, such as large boulders, waterholes, cataracts, and even individual trees." The desert nomads and the camel-breeders of the eastern

---

[52] I'll deal with most of these definitions in greater depth in the next two chapters, save for the very detailed definitions we find in the 1920s-1940s. One such definition had it that Palestine was "located on the Eastern shore of the Mediterranean Sea between 30/29 width and 15/33 north, and the length is 15/34 and 40/35...Palestine is divided from the Lebanese Republic by a line extending from Ras al-Naqura to the Palestinian village of Qadas, continuing along close to the village of Labuna and Ayta al-Sha'b and Yarun (Lebanese) and Malikiya (Palestinian). Then the border continues north at al-Mutilla (Palestinian), then passes along Hunin (Palestinian) and 'Adayssa (Lebanese), then the border veers east and south until it reaches Baniyas at the border with Syria. It continues south to the Banat Ya'qub Bridge located on the Jordan river, and further south, it aligns with the Jordan River and shores of Lake Tiberias, until it turns south east until the al-Hamma station, located on the Hijazi railway line between Samakh and Dar' by the Yarmuk River. The Hula and Tiberias lakes are therefore within Palestine's borders, including the eastern coast of the Hula lake. The Yarmouk River flows into the Jordan river, which divides Palestine from Transjordan, until it reaches the Dead Sea, where upon the Dead Sea itself constitutes the border directly down the middle from north to south, and the line continues in the Araba Valley until the Gulf of Aqaba. Palestine is divided from Egypt in the south by a line extending from Rafah (Palestinian) to the Gulf of Aqaba." See Wasfi 'Anabtawi and Sa'id al-Sabbagh, *Filastin wa-al-Bilad al-'Arabiyya wa-Sa'ir al-Buldan al-Sharq al-Adna wa-Hawd al-Bahr al-Mutawassit* (Jaffa: Maktabat al-Tahir Ikhwan, 1946), 9-10; for a similar although less elaborate description, see Rafiq al-Tamimi, Wasfi 'Anabtawi and Sa'id al-Sabbagh, *Hawd al-Bahr al-Mutawassat wa-Gharbi Uruba* (Jerusalem: Matba'at Bayt al-Maqdis, 1945), 10.

Great Indian Desert name individual rock outcrops that project above the sand at 20-mile intervals and vague undefined areas of the desert, "which seem to move as the sandhills move," as one observer recalled. Americans named fifty states, thousands of counties, and hundreds of thousands of cities. Our species named places wherever we went.[53]

But for how long have we been naming places like Palestine? We already said above that other species can name predators with generic symbols and can name one another with specific symbols for specific members of their species. We combined those two abilities. We don't know of any species that can do this in the wild, but Kanzi the bonobo, trained by primatologists, learned symbols to refer to 17 specific locations in the forest, each one home to a different food. Washoe the chimpanzee, also taught American Sign Language, learned to say and understand "where shoe?" and "where we go?" and could respond with "there" and "out." Apes harness a limited ability to name space. Over the course of the past few million years, we improved our ability to name spaces by many orders of magnitude. Exactly when that happened remains a mystery.[54]

* * *

---

[53] On the Yaghan, see José Ignacio Santos, María Pereda, Débora Zurro, Myrian Álvarez, Jorge Caro, José Manuel Galán, Ivan Briz i Godino, "Effect of Resource Spatial Correlation and Hunter-Fisher-Gatherer Mobility on Social Cooperation in Tierra del Fuego," *PLoS ONE* 10(4) (2015): 3; on the Solega, see Aung Si and Samira Agnihotri, "Solega Place Names and their Ecological Significance," *Anthropological Linguistics* 56(3-4) (2014): 389-414. For the quote, see ibid, 391; on the desert nomads and camel breeders, see Sidney Burrard, "Geographical Names in Uninhabited Regions and the Controversy over the Mount Everest Map," *Empire Survey Review* 3(16)(1935): 66-71.

[54] On the 17 locations in the forest, see Sue Savage-Rumbaugh and Roger Lewin, *Kanzi: The Ape at the Brink of the Human Mind* (New York: John Wily & Sons, Inc, 1994), 140-2; see also Sue Savage-Rumbaugh, Jeannine Murphy, Rose A. Sevcik, Karen E. Brakke, Shelly L. Williams, Duane M. Rumbaugh, Elizabeth Bates, "Language Comprehension in Ape and Child," *Monographs of the Society for Research in Child Development* 58(3/4) (1993): 87; R. Allen Gardner, Thomas E. Van Cantfort and Beatrix T. Gardner, "Categorical Replies to Categorical Questions by Cross-Fostered Chimpanzees," *The American Journal of Psychology* 105(1) (1992): 27-57. Having said that, when observed in the wild, vervet monkeys cannot signal which direction a predator is coming from even though that would greatly improve their chances of survival.

Stories. Palestine is not just any random space that we named. It's orders of magnitude more complex than a location in the forest with berries. That's because we tell complex stories about it. Try explaining the following story to Koko—the most gifted gorilla ever to learn American Sign Language—about one of the 17 locations she likes going to in the forest:

> Wondrous, you are, oh *location in the forest*. Your history dazzles with marvel. What land has played the role you have played? What land has attained what you have? You are small in size, rich in chronicles, great in transformations, and numerous in innovations. Your pride is overwhelming. Your history is recorded in the holy books, *location in the forest*, your geographical position is wondrous, you have a keen mind like Asia and intellect of Africa, and your children have gone to Europe. Oh, *location in the forest*—you are the heart of the world. *Location in the forest*, you are also distinguished by your varied climate. Bananas and dates are cultivated in the Jordan Valley. The world's best oranges are cultivated in Jaffa, a pleasant summer night's breeze reaches its mountaintops, while its highest peak, Mount Hermon, sparkles year-round with snow. Oh, *location in the forest*, your lowest point, the Dead Sea, is the deepest place on planet earth. It is without parallel. *Location in the forest*, you are the site of revelation, the birthplace of Judaism and Christianity and a Holy Land for Muslims, your land brings forth milk and honey. Your ancient inhabitants—the Hittites, Canaanites, Phoenicians, Philistines, and Israelites left behind so much celebrated history.[55]

Of course, this story was not told about one of Koko's locations in the forest. It was told about Palestine, and illustrated its greatness, beauty and wonder. It was written by Jubran Matar, an Arabic speaker from Beit Jalla in the summer of 1912. To understand how we told stories like *that* about Palestine, how we poured our hopes and prayers into our stories, we first need to explain how language got so complex.

Universal Grammar. If identities based on Palestine came into existence only after we could tell complex stories about the places we inhabited, when did we start telling such complicated stories? Let's have a brief look at the most complex form of animal language known to primatologists—vervet monkey warning calls—to see how far we've come. We already

---

[55] Jubran Matar was an Arabic speaking Christian Orthodox writer from Beit Jala. I've condensed and smoothened the prose of the original article. See Jubran Matar, "Filastin," *Filastin* 31 August 1912. On his place of origin, see *Filastin* 22 May 1912.

mentioned two vervet warning calls above—*leopard* and *hawk*. In fact, vervet monkeys have ten expressions: *snakes, hawks, eagles, leopards, baboons*, as well as *other predatory mammal, unfamiliar human, dominant monkey, subordinate monkey, watch other monkey*, and *see rival troop*. These calls include adjectives like *other*, *rival* and *dominant*, and assume a basic understanding of semantics: *other predatory mammal* excludes hawks, eagles, leopards and baboons. The rudiments of language are evident in their warning calls. Basic grammar and semantics helped monkeys deal with a minor nuisance in their lives: 75% of them get eaten by predators.[56]

Listening. In order to tell such complex stories about Palestine, we had to listen. The stakes were life and death, and so a knack for listening would have proven very useful. Perhaps *leopard* evolved into *leopard there*, *leopard right* or *leopard behind*, and then something slightly more complex like *leopard behind Veronica* or *leopard left Veronica*. Those who thought *leopard right* meant *leopard left* got eaten. Those who understood survived. Early hominids who learned to communicate locations in addition to predators would have had any enormous advantage in the African Savanna food chain. That's a single example of how natural selection might have led our species to go from warning calls to basic language to complex stories about Palestine. Alternatively, complex stories about Palestine might have evolved not as a result of natural selection but rather sexual selection. Females and males looked for partners who excelled at remembering, communicating, speaking, listening and related traits—social maturity, emotional intelligence and savanna smarts. We wanted to listen to each other before sex, and so learned to

---

[56] Robert Seyfarth and Dorothy Cheney, "The Assessment by Vervet Monkeys of their own and Another Species' Alarm Calls," *Animal Behavior* 40 (1990): 754-764; on the 75% figure, see Jared Diamond, *The Third Chimpanzee: The Evolution and Future of the Human Animal* (New York: Harper Perennial, 2006), 143-7.

remember, listen, speak, and hold in our farts. Those who couldn't figure out how to communicate got diluted from the gene pool.[57]

The idea that someone who excels at memory, communication, speech or language would have a reproductive advantage is evident everywhere around us. Consider how impressed we are when a long-lost crush remembers our name, or when a musician sings a beautiful song, or a politician delivers a riveting speech or an activist ignites a roaring crowd. Think about human sexual fantasies for a moment. Language is usually involved one way or another. Even the most open-minded people today wouldn't consider marrying someone with Downs Syndrome. We crave language competence in our sexual partners.[58]

* * *

To better understand how and when we learned to tell complex stories about Palestine, and therefore identify as Palestinian, I set out to observe a group of people who mirrored the Pleistocene environment (starting about 2.5 million ears ago) in which language first evolved: ideally, a group of 15-25 individuals who greedily enjoy lots of casual and intimate interaction. The San Francisco-based offices of the tech-company, Academia.edu, seemed like a good fit. Incidentally, I was also employed at the company during the entire period of fieldwork.

---

[57] On the importance of listening, see Michael A. Arbib and James Bonaiuto, "From Grasping to Complex Imitation: Mirror Systems on the Path to Language," *Mind & Society* 7 (2008): 43–64.
[58] Incidentally, the sexual scenario is more common among species with nervous systems, ears and eyes than among species without those things, and among those species that engage in courtship behavior. Based on the great lengths we go to curate our online imagine—it's fair to say humans excel in matters of courtship. Moreover, the sexual selection theory does a better job of explaining radical adaptations (i.e. language) in one species, Homo Sapiens, but simple warning calls in closely related species sharing similar environments. Whatever the case may be, evolution by either natural or sexual selection gave us a genetic or biological predisposition for language. See Geoffrey Miller, *The Mating Mind: How Sexual Choice Shaped the Evolution of Human Nature* (New York: Anchor Books, 2011), 8.

At Academia.edu, language evolved fastest in the foosball room. It therefore became necessary to play as much foosball as possible, something I swear I did not know before I began my fieldwork. But the laborious anthropological fieldwork paid off, since Academia.edu foosball players invented language ex nihilo in the foosball room. They accepted, rejected, accumulated and liberally used the arbitrary inputs of other players, including new verbs, nouns, phrases and adjectives, often co-opting pre-existing words when creating new ones. Phrases included *goal seekers, roonies, blood diamonds, full diamonds, back row billies, raptors, we got goosed, midflips, high quality games, black advantage,* and *it's tough at the top*. The dialect got so complex that a Github wiki page was compiled to acclimate new players to their adopted company's dialect (a small sampling):

> *Dreamliner* Hitting the ball directly into the opposing team's goal form the defensive handles at slow speed and a slight angle [...]
>
> *Great-Grandma* An extra slow push shot with the inner-most man of the 3 man handle
>
> *Goal-seeker* A serve involving a gratuitous amount of back- and side-spin, deflected by the serving team's middle men in an attempt to spin directly into the goal [...]
>
> *Goose* A loss of a point, game or match due to high-quality circumstances. If you lose, you can log your loss with raibo, we got goosed.

Having discovered the wiki, I realized I was an impoverished speaker of the language, being unfamiliar with *honk honks* [not mentioned above]. Had *honk honks* meant leopard—and had the 15 Academia.edu foosball players been a pack of Pleistocene homo habilis creatures a million years ago, I would have probably made for a tasty leopard dinner.

Aside from language, foosball players also proved adept at related behaviors like believing in fiction and developing arbitrary conventions, things that accompanied the invention of language during the Pleistocene (2,588,000 to 11,700 years ago). Players came to conclusions about who was the best player (a consensus was often not forthcoming), which pairs played best together, and which side of the table had an unfair advantage. They accepted arbitrary conventions as dogma, such as position switches each point in game two and high fives after matches regardless of who won—immutable holy grails of sorts. Academia foosball players invented language ex nihilo, believed in fictions and developed arbitrary conventions. To do this, they relied on creativity, proximity, memory, repeated interactions and cooperation—and they did it all totally instinctively. No one told them to make up words or stories about the greatest foosball shot in Academia history. They did it because of human nature. If language comes to our species instinctively, then it is almost certainly as old as the first modern humans who departed Africa about 100,000 years ago.

* * *

Neanderthals. So language is probably at least 100,000 years old, but it might be much older. A brief glance at the evolutionary history of our Neanderthal cousins may offer some preliminary clues as to just how old language might be. Neanderthals diverged from Homo Sapiens about a half million years ago when they departed Africa and settled in southern Europe. Then, about 40 thousand years ago when Homo Sapiens reached Europe, something awkward happened to the Neanderthal layers in the archeological record. They disappeared. Despite their hundreds of thousands of years head start adapting to Europe's harsh climate and conditions, Homo Sapiens prevailed, and Neanderthals went extinct.

The traditional explanation was that humans had already developed complex language and outsmarted the Neanderthals to extinction—hence language must be no older than our split from them some five hundred thousand years ago. To support this hypothesis, archeologists pointed to the abundance of sophisticated symbolic objects dating to the period only after Neanderthals were gone—musical instruments, cave paintings and shell necklaces, things that were traditionally much harder to find at Neanderthal sites. The traditional view was that art, face paint and music suggested we had language—and that their absence in the Neanderthal archeological layers suggested they lacked it.

Two things have happened in parallel that have changed this view. First, new archeological discoveries are suggesting Neanderthals were more sophisticated than previously thought. A recent find, for instance, shows they pierced holes in sea shells presumably to wear as ornaments. They engraved geometric patterns on rocks that could be construed to mean just about anything symbolic (see figure 4).

Figure 4. Neanderthal Geometric Pattern.

They may have used manganese dioxide, a black mineral, as crayons. They may have also cut wing bones off birds, potentially to use their feathers for decoration. They may have put iron ore, a red mineral often used as pigment, on sea shells. Neanderthals also cared for their sick and wounded, which is rare in the animal kingdom. Evidence is mounting that Neanderthals probably engaged in symbolic and emotionally complex behavior. [59]

Neanderthals also made complex tools, suggesting they could transmit information. In other words, they could communicate. They domesticated fire, made razor sharp flint tools and knives, butchered meat, scraped and stretched hide, and made leather and clothes. Neanderthals also made an adhesive from birch bark, the earliest known synthetic chemical in homo history. They used it to glue stone blades to wooden shafts. Scientists tried to reproduce it only using tools available to Neanderthals, and failed. After repeated lab experiments, scientists today (circa the 21st century) figured out that the bark needs to be heated to 750 degrees Fahrenheit in a closed chamber, such as a goose egg, to prevent the bark from igniting. So the Neanderthals must have placed the bark in something like a goose egg, then placed another closed chamber below it to catch the adhesive when it melts. Then, they sealed the two containers with mud to prevent the bark from igniting. They surrounded the sealed goose ends with hot coals, waited for the temperature to reach 750 degrees, and awaited their adhesive in the goose egg catch. It's difficult to imagine that Neanderthals learned these skills in isolation over the course of their own lifetime, and died without passing any information along to their offspring. If true that a single Neanderthal developed these sophisticated technologies in complete isolation, then he or she

---

[59] Joaquín Rodríguez-Vidala, Francesco d'Erricob and Francisco Giles Pacheco, et. al., "A Rock Engraving Made by Neanderthals in Gibraltar," *Proceedings of the National Academy of Sciences* 111(37) (2014): 13301-13306.

must have been on some seriously dank ganja, which is unlikely because Europe was experiencing an ice age at that time and marijuana thrives in tropical and temperate climates.[60]

The second development challenging the traditional view of Neanderthals is genetic evidence. In the past couple of decades, scientists have mapped out the entire human and Neanderthal genome, and determined that modern humans have 1-4% Neanderthal DNA! That means Homo Sapiens interbred with Neanderthals and produced fertile offspring. It seems plausible, therefore, that Neanderthals were capable of learning language, if indeed they lacked it. And if they were capable of learning language, Homo Sapiens may not have evolved all that much cognitively or anatomically during those 500,000 years of separation. If so, that would place the origins of language, and therefore stories about places like Palestine and identities like the Palestinians, more than a half million years ago![61]

* * *

---

[60] On caring for their young, see Thomas Wynn and Frederick L Coolidge, *How to Think like a Neandertal* (New York: Oxford University Press, 2012), 16-17; PBS, "Decoding Neanderthals," youtube.com (goo.gl/DFLn4x), 2013; on the adhesive, see "Neanderthal Apocalypse Did Campi Flegrei kill them off 2015" youtube.com, 22 May 2017 (https://goo.gl/UjbTyc) (~33:00 minutes); on the evidence linking use of cannabis with creativity, see Gráinne Schafera, Amanda Feildingb, Celia J.A. Morgana, et. al., "Cannabis Increased Verbal Fluency in Low Creatives to the Same Level as that of High Creatives," *Consciousness and Cognition* 21(1) (2012): 292–298.

[61] Wynn and Coolidge, *How to Think like a Neandertal*, 8. Another important genetic finding was that Neanderthals have the main human variant of the FOXP2 gene rather than one of the less common variants that can causes speech impediment and learning disabilities; Of course, most of our DNA does not come from Neanderthals, though. It comes from a few thousand Homo Sapiens who lived in Africa about a 100,000 years ago. The discovery that all modern humans descended from a small number of individuals in Africa has implications for anyone trying to understand the origins of language and complex stories about Palestine. It forces us to ask how we overwhelmed and out populated Denisovans in Asia, Neanderthals in Europe and Homo Heidelbergensis in Afro Euroasia? Judging by chimpanzee behavior as well as known cases of human population encounters, "overwhelm" and "out populate" may be euphemistic descriptions of what happened. (See, for instance, John C. Mitani, David P. Watts and Sylvia J. Amsler, "Lethal Intergroup Aggression Leads to Territorial Expansion in Wild Chimpanzees," *Current Biology* 20(12) (2010): 507-8). Some evidence suggests that early hominids frequently died violent deaths also. We don't know what gave us an evolutionary advantage that drove our hominid competitors to extinction.

Maps. Palestine is not just a place we named and told stories about. We also have an image of Palestine in our minds. This is because we made maps of it to help us visualize what our eyes cannot see. Maps make Palestine seem very real to us, which is important if we are going to identify with it. If we define maps broadly to include mental maps, then the ability evolved tens of millions of years ago. Consider that rats, slightly removed from us in evolutionary time, spent a lot of their history burrowing and navigating underground tunnels, and so scientists suspected they might help us understand the origins of mental maps. Their suspicions proved accurate. In a classic experiment, rats played around in Y-shaped mazes with food at one end and water the other. The rats were separated from the mazes, half made thirsty, the other half hungry. They were placed back in the mazes, and the thirsty rats went straight for the water, the hungry rats the food. This led more scientists to do more experiments, and it turns out that rats can navigate highly complex mazes and find the fastest way out without trial and error.[62]

Mental maps were an evolutionary adaptation among land mammals who hunted or borrowed. According to the natural selection scenario, the ability to make mental maps proved useful for finding water, food, shelter, prey and avoiding predators or rivals. According to the sexual selection scenario, the ability to make mental maps improved our chances of reproductive success. After all, what's sexier than roaming through the African Savannah with Tarzan two million years ago, who peers into the abyss of grass shrubs and says: turn left!

---

[62] The classical study on the topic is Edward C. Tolman, "Cognitive Maps in Rats and Men," *The Psychological Review* 55(4) (1948): 189-208; there is no scientific consensus on the topic, though. Andrew Bennet ["Do Animals Have Cognitive Maps," *The Journal of Experimental Biology* 199 (1996): 219–224] has argued no animal has been conclusively shown to develop a powerful memory of landmarks which allows novel short-cutting to occur, although concedes that animals can hold representations of space in their minds.

We were making mental maps for tens of millions of years. At some point, we learned to etch them as lines in the sand or commit them to fibrous materials. In the early 1900s, the Tuareg of the Sahara Desert constructed elaborate relief models in the sand of sifs, dunes, gravel flats and plateaus along the caravan routes in the desert. Potentially, their ancestors had been doing that for tens of thousands of years. Similarly, in the 1920s, Marshall Islanders made maps of their archipelago with shells bound to palm leaf midribs. Their ancestors might have doing that for tens of thousands of years as well.[63]

Maps first appeared in the fossil record about 20,000 years ago. Archeologists found a slab with seven semicircular motifs in Basque country Spain. They claimed hunter-gathers made huts in similar shapes and metrics, with "semicircular motifs," including the Kalahari Bushmen and Australian aborigines. It may have been a stretch to conclude that the semicircles etched into stone rock constituted a map, but claiming something is the world's oldest known map is how you get famous in the booming field of late Pleistocene rock art. For now, it's the oldest thing anyone has ever claimed was a map.[64]

* * *

Beauty. Beauty plays such a critical role in the stories we tell about Palestine and the maps we make of it that it's worth trying to understand how it came into existence also. Why have people

---

[63] On the Tuareg, see W. Dröber, "Kartographie Bei den Naturvölkern," *Deutsche Geographische Blatter* XXVII (1904): 29-46; on the Marshall Islanders, see H. Lyons, "The Sailing Charts of Marshall Islanders," *Geographical Review* LXXII (1928): 325-328.

[64] Marcos García-Diez and Manuel Vaquero, "Looking at the Camp: Paleolithic Depiction of a Hunter-Gatherer Campsite," *PLoS One* (2 December 2015).

distinguished Palestine by its virtuous wonders and proclaimed its grandeur and fertility? Why do we tantalize, paint, celebrate, design, fine-tune, commemorate and beautify? Scholars disagree over whether beauty is culturally relative or whether some things are universally beautiful. The traditional view had long been that "beauty is in the eye of the beholder," that it cannot be found in nature. It exists because we imagine it into existence. We imagine it because we can arbitrarily transform something ordinary into something special. This view has come under fire in recent decades as evidence mounts that all humans are born with beauty detectors. In one study, adults were asked to rate the beauty of hundreds of faces. 3-6-month-old babies were shown the same faces, and stared much longer at the faces adults found beautiful. Babies prefer looking at symmetry to asymmetry, touching soft to rough surfaces and listening to harmonious rather than dissonant music. These findings suggest beauty is not entirely a figment of our imagination.[65]

Archeologists have found thousands of thin, teardrop-shaped symmetrical stone blades or hand-ax tools across Asia, Europe and Africa from the Pleistocene (2,588,000 to 11,700 years ago). Why was everyone around the world making similarly symmetrical blades? There might have been something attractive about that shape, and perhaps also the hand ax artists who could make them. Beautiful blades might have marked their creators as fit, crafty and intelligent. Given their abundance in the archeological record, we might have competed over who made the best ones. As the old pick up line goes, "Would you like to swing by my cave so I can show you my collection of hand axes?" 1.4-million-year-old hand axes might have been the earliest form of

---

[65] For a defense of the beauty is culturally relative position, see Leon Botstein, "Art Now (Aesthetics Across Music, Painting, Architecture, Movies, and More." Youtube.com 10 October 2012 (https://goo.gl/jqbFqm); then see Nancy Etcoff, *Survival of the Prettiest: The Science of Beauty* (New York: Anchor Books, 1999), 31-2.

art. That's a fancy theory, admittedly, but such is how you get famous as an archeologist, apart from telling fantastic cavemen jokes—and calling semicircles "maps." These points suggest that we've been beautifying and adorning for millions of years. [66]

There are other reasons to believe our sense for beauty is very old. We tend to describe landscapes as beautiful that include open spaces, low grasslands, animal and bird life, water, a path, riverbanks, shorelines or diverse greenery interspersed with copses of trees that fork near the ground—i.e. the African savannah landscape we roamed for millions of years before leaving that continent to conquer the globe about 100,000 years ago.[67]

* * *

Identity. Palestine is a name, a symbol, and a place we tell stories about, make maps of and mark as special. But we also identify with Palestine, or develop an identity based on it. The underlying question of this dissertation is, why do we do that?

Family and Pack. Let's take a brief tour of the evolutionary history of our identities to understand why people did that. Our earliest social identities as a species revolved around family and pack. Chimps know their brothers from their cousins, and their cousins from members of other packs, and behave accordingly. Within their packs, vervet monkeys know who is related to whom, and treat their mothers, siblings and maternal grandmothers differently. When a vervet

---

[66] Denis Dutton, "A Darwinian Theory of Beauty," TED, youtube.com, 16 November 2010 (goo.gl/5bCocf)
[67] ibid.

monkey infant calls for help, other mothers in the pack turn to *that* vervet's mother to see how she reacts. Our family, extended family and pack identities have a long evolutionary history.[68]

Status. Status was one of our earliest identities as well. Vervet monkeys respond differently to dominant and subordinate members of their pack, as noted above. They even have symbols, or words, for *dominant* and *subordinate* in the wild. Similarly, male chimps zealously compete over status, and are even willing to kill their rivals if necessary. Status also has a long evolutionary history.

Culture. Culture, or arbitrary convention, or symbolic behavior, or what archeologists tend to call "behavioral modernity," by contrast, has a relatively short history. Culture might be 100,000 years old, or perhaps a few hundred thousand years old. Archeologists believe that artifacts such as art, jewelry, paint, sculptures and engravings suggest our species was anatomically modern, that we were cognitively the same as we are today. The earliest evidence for behavioral modernity, arbitrary convention or culture came in large quantities of ochre found about 100,000 years ago in caves known to have been inhabited by Homo Sapiens in South Africa. (Ochre has no demonstrated purpose other than as a decorative red dye). The first irrefutable evidence of culture, though, dates to about 82,000 years ago, when Homo Sapiens made a shell necklace in Morocco. About 70,000 years ago, decorative beads were found at a range of sites in Israel, Algeria and South Africa. We sculpted a lion's head onto a human body on an ivory mammoth tusk in Germany about 40,000 years ago—an even clearer indication that its creators were anatomically the same as we are today. We made an ivory flute, the world's oldest known

---

[68] Diamond, *The Third Chimpanzee*, 144.

musical instrument, also about 40,000 years ago. The cavemen who crafted it knew how far apart to carve the holes, how wide to make their circumferences and how narrow to make the pipe. It probably took about 100 hours to make, not including the time it took to figure out how to make it or play it. About 30,000 years ago, we placed 5,000 precious ivory beads along with 250 fox teeth in graves we dug for a twelve-year-old boy and ten-year-old girl. About 15,000-20,000 years ago, we painted murals of bird heads on human bodies in caves.[69]

Arbitrary behavior or culture depended on our belief in symbols. Just like we used words, grammar, morphology and syntax as symbols to communicate, we used body paint, necklaces and art as symbols too. With these symbols, we invented a wide range of beliefs, identities, ideologies, cultures and religions. Culture is one of our greatest assets as species, and one our most destructive ones too.[70]

Culture evolved out of the same process that all our other functions and faculties evolved out of: natural and sexual selection. Song, a classic example of an arbitrary human behavior or form of culture, has been found to increase the rate at which we form bonds of solidarity with strangers. Anyone who has ever listened to Lady Gaga's *Just Dance* on repeat, for instance, knows the importance of vocal talent to reproductive success. Religion, another example of culture or

---

[69] On the shell necklace, see Abdeljalil Bouzouggar et al., "82,000-year-old shell beads from North Africa and Implications for the Origins of Modern Human Behavior," *Proceedings of the National Academy of Sciences* 104(24)(2007): 9964-9969; on the beads, see Marian Vanhaeren, Francesco d'Errico, Karen L. van Niekerk, et. al., "Thinking Strings: Additional Evidence for Personal Ornament use in the Middle Stone Age at Blombos Cave, South Africa," *Journal of Human Evolution* 64 (2013): 500-517; see also Sish Advexon, "Great Human Odyssey - Documentary 2016," youtube.com 3 November 2016 (25:37) (goo.gl/W1YWYN); on the lionman and ivory flute, see ibid (57:12); on human birds, fox teeth and ivory beads see Yuval N. Harari, *Sapiens: A Brief History of Humankind* (London: Harvill Secker, 2014), 56-8.
[70] Stewart Guthrie, Joseph Agassi, Karin R Andriolo, et. al., "A Cognitive Theory of Religion" [and Comments and Reply], *Current Anthropology* 21(2) (1980): 181-203.

arbitrary behavior, has well-documented health benefits. Culture binds us closer together, and strong social bonds are one of the key factors keeping us alive and healthy, as the Harvard Adult Development Study has proven quite conclusively. Culture improved our chances of survival. No wonder it's universal.[71]

Tribes and Peoples. We roamed planet earth in packs of 15-20 at first, then as large as 150 as we improved our ability to cooperate in larger numbers. But eventually, owing to our ability to cooperate with people we do not know personally, we formed groups of many thousands, even tens or hundreds of thousands. Exactly when we stop calling such groups tribes and start calling them clans, ethnicities, peoples or nations seems somewhat arbitrary to me, but these variously small-ish to large-ish groups dominated planet earth for tens of thousands of years from the time we spread out of Africa into Europe, Asia and Australia and then North and South America.[72]

These groups thrived nearly everywhere until recently. The Amorite pastoralists of 18-19th century BC, for instance, consisted of 3 major tribal conferences in Mari, 10 in Hanean, 5

---

[71] See the Harvard Second Generation Study https://goo.gl/Uz3CEC. Researchers surveyed 148 studies on the topic and concluded that participants with stronger social relationships had an increased likelihood of survival. See Julianne Holt-Lunstad, Timothy B. Smith, J. Bradley Layton, "Social Relationships and Mortality Risk: A Meta-analytic," *PLOS Medicine* 27 July 2010; the most authoritative source on the research findings that link longevity and healthy living with religion is Harold G. Koenig, Dana E. King, and Verna Benner Carson (eds.), *Handbook of Religion and Health*, 2nd ed. (New York: Oxford University Press, 2012); see also Harold G. Koenig and Saad Al Shohaib, *Health and Well-being in Islamic Societies: Background, Research, and Applications* (Cham Switzerland: Springer, 2014); Jeff Levin and Michelle Prince, *Judaism and Health* (Woodstock, VT: Jewish Lights, 2013); Jeff Levin and Michele F. Prince, "Judaism and Health: Reflections on an Emerging," *Journal of Religious Health* 50 (2011): 765–777; for more on religion's evolutionary advantages, see David Sloan Wilson, *Does Altruism Exist?: Culture, Genes, and the Welfare of Others* (New Haven: Yale University Press; West Conshohocken, PA: Templeton Press, 2014); on song, see Eiluned Pearce, Jacques Launay, Robin I. M. Dunbar, "The Ice-Breaker Effect: Singing Mediates Fast Social Bonding," *Royal Society Open Science* 2(2015): 1-9.

[72] Most languages have a range of terms to describe these kinds of groups. Arabic, for example, uses the terms *milla, umma, ta'ifa, qabila, sha'b, qawm, 'irq*. For a nice survey of their usage in Arabic, see Ami Ayalon, *Language and Change in the Arab Middle East: The Evolution of Modern Political Discourse* (New York: Oxford University Press, 1987).

Benjaminites and 3 Suteas; Caesar mentioned some 100 Celtic tribes in Gaul when he conquered it; there were at least 40 tribes in Britain before it was conquered by Rome in the first century AD; Tacitus mentioned some 50 tribes in his *Germania*; Ptolemy identified 69 tribes; Herodotus and other Greek writers mentioned between 50-100 Thracian tribes in today's Bulgaria; European settlers encountered some 27 tribal confederations on the Great Plains of North America; they found some 40 tribes in New Zealand when they conquered it. Some 25 tribes made up the Dinka in South Sudan, 20 tribes the Logoli and Vugusu Bantu of western Kenya. Tribes were everywhere. When they got too large, or when someone got power hungry, or when war broke out, or when resources grew scarce, they divided, subdivided, relocated or were slaughtered *en masse*.[73]

Tribes and their larger outgrowths varied in size, nature, composition and cohesion. They could combine arbitrary behaviors such as dietary restrictions, musical tastes, dance styles and body mutilation with a perception of shared lineage, heritage or origin. They could be based on language, race, religion, leader or place of birth. These groups were often as much obsessed with how they differed from other groups as they were about what made them unique.[74]

They defined themselves inconsistently over time depending on who was doing the defining. The Arabs, for example, evolved to mean dozens of different things in the past millennium: a group of people sharing a language, history, common origin, or parent who could speak the language.

---

[73] Azar Gat, *Nations: The Long History and Deep Roots of Political Ethnicity and Nationalism* (Cambridge: Cambridge University Press, 2013), 45-7; Kristian Kristiansen, *Europe Before History* (Cambridge: Cambridge University Press), 193-195.
[74] On their obsession with boundaries, see Fredrik Barth, *Ethnic Groups and Boundaries: The Social Organization of Cultural Differences* (Boston: Little, Brown, 1969).

Arab could refer to a descendant of an Arab tribesman on the father's side only, a Muslim, an Arabic speaker, an Arabic speaker loyal to Caliph, or a nomadic or semi-nomadic Arabic speaker generally known today as Bedouin. This is one of the most defining characteristics of tribes, clans, peoples, ethnicities and nations in history. They are defined arbitrarily and change a great deal over time.[75]

This is why so many writers have gotten famous insisting our identities were imagined, invented and constructed. W.E.B. Du Bois famously argued that the constructed differences between races

---

[75] In the 7th-8th centuries, the term Arab most commonly referred to a descendant of an Arab tribesman on the father's side. Some of those who opposed Arab rule in Khurasan, though, used in to mean "a bigoted member of the Umayyad establishment who ascribed religious and political significance to his descent." By the Abbasid period, Arab could mean anyone "who professed Islam, spoke Arabic (well or badly) and saw himself as a member of the polity ruled by the caliph." See Michael Cooperson, ""Arabs" and "Iranians": The Uses of Ethnicity in the Early Abbasid Period," pp.364-387 in *Islamic Cultures, Islamic Contexts: Essays in Honor of Professor Patricia Crone* Asad Q. Ahmed, Behnam Sadeghi, Robert G. Hoyland, Adam Silverstein (eds.) (Leiden, Brill: 2015), 365; see also Patricia Crone, *The Nativist Prophets of early Islamic Iran: Rural Revolt and Local Zoroastrianism* (New York: Cambridge University Press, 2012), 273;
Haim Gerber ["The Limits of Constructedness: Memory and Nationalism in the Arab Middle East," *Nations and Nationalism* 10(3) (2004): 259] suggested that Ibn Khaldun (d.1406) used the term Arab "in the proto-national sense, in addition to using it to refer to Arabs of the desert"; Steve Tamari ["Arab National Consciousness in Seventeenth and Eighteenth-Century Syria," pp. 309-321 in *Syria and Bilad al-Sham under Ottoman Rule: Essays in honour of Abdul-Karim Rafeq*, Peter Sluglett; Stefan Weber (eds). (Leiden: Brill, 2010), 312] claimed that "members of the Arab 'ulama of the Empire were conscious and proud of their identity as Arabs." He further specifies that this Arab identity included a "presumption of spiritual chosen-ness; myth of common origin; and an innate capacity to understand Arabic, the language of God."; Abdul-Karim Rafeq ["Social Groups, Identity and Loyalty and Historical Writing in Ottoman and post-Ottoman Syria," pp. 79-93 in *Mondes Contemporains: Les Arabes Et L'Histoire Créatrice* Dominique Chevallier (ed.) et al (Paris: Presses de l'Université de Paris-Sorbonne, 1995), 80] argued that people who wrote in Arabic from the 16th through the 19th century "identified their own people as *Awlad al-'Arab* or *Abna' al-'Arab* [children of the Arabs], a term which the Ottoman state also used in the official documents for its urban Arab subjects." He also wrote that "Egyptian chroniclers referred to urban Egyptians as *Awlad al-'Arab* while what we called Bedouin today were referred to by local and Ottoman sources alike as *'Arab, A'rab* and *'Urban*"; Hananiyya al-Munayyir (d.1823) [*al-Durr al-Marsuf fi Tarikh al-Shuf* (n.p.: Dar al-Ra'id al-Lubnani, 1984), 23] believed that the term Arab referred to only nomadic Arabic speakers of the desert; Rifa'a Rafi' Tahtawi (d.1873) [*Kitab al-Ta'ribat al-Shafiyya li-Murid al-Jughrafiya* (Bulaq: Dar al-Tiba'a al-Khidyawiyya, 1838), 150] differentiated between nomadic Arabs of the wilderness and Arabs who tilled the soil; By the early 20th century, as race science grew in popularity, some folks like Negib Azoury explicitly excluded Egyptians from "the Arab race" because they were apparently of African Berber origin. See Adeed Dawisha, *Arab Nationalism in the Twentieth Century: From Triumph to Despair* (Princeton: Princeton University Press, 2016), 25; As late as 1935, folks known as Bedouins today reportedly still used the term Arab to denote only themselves. See Mikha'el Asaf, *Toldot Ha-Shilton Ha-'Aravi Be-Erets Yisrael* (Tel Aviv: Dvar, 1934/5), 279, note 24; The Greek Orthodox Patriarch of Jerusalem liked to call its Arab laity Arabic speakers rather than Arabs to emphasize that they were ethnically or originally Greek. See Jacob William Albert Young, *The Orthodox Patriarch of Jerusalem* (London: H. Milford, Oxford University Press, 1926), 25.

"infinitely transcended" the physical differences between them. Frederik Barth explained that ethnicity is primarily about differences "believed" to exist between groups. Benedict Anderson famously claimed nations were "imagined communities"; Shlomo Sand argued the Jewish people were an invention; Wilfred Cantwell Smith suggested religion was also a modern human invention. Yuval Harari claimed our ability to imagine in the first place is what led to all our other imagined identities. You don't need to be an academic to know that race is a social construct, nations are imagined communities or religion was a human invention.[76]

The genre of "invention" literature is almost becoming a caricature of itself. Walk into a bookstore in San Francisco and you'll find books like David Wootton's *The Invention of Science*, Andrea Wulf's *The Invention of Nature*, Jessica Helfand's *The Invention of Desire* and Glenn Adamson's *The Invention of Craft*. These books were written for broader audiences. Academics go much further: there is Anis Bawarshi's *The Invention of the Writer*, Judith Veronica Field's *The Invention of Infinity*, James Dougal Fleming's *The Invention of Discovery*, Simon Goldhill's *The Invention of Prose* and, to be sure, Thomas Römer's *The Invention of God*. I got lucky that no one had already claimed Palestine was an invention. Pro-tip: if someone has already snatched up your invention, re-invent it, as in, Timothy Mitchell's "The Invention and Reinvention of the Egyptian Peasant," or Elizabeth Shove and Mika Pantzar's "the Invention and Reinvention of Nordic Walking," or Matti Goksøyr's "The Invention and Reinvention of Norwegian Polar Skiing."[77]

---

[76] See W. E. B. Du Bois, "The Conservation of Races" (American Negro Academy, 1897); Barth, *Ethnic Groups and Boundaries*; Shlomo Sand, *The Invention of the Jewish People* (London: Verso, 2010); Wilfred Cantwell Smith, *The Meaning and End of Religion: A New Approach to the Religious Traditions of Mankind* (New York: New American Library, 1965); Benedict Anderson, *Imagined Communities: Reflections on the Origins and Spread of Nationalism* (London: Verso, 1991); Harari, *Sapiens: A Brief History of Humankind*.

[77] Anis S Bawarshi, *Genre and the Invention of the Writer: Reconsidering the Place of Invention in Composition* (Logan: Utah State University Press, 2003); Judith Veronica Field, *The Invention of Infinity: Mathematics and Art in*

In short, we first evolved to identify with our families, packs, and statuses, and we did that long before we were humans. Later, we developed identities dependent on learned symbols, complex language, sophisticated social relations, abstract thought and arbitrary convention—i.e. things like religions, tribes, peoples, clans, ethnicities or nations.

* * *

Places. Now let's zoom in on identities based not on family, status, tribe or culture, but on places such as Palestine. You might believe that a Palestinian identity isn't just about Palestine—since it implies something about a person's religion (i.e. Christian or Muslim), ethnicity (i.e. Arab) and culture (hummus and tahini). Those things might be true today, but a Palestinian identity has not always implied Arab, Christian or Muslim in the past, as we discovered in the previous chapter, and might not in the future. What makes a Palestinian identity different than some of the other identities discussed above is that "Palestinian" is an identity based on Palestine, a place, rather than an arbitrary culture, religion, behavior, song or dance.

Identities of this sort are very old, probably tens of thousands of years. Before we domesticated crops, we settled down along the seasonal migration routes of fish, birds and large animals, as well as in wetlands. The sources of food came to us, not the other way around. These settled

---

the Renaissance (Oxford [u.a.]: Oxford University Press, 1997); James Dougal Fleming (ed.) *The Invention of Discovery, 1500-1700* (Abingdon, Oxon: Routledge, 2016); Simon Goldhill, *The Invention of Prose* (Oxford: Oxford University Press, 2002); Anthony M Platt and Miroslava Chavez-Garcia, *The Child Savers: The Invention of Delinquency* (New Brunswick, N.J. : Rutgers University Press, 2009); Thomas Römer, *The Invention of God* (Cambridge, Massachusetts: Harvard University Press, 2015); Glenn Adamson, *The Invention of Craft* (Oxford: Berg, 2013); on the essay, see Timothy Mitchell, *Rule of Experts: Egypt, Techno-Politics, Modernity* (Berkeley, CA: The University of California Press, 2002).

peoples probably had identities similar enough to "Palestinian." The Yaghan people, hunter-gatherers who inhabited the channels and islands of the southernmost part of Tierra del Fuego (Argentina-Chile), called themselves *Yahgashagalumoala*, meaning "people from mountain valley channel." The Awabakal, similarly a hunter-gatherer people who eat lots of fish and who inhabit the Mid North Coast region of New South Wales, Australia, use the same word to describe themselves and Lake Macquarie, meaning flat or plain surface. Since both groups fished, they built more permanent dwelling places, and thus were greatly invested in their places of subsistence, even deriving their own self-appellations from it. I'd bet similar groups of hunter gatherers tens of thousands of years earlier also had identities similar to "the Palestinians."[78]

Since Palestine exists in our minds, not in reality, the identities that developed around it were also subject to arbitrary definition and evolution over time. In the 10th century, at least one Arabic speaker from Jerusalem used the term Palestinian to refer to himself, as we shall discover in the next chapter. Other Muslims described hadith transmitters as "Palestinian," although they never used the term in its collective (i.e. "the Palestinians.") In 19th century Europe, Palestinian usually referred to someone who lived during the times of Jesus. But by the 1870s, some Americans, British and Germans started using it in new ways: to refer to the land's modern Arabic speakers, or to mean a "Jew, Syrian or Arab" from Palestine, in one case. Then, beginning in roughly 1898, Arabic speaking Muslims and Christians used it to refer only to themselves, although some thought it could include Jews. From the 1920s onwards, British,

---

[78] E. Lucas Bridges, *Uttermost Part of the Earth: A History of Tierra del Fuego and the Fuegians* (London: Hodder & Stoughton, 1949), 62; for more on the Awabakal, see Lancelot Edward Threlkeld, *An Australian Grammar: Comprehending the Principles and Natural Rules of the Language as Spoken by the Aborigines in the Vicinity of Hunter's River, Lake MacQuarie, &c. New South Wales* (Sydney: Printed by Stephens and Stokes, 1834). On sedentary life before agriculture, see James C. Scott, *Against the Grain: A Deep History of the Earliest Sates* (New Haven: Yale University Press, 2017), 10, 47-57.

Zionists and even Arabs used it to refer to all subjects of the British Mandatory Government of Palestine. In the 1930s, the Greek Orthodox Patriarch of Jerusalem, and the Fraternity of monks who controlled it (all Greek speakers) were embroiled in a struggle over the Church with their own Arab congregants—and to assert their legitimacy, the Greek speaking Orthodox clergy *also* insisted they were Palestinian. The term also retained its meaning to refer to people who lived in Palestine during the times of Jesus. At least one Muslim Arab writer during the 1940s also used the term to refer to any Muslim in any period of history. The term Palestinian meant a range of different things over the years.[79]

Today, a Palestinian can mean an American kid who proclaims him or herself an atheist and does not speak a single word of Arabic—so long as a parent or even grandparent defined him or herself a Palestinian. In practice, if you say you are Palestinian, most everyone will accept it at

---

[79] James Finn, the 19th century British consul in Jerusalem, used the word Palestinian to refer to the land's modern inhabitants in his 1870 memoir, complaining that the Ottoman governor of Jerusalem during the Crimean War (1853-1856), Muhammad Hafiz, was too old and ill prepared to govern and was "unaccustomed to the rough manners of the Palestinians." See James Finn, *Stirring times, or, Records from Jerusalem Consular Chronicles of 1853 to 1856* (London: C. Kegan Paul, 1878), 248. Finn (ibid, 414) also added that a certain 'Akeeli Aga from the Galilee, who had accompanied the 1848 American Scientific Expedition to the Dead Sea, was "originally an Arab of Algiers, or some adjacent country, who had gathered to himself a band of rievers of African origin whom the Palestinians declared to be Indians." Ludwig Schneller [*Kennst du das Land?: Bilder aus dem Gelobten Lande zur Erklärung der Heiligen Schrift* (Leipzig: 1899 [1889])] wrote a book about Palestine's people, customs, food, clothes, weddings, music, holidays, tribes and gender roles, frequently compared the modern inhabitants of Palestine to their Biblical predecessors. "The olive tree plays a major role in the lives of the Palestinians," he noted in one instance, using the German word, *Palästinenser*. While the main meal of the day in the West was lunch, "the Palestinians" preferred to feast in the evening, owning to the heat of the midday (Ibid, 107); for further examples, see ibid, 127, 156; James Wells [*Travel-pictures from Palestine* (New York: Dodd, 1896), 148] was told on his travels to Palestine that the striped cloaks worn by the local peasants could be seamless, much as they were during Biblical times. "If such a coat fell into the hands of a company of modern Palestinians," Wells noted, "they would probably 'cast lots for it'; for as you may see in every market-place, they are inveterate gamblers."; Adela E. Orpen [*The Chronicles of the Sid: Or, the Life and Travels of Adelia Gates* (New York: Fleming H. Revell Co, 1897), 301-2] traveled from New York to Nablus in 1897, writing that "I was too much interested in the things that marked the approach to Sychem, Shechem, Naplous, or Nablus, whatever it may best suit one to call it." She added that "I like the name Shechem best, though Palestinians, whether Christian, Jew, Syrian or Arab, now say Nablus;" on the Greek Orthodox Patriarch and Fraternity in the 1930s, see Merav Mack, "Orthodox and Communist: A History of a Christian Community in Mandate Palestine and Israel," *British Journal of Middle Eastern Studies* 42(4) (2015): 392.

face value, no background check necessary. I, for example, have pretended to be Palestinian a lot, and no one in Damascus, Ramallah, Cairo, Irbil, Tunis or Beirut knew I was full of myself. To the contrary, they greeted me a hero's welcome out of solidary. I am living and breathing evidence the identity is a total fiction. I invented it out of thin air, and no one had any way of proving me wrong.

All identities based on places like Palestine are determined arbitrarily. The 8th century chronicler Isidor Pacensis used the term *Europeans* in Latin to refer to the Romani-Gallic and barbarian forces who fought together against Muslims in the battle of Tours in 732—but not Sarmatians, Lombards and Vikings, even though they also lived in what we think of as Europe today. Membership in an Aztec city-state, or *altepetl*, was defined by the personal relationship between the ruler and subject, not by location, such that subjects of various and even rival *altepetl*s lived interspersed. German speaking Jews born and raised in Germany struggled to become Germans in the 19th century. The *Matawila* of Jabal 'Amal, or Shi'a in today's parlance, were at first not considered Lebanese when that term gained popularity in the 19th and early 20th centuries. Some Arabic speakers in the mid-19th century did not consider Muslims or Kurds Syrians, a term they reserved for Christians. An Austrian statesman once asked a Hungarian nobleman in 1829, "what do we mean by the *Greeks*? Do we mean a people, a country, or a religion?" Not everyone living in the United States of America is considered an American, just as not everyone living in Israel is considered Israeli, just as not everyone living in Palestine is considered Palestinian. The point was better made by the comedian Sebastian Maniscalco, "I'm half Italian, half Sicilian." His dad apparently disagreed: "you are Sicilian!" In short, we arbitrarily define our relationships to places like Europe, *altepetl*s, Germany, Lebanon, Syria, Greece, America, Israel, Palestine, Italy, Sicily and millions of other places.[80]

* * *

Agriculture. Now on to the history of identities like "Palestinian" after the Agricultural Revolution. The Agricultural Revolution marked an important milestone in this history. Although permanent settlement existed before the Agricultural Revolution among peoples who subsisted off fish, migratory birds and lived in wetlands, as noted above, sedentary life expanded rapidly after the spread of agriculture as a means of subsistence. Beginning around 10,000 years ago, groups of humans in at least four separate times and places gradually started to farm and domesticate animals in addition to hunt and gather. This new way of life spread and made sedentism the dominant human lifestyle everywhere. Instead of moving around every few weeks or season to follow the hunt and wild vegetation, we toiled small plots of land our entire lives.

Sedentary lifestyle had many tantalizing effects on our identities. As settled peoples, we came to identify with our places of settlement, and identified others with their places of settlement—and also figured out ways of recording how we identified. The Akkadians lived in the region of Akkad, Amorites the land of the Amorites, Aramaeans Aram, Assyrians Assyria, Chaldaeans *Mat Kaldi*, or the land of Chaldeans, and Persians Persia. The ancient Israelites conflated the

---

[80] On the Europeans, see Denys Hay, *Europe: The Emergence of an Idea* (Edinburgh: Edinburgh University Press, 1957), 25; on use of the term Palestinian in the early Islamic period, see chapter 3; on the Aztec city-states, see Michael E. Smith, "Aztec Urbanism: Cities and Towns," pp. 201-217 In *Oxford Handbook of the Aztecs*, (eds.) Deborah L. Nichols and Enrique Rodríguez-Alegría (New York: Oxford University Press, 2016), 211-212; on the Greek anecdote, see Dimitris Livanios, "The Quest for Hellenism: Religion, Nationalism and Collective Identities in Greece (1453-1913)," *The Historical Review / La Revue Historique* 3(2006): 33; then see Sebastian Maniscalco, "Aren't You Embarrassed?" *Netflix* 28 July 2015.

land of the Philistines [*Plishtim*] and Philistine [*Pleshet*], as well as "all Edom" and "all the Edomites." The Vietnamese called China Ch'ing Country (*Thanh-quoc*) because Ch'ing people (*Thanh-nhan*) lived there. The Arabs called southern Lebanon the Land of the *Matawila* (known as Shi'a today) because *Matawila* lived there. They called northern Iraq "the Land of the Kurds," because Kurds lived there. They called Arabia or the Land of Sham "the Land of the Arabs," because Arabs lived there. They called the Hawran "the Land of the Druze" because Druze lived there and they called parts of Lebanon "the Land of the Maronites" because Maronites lived there. We became much more important parts of the places we lived in when we lived in them all year round, from generation to generation.[81]

This is part of the reason why there is so much confusion over the terms *nations* and *nationalism* among academics. The conventional wisdom a few decades ago was that the French Revolution inspired an era of nationalism in Europe and then the rest of the world. Classicists and medievalists left this idea alone for a while, focusing on more pressing issues like paleographic manuscript marginalia. But then modernists read history and pre-modernists read about nations. A fascinating cross-fertilization ensued. Nations were found in 16th century France, 14th century

---

[81] On the ancient Israelites, see Steven Elliott Grosby, *Biblical Ideas of Nationality: Ancient and Modern* (Winona Lake, Ind: Eisenbrauns, 2002), 124; on the "land of the Arabs," al-Hasan ibn Muhammad al-Burini (d. 1615), *Tarajim al-A'yan min Abna al-Zaman* (Damascus: al-Majma' al-'Ilmi al-'Arabi, 1959-62), 214; Makariyus the Antiochean (d.1672), cited in see Radu, "Voyage Du Patriarche," 57; Abu Salim 'Abd Allah bin Muhammad al-'Ayyashi (d.1679), *al-Rihla al-'Ayyashiyya lil-Baqa' al-Hijaziyya: al-Musamma Ma' al-Mawa'id* (Beirut: Dar al-Kutub al-'Ilmiyya, 2011), II, 400; Istifan al-Duwayhi (d.1704), *Tarikh al-Ta'ifa al-Maruniyya* (Beirut: al-Matba'a al-Kathulikiyya lil-Aba' al-Yasu'iyyin, 1890), 71; Mikha'il Burayk (d. after 1782), *Tarikh al-Sham, 1720-1782* (Beirut: Dar al-Qutaybah, 1982), 58, 68-69; 'Abd al-Qadir Abi al-Sa'ud, *Min Misr ila Islambul* (written around 1840-1) (Dar al-Kutub Manuscripts, Bab al-Khalq, Cairo, Egypt, #755), folio 49; Jurji Yanni, *Tarikh Suriya* (Beirut: al-Matba'a al-Adabiyya, 1881), 175; for more on this term, see Rafeq, "Social Groups, Identity and Loyalty;" on 'the land of the *Matawila*,' see Burayk (d. after 1782), *Tarikh al-Sham*, 23; on the land of the Maronites, see Rifa'a Rafi' al-Tahtawi, *Jughrafiyat Bilad al-Sham* (date unknown) (Dar al-Kutub Manuscripts, Bab al-Khalq, Cairo, Egypt, MS#42), folio 34; on the Vietnamese, see Alexander Woodside, *Vietnam and the Chinese Mode: A Comparative Study of Nguyen and Ch'ing Civil Government in the First Half of the Nineteenth Century* (Cambridge, MA: Harvard University Press, 1971), 19; for further examples of this, see also D. Roden, "Some Geographical Implications from the Study of Ugandan place-names." *EastAfrican Geographical Review* 12 (1974): 79-80.

North Africa, 13th century Greece, medieval Netherlands and among the Anglo-Saxons and Irish in the 11th and 8th centuries. Strands of nationalism were found among the Arabs in the 13th and 16th centuries, among the Byzantines (*Romaioi*) from the 5th through 16th centuries; in 7th century Tang Dynasty China, and among the ancient Athenians, Hebrews, Moabites, Edomites, Assyrians and Egyptian Pharoaic states more than two millennia ago. To one prominent archeologist, the Iron Age, which began some 3,200 years ago, initiated the "era of nation-states." Nations and nationalism existed everywhere. No wonder one of world's most famous scholars in the field, Eric J. Hobsbawm, wrote some three decades ago in a line that should be more famous than it is that "I adopt no *a priori* definition of what constitutes a nation." The word nation, he claimed, was "used so widely and imprecisely that the use of the vocabulary of nationalism today may mean very little indeed." Essentially, scholars found nations wherever we have records that speak to how people identified. Wherever we settled, we developed ties to our places of settlement. Those ties appear universal among our species.[82]

---

[82] On the Iron Age, see Assaf Yasur-Landau, *The Philistines and Aegean Migration at the End of the Late Bronze Age* (Cambridge: Cambridge University Press, 2014), 1; on the ancient Egyptians, see Gat, *Nations: The Long History*, 85-89; on the Hebrews, Moabites and Assyrians, see Steven Grosby, "Borders, Territory and Nationality in the Ancient Near East and Armenia," *Journal of the Economic and Social History of the Orient* 40(1) (1997): 1–29; on the Athenians, see Aviel Roshwald, *The Endurance of Nationalism: Ancient Roots and Modern Dilemmas* (Cambridge: Cambridge University Press, 2006); on the Anglo-Saxons, see Adrian Hastings, *The Construction of Nationhood: Ethnicity, Religion and Nationalism* (Cambridge: Cambridge University Press, 1997); on the Greeks, see Stephen G. Xydis, "Mediaeval Origins of Modern Greek Nationalism," *Balkan Studies* 9 (1968): 1-20; on the Byzantines, see Anthony Kaldellēs, *Hellenism in Byzantium: The Transformations of Greek Identity and the Reception of the Classical Tradition* (Cambridge: Cambridge University Press, 2007), ch. 2; on the Tang Dynasty, see Gat, *Nations: The Long History*, 93-103; on medieval Netherlands, see Philip Gorski, "The Mosaic Moment: An Early Modernist Critique of Modernist Theories of Nationalism," *American Journal of Sociology* 105 (2000): 1428-1468; on religious nationalism during the Reformation period, see Philip Gorski, *The Disciplinary Revolution* (University of Chicago Press, 2003); on the 13th century Arabs, see Zayde Antrim, "Waṭan before Waṭaniyya: Loyalty to Land in Ayyūbid and Mamlūk Syria," *Al-Masaq: Journal of the Medieval Mediterranean* 22(2) (2010): 174; on 14th century North Africa, see Haim Gerber ("The Limits of Constructedness," 259; on 16th century France, see Anthony Marx, *Faith in Nation: Exclusionary Origins of Nationalism* (Oxford: Oxford University Press, 2003); on the 16th century Arabs, see Haim Gerber, "The Limits of Constructedness," 252; for a further critique of modernist interpretations of nationalism, see Steve Tamari, "Arab National Consciousness," 309-321; then see Eric J. Hobsbawm, *Nations and Nationalism since 1780: Programme, Myth* (Cambridge: Cambridge University Press, 1990), 8-9.

Settled peoples invested more resources in material possessions than hunter-gatherers. We built complex structures, places of worship and seats of government. With walls everywhere, we started drawing maps on them. In the 1960s, archeologists discovered one of the earliest known sites of wheat cultivation in Çatalhöyük, Central Anatolia, Turkey, dating to 8,500 years ago. These ancient settled peoples drew a map on the interior side of a wall in a dwelling place. The map depicted an explosive summit eruption of the Hasan Dağı twin-peaks volcano located about 130 km northeast of Çatalhöyük with a bird's eye view of a town plan in the foreground. Permanent settlement led us to project our maps onto walls, floors and movable objects. Permanent settlement was probably the greatest victory for maps in human history. And maps made the places of our lives feel real and important.[83]

States. We produced a lot more food by domesticating plants and animals than by gathering or catching them. This led to large permanent settlements, population growth and surpluses. That incentivized conquest, and conquest gave rise to states. States were groups of people who agreed amongst themselves on a chain of command, claiming that chain of command had a monopoly on the use of force in a certain area. Chains of command did not usually farm or hunt and so they needed to collect taxes to feed themselves. In order to collect taxes, places like Palestine flourished. You couldn't ask your subjects to pay taxes to the governor of "the fourteen-mile expanse of land due east from the southern-most hilltop of the rugged terrain south of Hebron to the land extending north for eighteen miles until the narrow valley past the third river." You couldn't maintain tax collection records if you had to describe the physical attributes of the district, rather than using its name. You couldn't distribute salaries, conscript soldiers or instill

---

[83] AK Schmitt, M Danišík, E Aydar, E Şen, İ Ulusoy, OM Lovera, "Identifying the Volcanic Eruption Depicted in a Neolithic Painting at Çatalhöyük, Central Anatolia, Turkey." *PLoS ONE* 9(1) (2014): e84711

loyalty in subjects. The same went for everyone else: scholars, priests, merchants and hair dressers needed to use the names the state chose to make themselves understood and to describe events accurately. "Khalid bin Walid controlled Qanasrin, Yazid governed Damascus, Muʻawiya governed Jordan, Amlaqa bin Mujazzin governed Palestine and the coast was ruled by ʻAbd Allah ibn Qays." That's how the great historian, Ibn a-Athir (d.1233) described it. Places like Palestine facilitated governance. They made it easier for states to conscript soldiers, commanders to give orders to subordinates, bureaucrats to convey information to governors and scholars to relay scholarly information to readers. States needed to divide the world into places like Palestine, and that gave rise to identities having to do with those places.[84]

To fully understand the lure of conquest or governance as a means of subsistence, and thus the proliferation of states around the globe, and thus the proliferation of places like Palestine, and thus the popularity of identities like the Palestinians, consider Stephen Colbert's 2011 address before the United States Congress, where he shared his vast experience spending one day as a migrant farm worker. "I certainly hope my star power can bump this hearing all the way up to CSPAN1," Colbert explained. This was part of Colbert's ongoing series, *Stephen tries other things and realizes, my job is much better*. The comedian participated in the United Food Workers Take Our Jobs Campaign, claiming to have been 1 of 16 people in the United States that year to take up the challenge. "After working with these men and women—picking beans, packing corn, for hours on end, side by side, in the unforgiving sun," Colbert proclaimed in a tender voice as if his shift had just ended, "please don't make me do this again. It is really, really, hard." Colbert started to cry. "For one thing, when you are picking beans, you have to spend all

---

[84] See ibn al-Athir, *al-Kamil fi al-Tarikh* (Beirut: Dar al-Kitab al-ʻArabi, 1983), II, 375.

day bending over. It turns out, and I did not know this, most soil is at ground level. If we could put a man on the moon," Colbert said in total exasperation, "why can't we make the earth waste high? This helped me understand why so few Americans are clamoring to begin an exciting career as a seasonal migrant fieldworker." Places like Palestine facilitated conquest, defense and governance, and governance meant you could spend the day sitting rather than bending over.

Some states tried to enforce these places as canonical. An example of this, as we learned in the previous chapter, was when the Israeli military sought to ban use of the word Palestine in company or newspaper names in the occupied territories in the 1980s. The group variously known as I.S.I.S. or I.S.I.L. or I.S. was probably annoyed that everyone was using different names for the group. Americans chose I.S.I.L or I.S.I.S., the Turks İşit, Arabs and Israelis *Da'sh*, so the group changed its name in July 2014 to "the Islamic State," now often called just "I.S.," even though the earlier names still persist.[85]

States thus played a critical role in the rise and fall of places like Palestine and the identities that sprung forth from them. Few Arabs before the 1850s had heard of the Arabic word *Suriya* (Syria). As Assad Kayat explained in his 1847 memoir, "first we begin with the general name of the country. It is called 'Bar Alsham,' or the country of Shem [sic]." But, in the 1860s, the Ottoman state introduced a new district called Syria. From that point onwards, the term Syria gained in popularity. By the late 19th century, the term *Suriya* appeared as frequently in Arabic as the term *Sham*. (Syria arose in popularity for other reasons, as well, such as its usage by

---

[85] Patrick J. Lyons and Mona al-Naggar, "What to Call Iraq Fighters? Experts Vary of the S's and L's," *New York Times* 18 June 2014 (https://goo.gl/6BSTQp)

foreign missionaries, travelers and diplomats. In fact, this was part of the reason why the government changed it to *Syria* to begin with).[86]

The French conquered the place in 1920, making Syria even more important than it ever had been—at the expense of Sham. "What we mean by Land of Sham," explained the activist Muhammad 'Izzat al-Darwaza in 1924 in a lengthy footnote to the word Sham, "were the countries of Syria and Palestine, and the wilderness that connects it to Najd and Iraq, known as the wilderness of Sham." Arab geographers in the 1940s explicitly claimed that the phrase "the Land of Sham" sounded outdated. One of the most popular geographical terms in Arabic for more than a millennium needed clarification, seemingly in large part because it fell from administrative use.[87]

Name changes could be slow to settle in where states invented places ex nihilo. Prior to the 1920s, Jordan was variously known as *Eastern Palestine, that which is across the Jordan, the eastern bank of the Jordan, the wilderness of Sham, that which is behind the Jordan, the southern part of the Vilayet of Syria, behind Palestine* and *the Arab East*. It wasn't a coherent

---

[86] See Assad Y. Kayat, *A Voice from Lebanon* (London: Madden and Co., Leadenhall-Street, 1847), 325-6; having said that, it was not so easy to completely displace Sham. Shahin Makariyus [*Hasr al-Litham fi Nakbat al-Sham* (Cairo: n.p., 1895), 4] noted that "the land is still called by its Roman name [i.e. Syria] among the Europeans and it is still called by its Arab name [*al-Sham*] among the Arabs." On the rise in popularity of the term Syria, see Fruma Zachs, *The Making of a Syrian Identity: Intellectuals and Merchants in Nineteenth Century Beirut* (Leiden: Brill, 2005).
[87] See Muhammad 'Izzat Darwazah, *Mukhtasar Tarikh al-'Arab wa-al-Islam* (Cairo: al-Matba'a al-Salafiyya, 1924), I, 81; S. Hadhwah [*Tarikh al-Umma al-'Arabiyya: Qadiman wa-Hadithan* (Jerusalem: Matba'at al-Ard al-Muqaddasa, 1945), 41, 115] added the word "Syria" in parenthesis when writing about Sham, presumably for clarification, and added the words "Syria, Palestine and Transjordan" in parenthesis when writing about *Bilad al-Sham*; Wadi'a Talhuq [*al-Salibiyya al-Jadida fi Filastin* (Damascus: Matba'at al-Nidal, 1948), 55] also added the word "Syria" in parenthesis when writing about Sham during the Fatimids and Abbasid periods. Wadi'a Talhuq [*Filastin al-'Arabiyya: Fi Madiha wa Hadiruhu wa-Mustaqbaluhu* (Beirut: Majallat al-'Alman, 1945), 77] explained elsewhere that "Palestine was considered a part of Greater Syria – of the Shami Country (*al-qutr al-Shami*), to use the old term (*'ala hadd al-istilah al-qadim*)." For further examples, see al-Sabbagh, *Filastin wa-al-Bilad al-'Arabiyya*, 2.

place in people's minds, but rather a geographical area appended to or defined by some other place—Sham, Syria, Palestine or the Jordan River. The British debated calling the place "Belka" or Trans Jordania, but decided on Transjordan in the end. King 'Abdullah himself debated between calling it *Sharq al-Urdunn* (East of the Jordan) or *al-Sharq al-'Arabi* (the Arab East)—a name that was in fact used during the 1920s (see figure 5). No wonder people called it different things during the 1920s, 1930s and 1940s despite British political fiat. Transjordan eventually won out in English, and other terms like *Eastern Palestine* fell out of use. Soon enough, though, the state changed its name to the Hashemite Kingdom of Jordan. Just as quickly, *Transjordan* sounded as outdated as *Eastern Palestine*. The state decided it was Jordan, and the rest of us went along with it.[88]

---

[88] On "Eastern Palestine" and "that which is across the Jordan" (*fi 'abr al-Urdunn*), see "Takhtit Sharqi Filastin," *al-Muqtataf* 6 (1881): 272; on "the Arab East" (*al-Sharq al-'Arabi*), see "Southern Syria, or Palestine and the Arab East," in Sa'id Sabbagh, *Jughrafiyat Suriya al-'Umumiyya al-Mufassala* (Saidon: Matba'at al-'Irfan, 1924), 128; on "Jordan" and "Eastern Palestine," see Shukri Khalil Suwaydan, *Tarikh al-Jam'iyya al-Imbaraturiyya al-Urthudkuksiyya al-Filastiniyya* (Boston: Matba'a Suriya al-Jadida, 1912), 120, 123; on Eastern Palestine, see Salah, *Filastin wa-Tajdid*, 13, 18; on the "eastern bank of the Jordan" (*daffat al-Urdunn al-sharqiyya*), see *Filasitn* 24 January 1912; on "the wilderness of Sham," see As'ad Mansur, *Murshid al-Tullab ila Jughrafiyat al-Kitab* (n.p., 1905), 1-2; on "behind Palestine" (*wara' Filastin*), see *al-Hilal* 10(6) (1901): 184; on "that which is behind the Jordan," see 'Isa Iskandar al-Ma'luf, "Haywanat Ghariba fi ma wara' al-Urdunn," *al-Athar* 1(5) (1911): 155; on the confusion, see Maktabat Bayt al-Maqdis, *al-Mukhtasar al-Jughrafi* (Jerusalem: al-Tiba'a al-'Asriyya, 1945), 97; Yusuf Sufayr, *Jughrafiyat Lubnan al-Kabir wa-Hukumat Suriya wa-Filastin* (Beirut: Matabi' Kuzma, 1924), 84; Interestingly, Sahil al-Sayyid [*al-Murshid al-'Arabi, Filastin* (Jerusalem: al-Matba'a al-'Asriyya, 1936), 10] claimed Transjordan was part of Palestine based on his view that the British colonial division of Palestine and Transjordan was illegitimate; on the British debates, see Joseph A. Massad, *Colonial Effects: The Making of National Identity in Jordan* (New York: Columbia University Press, 2012), 23-4.

Figure 5. Map of "Southern Syria, or Palestine and the Arab East."[89]

Some places, admittedly, survived the test of time without any state guarantors. Palestine survived for centuries without one, as we shall discover in the next chapter. Not surprisingly, though, it lived in a state of neglect for much of that period and could have remained an antiquated place of the past like Mesopotamia or Transjordan. Palestine did have some things going for it, though. Prior to its disappearance from administrative parlance in the 11th century, Palestine had political status in Roman, Byzantine and Arab civilizations, and a variation of the term (*Pleshet*) appeared in the most the popular series of books in European and Middle Eastern history: the Bible. Those laurels helped Palestine survive when it fell from political use. Palestine's rise, fall and rise again is the subject of the next chapter.

---

[89] Cited in Sa'id al-Sabbagh, *Jughrafiyat Suriya al-'Umumiyya al-Mufassala* (Saidon: Matba'at al-'Irfan, 1924), 128

Cities. The Agricultural Revolution had another important effect on identities like Palestinian. It brought cities into the world. We associated cities with the larger areas in which they were situated, in part, because it made it easier to communicate information. "Sus is an area at the edge of the Maghreb. Tripoli is on the coast of Damascus, Beirut is a city in Damascus, Ashkelon is a city on the coast of Palestine, Manbar is in Balkh, and Rumayda is a city in the Maghreb." These were the words of the famous Arab geographer, al-Muqaddasi (d. 991), who continued like this for pages on end. It was much easier to keep track of cities when each one is situated within its own parent region.[90]

We also combined cities and lands into phrases. Arabs called Tripoli "the Tripoli of Sham," Caesarea "the Caesarea of Palestine," Sabastia "the Sabastia of Palestine," Ramla "the Ramla of Palestine," Damascus the "Damascus of Sham," Baghdad "the Baghdad of Iraq" and Cairo "the Cairo of Egypt." We did this when cities became prominent parts of the larger areas in which they were located. Damascus was the political center of Sham; Cairo was Egypt's hub; Baghdad dominated Iraq; and Ramla ruled Palestine.[91]

We also conflated cities and regions. The 7th century Muslim conquerors initially called Jordan *Tiberias*. Some Muslims thought Palestine referred to the city of Ramla. The town of Sabastia (near Nablus) was also known as Palestine. To this day, Egyptians use the word *Misr* for both *Cairo* and *Egypt*. Syrians use the term *Sham* for *Syria* and *Damascus*. Arabic and English

---

[90] Muhammad ibn Ahmad al-Muqaddasi (M.J. De Goeje ed.), *Kitab Ahsan al-Taqasim fi Ma'rifat al-Aqalim* (Leiden: E.J. Brill, 1906), 24.
[91] The Arabic terms used were: *Tarabulus al-Sham, Kaysariyyat Filastin, Sabastiyat Filastin, Ramlat Filastin, Dimashq al-Sham, Baghdad al-'Iraq* and *Kahirat Misr.*

speakers use the word "Gaza" or "Ghazza" for the city and the strip. Lots of people also conflated Jerusalem and Palestine, or described Palestine as "the Land of Jerusalem" or used the two terms interchangeably, especially in the late 19th and early 20th centuries.[92]

In the Middle East, as in other parts of the world, the conflation is obvious from a look at the language itself. The Arabic words *balad*, *ard*, and *watan* denoted cities and regions, or cities plus the towns, villages, agricultural lands surrounding them. *Ard* referred to regions such as the *Holy Land* as well as cities like Damascus or Gaza. *Balad* and its plural, *bilad*, referred to Palestine and Syria as well as Jaffa and Nablus. *Watan*, or homeland, referred to villages, cities and lands as well.[93]

---

[92] On Sabastia's conflation with Palestine, see ʿAbd al-Ghani al-Nabulusi (d.1731) *Rihla ila al-Quds* (Cairo, 1902), 6-7; Muhammad bin Jaʿfar bin Idris al-Kitani (d.1903) *al-Rihla al-Samiyya ila Iskandariyya wa-Misr wa-l-Hijaz wa-Bilad al-Sham* (al-Dar al-Bayda, Morocco: Markaz al-Turath al-Thaqafi al-Maghribi, 2005), 307; on the conflation of Palestine and Ramla, see Zachary Foster, "Was Jerusalem Part of Palestine? The Forgotten City of Ramla, 900–1900," *British Journal of Middle Eastern Studies* 43(4)(2016): 575-589; on the conflation of Palestine and Jerusalem, see *Daʾirat al-Maʿarif* 10 (1898), 196; *Filastin* 13 April 1912; *Filastin* 27 June 1912; *Filastin* 30 September 1911; Abi al-Saʿud Affandi, *Kitab al-Dars al-Tamm fi al-Tarikh al-ʿAmm* (Cairo: Matbaʿat Wadi al-Nil, 1872/3), 66); Rashid Khalidi, *Palestinian Identity: The Construction of Modern National Consciousness* (New York: Columbia University Press, 1997), 59, n. 84; "Anadolu Taksimat-i Idariye" and "Suriye ve Beyrut Vilayetleri" in Mekatib-i Ibtidaʾiye, *Juğrafiya-i Osmani* (Matbaa-i 'Amire, 1913/1914), 98, 193, respectively; Michelle Campos, "Making Citizens, Contesting Citizenship in Late Ottoman Palestine," pp.17-33 in *Late Ottoman Palestine: The Period of Young Turk Rule* Yuval Ben-Bassat and Eyal Ginio (eds.) (London: I.B. Tauris, 2011), 24, 27; Johann Büsso, *Hamidian Palestine: Politics and Society in the District of Jerusalem 1872-1908* (Leiden; Boston: Brill, 2011), 479.

[93] On the Land of Jerusalem (*Ard al-Quds*), see, for instance, n.a., *Nisba Sharifa Muttasila bi-Tamim al-Dari* [Manuscript Section of the National Library of Israel, JER NLI AP Ar. 593, 1860), 20, 23, 24; on Damascus, see Ibn al-Wardi (d.1348), *Kharidat al-ʿAjaʾib wa-Faridat al-Gharaʾib* (Cairo: Mustafa al-Babi al-Halabi wa-Awladihi, 1923), 29; on Ashdod, see Khalil Sarkis, *Kitab Urshalim, ayy al-Quds al-Sharif* (Beirut: Matbaʿat al-Maʿarif, 1874), 17; on Gaza, see Niqula ibn Yusuf al-Turki (d. 1828), *Dhikr Tamalluk Jumhur al-Faransawiyya: al-Aqtar al-Misriyya wa-l-Bilad al-Shamiyya* (*Histoire de l'Expedition des Français en Égypte*) (Paris: Royale, 1839; Beirut: Dar al-Farabi, 1990), 136; on Sidon, see Haydar Rida al-Rukayni (d.1783), *Jabal ʿAmil fi al-Qarn*, 1163-1247H/1749-1832M (Beirut: Dar al-Fikr al-Lubnani, 1997), 69; see also n.a., *Salname-yi Vilâyet-i Suriye* (Suriye [Syria]: Suriye Vilâyet Matbaasında tabʿ Olunmuştur, 1887-8), 239; on the conflation of Tiberias and Jordan, see Abu ʿUbayd al-Bakri (d.1094), *al-Masalik wa-l-Mamalik* (Qartaj: al-Muʾassasa al-Wataniyya lil-Tarjama wa-l-Tahqiq wa-l-Dirasat, 1992), I, 498; Amikam Elad, "Two Identical Inscriptions from Jund Filasṭīn from the Reign of the ʿAbbāsid Caliph, Al-Muqtadir," *Journal of the Economic and Social History of the Orient* 35(4) (1992): 334-5; on *watan*, see, for instance, the 18th century Sufi traveler Taha al-Kurdi (a.k.a. Muhammad Taha ibn Yahya Sahih al-Din al-ʿIraqi) (d.1800) [*al-Rihla* (Yale University, Manuscript Division, Landberg #220), folio 2a] who wrote in his travelogue that "I left my homeland (*watan*)," which was in the "village of Balisan, in the Land of the Kurds, within the city of Baghdad." His homeland was the village of Balisan, the city of Baghdad and the land of the Kurds – i.e. a land inside of a city inside of a homeland!

The Arabs were not exceptional. In ancient Egypt, the rulers of the New Kingdom occasionally called Gaza *the City of Canaan* or even simply *Canaan*, even though *Canaan* also referred to a much larger region from Nahr al-Kabir to Gaza. The Akkadian Empire was based in the city of Akkad and its surrounding region, also known as Akkad, or the land of Akkad (*Mat Akkadi*). Asssyria was named after its capital city, Aššur. The phrase *King of Aram*, a region, referred to the rulers of kingdoms like Damascus.[94]

No surprise that historians love the phrase "city-state." Scholars of ancient Mesopotamia often describe the smaller kingdoms that thrived in the region in the 3rd century BC as city-states, since they often included one or two major urban centers as well as the surrounding rural areas. The Aztecs had the *altepetl*, the ancient Greeks had *polis*, Renaissance Europeans had Venice, Milan, Florence, Genoa, Pisa, Siena, Lucca, Cremona. All are called city-states in modern English.[95]

In 21st century North America, cities usually subsume their outlying areas: the Detroit Area, the Bay Area, the Tri-State Area, the Greater Toronto Area and Chicagoland. In many cases, we even add the word *area* to the name of the city itself to imply it is more than just the city. People from Pontiac, Waterford or West Bloomfield, Michigan will say they are from the Detroit Area, for example, when talking to San Franciscans. It makes ourselves and our places of origin

---

[94] On the phrase, *King of Aram*, see Bruce Routledge, "The Antiquity of the Nation? Critical Reflections from the Ancient Near East," *Nations and Nationalism* 9(2) (2003): 226-7; on Canaan, see Robert Drews, "Canaanites and Philistines," *Journal for the Study of the Old Testament* 23(81) (1998): 47-8.

[95] On ancient Mesopotamia, see Piotr Michalowski, "The Presence of the Past in Early Mesopotamian Writings" pp. 144-168 in *Thinking, Recording, and Writing History in the Ancient World* Kurt A. Raaflaub (ed.) (Chichester, West Sussex; Malden, Massachusetts: Wiley Blackwell, 2014), 150; on the prevalence of city-states in global history, see Gat, *The Long History*, 67-83.

intelligible to other people. It facilitates basic communication. That's why cities and regions have long formed a spectrum in thought and language.

How did cities—and their conflation with regions—affect identities like "Palestinian"? Since there was never a clean break between regions and cities, identities related to regions and cities have also been fluid: city dwellers, townspeople, villagers and country folks alike all see the areas around them as natural extensions of their places of origin. Our ties to cities have often been closely linked to our ties to regions. Today, think of the importance that Jerusalem plays for Palestinians, Damascus to Syrians, Cairo to Egyptians and Baghdad to Iraqis. Our identities based on cities and regions have evolved to become quite similar in nature, content and form. Most everything that has been said in this chapter about Palestine could have been said about cities, towns and villages.

* * *

Conclusion. We identify with Palestine because it seems real to us. It seems real to us because we named it, told stories about it and made maps of it. We also made Palestine beautiful owing to our aesthetic tastes. We painted colorful maps of its peaks and valleys, wrote eloquent poems commemorating its martyrs and threw extravagant parties celebrating its independence. The rest of this dissertation will pick up when Palestine first entered the historical record, moving from the ancient to the modern world. Why did Palestine become so important that people came to identify with it and even sacrifice their life for it?

CHAPTER THREE

The Pre-Modern World

Most people writing about Palestine don't obsess over its name, even if I implied that previously. As an academic, I've been trained to inflate the importance of my topic. Instead, most people writing about Palestine assume it's real, which is okay. It's difficult to write history without assuming places like Palestine are real.

But as far as name controversies go, as we discussed in chapter one, Palestine handily defeats its competitors. To quantify the obsession with Palestine, consider that the Wikipedia page, *Timeline of the History of the Name Palestine*, has accumulated some 30,000 words and 401 footnotes as of August 2017. These figures eclipse even other highly controversial name disputes like Macedonia, and they dwarf others like Denali–Mount McKinley, the Persian/Arab Gulf, Kosovo/a, the Sea of Japan, Khuzestan and Anatolia by an order of magnitude.[96]

Palestine entered the historical record about 3,000 years ago. In the ancient Near East, the term was closely associated with the land settled by the Philistines, the peoples mentioned by the ancient Egyptians, Assyrians and Hebrews. The land they inhabited long survived the Philistines themselves, as the term entered Greek and Latin, probably through Aramaic, and came to denote

---

[96] On Macedonia, see the Wikipedia page titled, "Macedonia naming dispute." For a survey of other name disputes, see the Wikipedia page titled, "Geographical renaming." For a survey of references to the term Khuzestan, see the Wikipedia page, "Origin of the name Khuzestan." On the Anatolia debate, see Christopher Markiewicz, "The Crisis of Rule in Late Medieval Islam: A Study of Idrīs Bidlīsī (861-926/1457-1520) and Kingship at the Turn of the Sixteenth Century" (Ph.D. Dissertation, University of Chicago, 2015), xvi-xvii.

a larger region, including both the mountainous interior and coastal plain of the surrounding area. After the Arab conquest, it also came to mean the city of Ramla, the city of Sabastia, the city of Ramla and its surroundings, the city of Gaza, the city of Gaza and its surroundings, the coastal plains up until the mountainous interior, the area around Jerusalem, the District of Jerusalem, a land stretching from Rafah to Lajjun and Jaffa to Jericho, a land equivalent to the Holy Land, and many other areas. In this sense, Palestine was a typical place. It has come in and out of fashion and has meant different things to different people in different time periods.[97]

Some of this history is not without controversy. The most infamous incident was the alleged name change from Judaea to Palestine in 135 CE. Most scholars believe the Roman Emperor Hadrian changed the provincial administrative name of Judaea to Palestine to erase the Jewish presence in the land, a point often seized by Israel apologists because it squares nicely with the theory that Jews have faced millennia of uninterrupted persecution. What Israel apologists don't know is that it's equally likely the name change had little to do with Jew hatred and more to do with Hadrian's romance with ancient Greece. It's also possible Judaea gradually fell from use out of derelict rather than spite. These theories are little known even among scholars because they serve no political agenda. Regrettably, it seems too many historians of Hadrian and the Jews of the Roman Empire have fallen victim to the propaganda.

From the 2nd to the 7th centuries, the Romans and Byzantines used the word Palestine in administrative parlance. Thereafter, Palestine experienced a period of retreat in the medieval

---

[97] In the 19th and 20th centuries, Palestine went global, referring to Palestina, Alagoas (Brazil), Palestina, São Paulo (Brazil), Palestina de Goias (Brazil), Palestina, Caldas (Colombia), Palestina, Huila (Columbia), Palestina de Los Altos (Guatemala), Palestina (Ecuador) and Palestine, Texas (United States).

Latin west, but was revived when Renaissance Europeans re-discovered the ancient Greek and Latin texts, most of which called the place Palestine. They brought these texts out of manuscript, translated them into European vernaculars and published them repeatedly with the aid of the printing press. They also illustrated Palestine on maps and told stories about its history and geography. The classical texts became popular in Europe because they offered independent accounts of the events described in the Holy Books, almost as if God had left behind clues to understanding the scriptures.

The Arabs conquered Palestine from the Byzantines in the 7th century, and preserved the word Palestine—*Filastin* in Arabic—in administrative nomenclature for three centuries. The Crusaders, who conquered parts of the region from the 11th through 13th centuries, preferred other terms to Palestine. Meanwhile, though, the Arabs continued to tell stories about Palestine for the same reason people today tell stories about Mesopotamia, Transjordan and Cilicia. They preserved place names of the past, even if those words fell from everyday usage. There were exceptions, though, such as the people of Ramla and its surroundings, who remembered and used the term Palestine in their day-day lives.

The final section of this chapter looks at whether a Palestinian identity existed before the modern period, as some have claimed. I stated that permanent settlement, the rise of states and agricultural surplus led people to identify with places like Palestine. Most Arabic speakers who inhabited the region were sedentary, so this held promise that some of its inhabitants might identify with it—and, indeed, at least one did. But the state was a comparatively small institution until quite recently, and Palestine was only incorporated in it from the 7th through the 11th century, not after. As far as the surplus goes, most Arabs in history were farmers, not geographers, journalists or educators. This made it harder for identities like the Palestinians to flourish, since they were greatly dependent on people telling stories about it, writing its history and making maps of it. Thus, although at least one Muslim did identity as Palestinain in the 10th century, ties to Palestine were weak before the 19th century.

* * *

The Egyptians (1150 BC - 900 BC). Palestine first appeared in the historical record as *Peleshet* in the Papyrus Harris hieroglyphics, a text totaling some 1,500 lines dating to 3,100 years ago. "I extended the boundaries of Egypt. I overthrow those who invaded Egypt from their lands." So said an Egyptian Pharaoh, who was not humble about his military prowess. "The *Peleshet* were made into ashes." The Egyptians also left behind three inscriptions in the Medinet Habu reliefs located at the Mortuary Temple of Ramesses III in Luxor that bear the name *Prst*. (Egyptologists disagree over how to transcribe the word, since we do not know how Egyptian sounded). The *Prst* are described as peoples of the sea who invaded Egypt by land and sea. An inscription from roughly the same time was also found on the famous Padiiset's Statue (figure 6) stating that an envoy named Pa-di-Eset came from Canaan and *PeLeSeT*. Finally, the Onomosticon of Amenope, a hieroglyphics catalogue of objects, towns, offices, buildings, types of land, produce, beverages and also peoples, mentioned the *Pelesti* cities of Ashkelon, Ashdod and Gaza. In short, at least five separate Egyptian hieroglyphic sources mention these people, variously known among as *Peleshet, Prst* or *PeLeSeT*.[98]

---

[98] Egyptologists variously transliterate the group as *pw-r-s-ty*, *PuReST*, *PuLeST*, *PeLeSHeT*, *Prst* or *Plst*, depending on the source text and language. See Nissim R. Gangor, *Who Were the Phoenicians?* (KIP: Katarim International

Figure 6. Padiiset's Statue.

The Assyrians (800 BC-600 BC). The Assyrians were the second oldest peoples to mention the Philistines. A slab of rock was found buried amidst the ruins of the prosperous Assyrian city, Nimrud, 30 kilometers south of Mosul, dating to about the 9th century BC. "I ruled from the

---

Publishing, 2009), 110; Nur Masalha, "The Concept of Palestine: The Concept of Palestine from the Late Bronze Age to the Modern Period," *Journal of Holy Land and Palestine Studies* 15(2) (2016): 144-5; for an authoritative survey of the sources on the Philistines, see Trude Dothan, *The Philistines and their Material Culture* (New Haven: Yale University Press, 1982), 1-24; on the Papyrus Harris, see ibid, 3; on the Medinet Habu reliefs, Padiiset's Statue and the Onomosticon of Amenope, see Carl S. Ehrlich, *The Philistines in Transition: A History from ca. 1000-730 BC* (Leiden: Brill, 1996), 65; Dothan, *The Philistines and their Material Culture*, 3-5; James Henry Breasted, *Ancient Records of Egypt* (Urbana: University of Illinois Press, 2001), 24; Georg Steindorff, "The Statuette of an Egyptian Commissioner in Syria," *The Journal of Egyptian Archaeology* 25(1) (1939): 30-33; Niels Peter Lemche, *The Canaanites and Their Land: The Tradition of the Canaanites*, (Sheffield, U.K.: Sheffield Academic Press, 1999), 54.

beginning of my reign, from Dur-Kurigalzi, Sippar of Shamash, Pasitu of the Dunanu." Seemingly, the *Pasita* were the same people as the *Peleseti* or *Prst* in the Egyptian sources.[99]

Another Assyrian King, Sennacherib, had stories of his campaign against the Kingdom of Israel and the Kingdom of Judah etched into multiple clay prisms, each with this same modest inscription: "I, King of the Universe, King of Assyria [Assur], gave my thought and brought my mind to accomplish this work according to the command and will of the Gods." King Sennacherib reportedly snatched away "from their lands people who had not submitted to my yoke, including the people of Kaldu (Chaldea), the Aramaeans, the Mannai, (the people of) Kue and Hilakku, (of) Philistia [*Pi-LiS-Ti u*] and Tyre. I made them carry the basket and mold bricks." Molding bricks doesn't sound pleasant.[100]

Hundreds of 8th century BC neo-Assyrian clay tablets were also discovered in the waste deposits of the Assyrian foreign ministry offices. The tablets described the affairs of the Assyrian state in cuneiform script. On one tablet, a servant told the King he had collected taxes in Tyre, Lebanon and Sidon and forced the people there to submit to the rule of the Kingdom. "Bring your lumber, do your work on it," wrote the local governor to the people of the Lebanon, but "do not deliver it to the Egyptians or Palestinians [*pa-la-as-ta-a-a*]," the same Philistines mentioned in the Egyptian sources.[101]

---

[99] Hayim Tadmor, "An Ancient Scribal Error and Its Modern Consequences: The Date of the Nimrud Slab Inscription," *Anatolian Studies* 33 (1983): 199-203. According to a much earlier translation, the text was rendered: "From over the river Euphrates, Syria, and Phoenicia, the whole of it, Tyre, Zidon, Omri Edom and Philistia...I have subjugated" (edited for clarity). See George Smith, *The Assyrian Eponym Canon* (London: Samuel Bagster and Sons, 1875), 115.
[100] Daniel David Luckenbill, *The Annals of Sennacherib* (Chicago: University of Chicago Press, 1924), 104.
[101] For background on the tables, see the many articles published in the 1950s by M. E. L. Mallowan in the journal, *Iraq*. For a transcription and translation of the tablet, see Henry W.F. Saggs, *The Nimrud Letters, 1952* (London: The British School of Archeology in Iraq, 2001), 156-7.

The Israelites (1000BC-130 AD). The Egyptian and Assyrian statues, inscriptions, slabs and papyri were only recently rediscovered and deciphered in the 19th and 20th centuries. The Hebrew texts, by contrast, have been known for millennia. They mention the Philistines or Philistia, known in Hebrew as *Plishtim, Eretz Plishtim* or *Pleshet*, some 280 times and have more to say about the Philistines than all the Egyptian and Assyrian texts combined.

The Bible described the Philistines as the most wretched of all the enemies of the Children of Israel. They lived in Gaza, Ashkelon, Ashdod, Ekron, and Gath—i.e. the southwest flank of the Israelites—and reportedly fought the Israelites in the Battle of Shephelah, the Battle of Aphek, the Battle of Eben-Ezer, the skirmish at Michmash, the fight near the Valley of Elah, the battle at Mount Gilboa and more. They even occupied Hebrew cities and garrisoned Bethlehem. The Hebrews described them as pagan idol worshipers who did not circumcise their young and consumed unclean animals. Delilah the Philistine woman infamously cut Sampson's hair, usurping his supernatural strength. The Philistine giant Goliath even more infamously caused King Saul's troops to tremble until David killed him with a single slingshot. Without corroborating evidence, of course, we don't have any way of verifying or refuting these stories. What's fair to assume is that the stories would have been very different had Philistine texts survived instead of Egyptian, Assyrian and Israelite ones.[102]

Philistine Identity. Scholars today use the term Philistine as an archeological rather than ethnic label to refer to the period of permanent settlement in the Gaza region that began around 1200

---

[102] See 13 Joshua; 1 Chronicles; 2 Samuel.

BC. The artifacts found at Philistine sites resemble a mix of Aegean and other cultures. Philistine clay pots, pans, wine juglets, red and black cups, and figurines of goddesses, resemble Greek, Aegean and Minoan culture as well. Moreover, Egyptian reliefs of Philistine ships, shields, and body armor look like Aegean ones. Philistine culture also supported a wealth of professions and trades much as Aegean culture had, including warriors, farmers, sailors, musicians, dancers, merchants, shamans, priests, artisans, and architects. Textual evidence supports this as well: Biblical descriptions of Philistine pillared temples also match Aegean Megaron architecture.[103]

The Aegean origins theory is now being subjected to genetic testing. In July 2016, archeologists uncovered a large cemetery just outside the walls of Ashkelon in the Philistine heartland, a site that was in use in the late 11th century BC and early 8th century BC according to radiocarbon dating of other objects found there. The site was thus in use during a time when Philistines are believed to have inhabited that area. Forensic specialists are now extracting DNA samples from the bones in the cemetery to understand their degree of genetic similarity to Aegean bones from the same period.[104]

But without written records from the Philistines themselves, it's difficult to know how they self-identified. As for the word *Philistine* itself, DNA evidence cannot answer this question, and so etymological gymnastics reign supreme. Before the archeological record started pointing to the

---

[103] On the amorphous Philistine identity, see S Maeir, A. M., Hitchcock, L. A., and Horwitz, L. K. "On the Constitution and Transformation of Philistine Identity." *Oxford Journal of Archaeology* 32(1) (2013): 1–38; Jeff Emanuel, "'Dagon Our God': Iron I Philistine Cult in Text and Archaeology," *Journal of Ancient Near Eastern Religions* 16(1) (2016): 24-5; on the archeological similarities to Aegean peoples, see ibid, 29; Dothan, *The Philistines and their Material Culture*, 7-11; David Ben-Shlomo, *Philistine Iconography: A Wealth of Style and Symbolism* (Göttingen: Academic Press Fribourg, Vandenhoeck & Ruprecht, 2010), 16.
[104] See Kristin Romey, "Discovery of Philistine Cemetery May Solve Biblical Mystery," *National Geographic* 10 July 2016 (goo.gl/7Lhkq3).

Aegean, scholars related the word Philistine to the Sanskrit *valaksa*, meaning *white*; the Ethiopian verb *falasa*, meaning to wander. Some said *Philistia* morphed out of the nearby Biblical region known as *Shephelah* in the Judean foothills. Archeologists also found a Hieroglyphic Luwian inscription in an Aleppo citadel by a ruler, "Taita, the Hero of Palistinean"—certainly an interesting find, although it's unclear if or how the ruler had any relation to the Philistines.[105]

Today, the most popular etymological theories trace the term to the Aegean. The Philistines could be related to the Pelasgians—the Greek term to refer to the inhabitants of the Aegean Sea region before the Greeks. It might also come from the river Strymon in Macedonia, which had previously been called Palaistinos. Perhaps it came from the Pylian Kingdom [known as *Pylos*, originally *Pylosten*, or *Pu.le.se.te* in Egyptian], an ancient state in what is now southern Greece whose people also specialized in metalwork and armoire, boasted similar social organization and were conquered, destroyed and dispersed by invaders. Perhaps they were the Philistines. Now let's move from the ancient Near East to antiquity.[106]

* * *

Judaea or Palestine? (500BC-4th century AD). The nice thing about the Philistines is that propagandists haven't been interested in them. That is not the case once we reach antiquity.

---

[105] On the *Shephelah* theory, see Gustav Moritz Redslob, *Die Alttestamentlichen Namen der Bevölkerung des Israelitenstaates* (Hamburg: Meissner, 1846), 4-5; on the other theories, see A.S. Macalister, *The Philistines: Their History and Civilization* (S.l: Oxford University Press, 1914), 3-4; Guy D. Middleton, "Telling Stories: The Mycenaean Origins of the Philistines," *Oxford Journal of Archaeology* 34(1) (2015): 45–65; on the Aleppo citadel finding, see J.D. Hawkins, "The Inscriptions of the Aleppo Temple," *Anatolian Studies* 61 (2011): 35-54.
[106] On the Pylian Kingdom theory, see Othniel Margalith, "Where Did the Philistines Come From?," *Zeitschrift für die Alttestamentliche Wissenschaft* 107(1) (1995): 104, 109.

From the 2nd century AD onwards, propagandists have hijacked the history of Palestine. The Roman Emperor Hadrian is claimed to have replaced the district of Judaea with Palestine to erase the land's Jewish identity after crushing the Bar-Kokhba revolt in 135 AD, what we might call the erasure hypothesis. Many Israel apologists know this fact because it fits into their narrative of world history, which is that Jews have faced millennia of uninterrupted persecution.[107]

Recently, it was Malcolm Hoenlein, the executive vice-president of the Conference of Presidents, who told a meeting of Israel lobby operatives in New York that the Boycott, Divestment and Sanctions (BDS) movement had its roots in the ancient world. "We let this cancer metastasize until now on campuses across the United States," Hoenlein said. "This started when the Romans changed the name of Judaea to Philistia. That was the beginning of BDS." As

---

[107] Bernard Lewis was an early and prominent advocate of the erasure hypothesis, popularizing it for wider audiences. He wrote in Commentary Magazine in 1975 that "the name "Palestine" is first attested in the history of Herodotus, and appears in the works of later Greek and Latin writers.... in normal classical usage Palestine Syria (Syria Palaistinê) seems to have meant the coastline formerly inhabited by the Philistines.... [it] did not, however, include the land of Judea, which was usually and officially known in Roman times by that name. The official adoption of the name Palestine in Roman usage to designate the territories of the former Jewish principality of Judea seems to date from after the suppression of the great Jewish revolt of Bar-Kokhba in the year 135 C.E. After this revolt, which caused great trouble to the Roman Empire, the Emperor Hadrian made a determined attempt to stamp out the embers not only of the revolt but of Jewish nationhood and statehood. The city of Jerusalem was destroyed and then rebuilt with a new name, as Aelia Capitolina; it would seem that the name Judea was abolished at the same time as Jerusalem and the country renamed Palestina or Syria Palestina, with the same intention—of obliterating its historic Jewish identity. The earlier name did not entirely disappear, and as late as the 4th century C.E. we still find a Christian author, Epiphanius, referring to 'Palestina, that is, Judea.' It had, however, ceased to be the official designation of the country." See Bernard Lewis, "The Palestinians and the PLO," *Commentary Magazine*, 1 January 1975; Lewis repeated this idea as late as 2010 when he was asked about the "Palestinian issue." See Jerusalem Conference, "Bernard Lewis Speaks at the Jerusalem Conference 2010 Part 2," *youtube.com,* 1 February 2011 (goo.gl/sZHzoL); The first problem with Lewis's remarks is that his chronology of events is awkwardly out of order. Lewis claimed the name changes of Jerusalem and Judaea took place "at the same time," both putatively in response to the revolt. But Hadrian visited Jerusalem in the early spring of 130, and scholars agree he changed the name of Jerusalem during this trip. The Jewish revolt happened *afterwards*, in 132. How could Hadrian have changed the name of Jerusalem in 130 in response to a revolt that happened in 132? On the 130 date of name change of Jerusalem to Aelia Capitolina, see William F. Stinespring, "Hadrian in Palestine, 129/130 A. D.," *Journal of the American Oriental Society* 59(3)(1939): 361; David Golan, "Hadrian's Decision to supplant "Jerusalem" by "Aelia Capitolina" *Historia: Zeitschrift für Alte Geschichte* 35(2) (1986): 226-239; Hannah M. Cotton, "The Impact of the Roman Army in the Province of Judaea/Syria Palaestina," pp.393-408 in *The Impact of the Roman Army (200 BC-AD 476)*, Lukas de Blois, Elio Lo Cascio and Olivier Hekster (eds), (Leiden: Brill, 2007), 399-400.

the Roman Emperor Hadrian famously said, "we must quell Jewish rebellion by means of peaceful, nonviolent resistance: boycott, divestment and slaughter of Jews by sword and fire."[108]

A Jerusalem Post blogger echoed these statements after having visited the Hadrian exhibition at the Israel Museum in January 2016.

> The most important little tidbit I gleaned from that movie [about Hadrian] was that in his efforts to defeat the Jewish People and Nation, he changed the name of the Land from Judea to "Palestine," sic. The invention was an ancient one, and the aim was the same as the more modern use of the word. It's a simple tool to deny Jewish History and Jewish rights to our Land. That is why the word "Palestine" appears on all sorts of maps over the ages...[109]

Some of the most respected proponents of the erasure hypothesis, though, are openly biased about their approach to the question. The historian Louis Feldman, for instance, explicitly described evidence that refuted the erasure hypothesis as a "problem" requiring thought experiments to resolve. At one point, he even wrote that "the name Palestine, as we can see from the Bible is correctly used only when applied to the land of the ancient Philistines along the coast of the Mediterranean [...] were it not for Hadrian's deliberate attempt to eliminate all traces of Jewish sovereignty, the name would have remained *Judea*." First, the Bible's geographical lexicon is no more correct or incorrect than Greek or Latin lexicons. Geographical lexicons can be intelligible or unintelligible, but not correct or incorrect, at least from a historian's point of view. Second, Feldman's counterfactual claim that Judaea *would* have remained (had it not been erased) says a lot more about Feldman than his sources—which, perhaps to Feldman's surprise,

---

[108] Ali Abunimah, "Israel Lawfare Group Plans 'Massive Punishments' for Activists," *The Electronic Intifada* 25 June 2016 (goo.gl/9hpAgW).
[109] Batya Medad, "Who Invented "Palestine?" HADRIAN!" *Jerusalem Post* 16 January 2016 (goo.gl/vta4br); for further examples, see, for instance, David Bukay, "The Origin and Essence of "Palestine" and "Palestinians" as Political Entities," *Modern Diplomacy* 12 August 2016 (goo.gl/D8NJDA); Uri Dromi, "Hadrian's Lessons for Modern-Day Israel," *Miami Herald* 25 February 2016 (goo.gl/0HJR86); Simcha Jacobovici, "Palestine: History of a Name," *Times of Israel Blogs* 8 August 2013 (goo.gl/ijS1zV); Matthew M. Hausman, "The UN Fails History 101," *Arutz Sheva* 6 June 2016 (goo.gl/egVs5z).

cannot predict the future. Regrettably, this has generally been the tone of scholarship on the issue: assume the erasure hypothesis is fact, and look for evidence to support it.[110]

Before we get into the evidence for and against the erasure hypothesis, let's clear up one common misconception about the alleged name change. Historians do not believe that Hadrian preserved the administrative boundaries of Judaea and simply rename the province Palestine. Instead, the consensus is that the district was abolished altogether and replaced not with Palaestina, but with *Syria-Palaestina*. Palaestina, to repeat, was *not* the name of a Roman administrative province beginning in 135.[111]

Now let's discuss the evidence in support of the erasure hypothesis. Recall that the Romans banned circumcision, hellenized Jerusalem and levied a half-shekel tax on the Jews to pay for it. This inspired rebellion. The leader of the rebellion, Bar Kokhba, took complete control of Judaea (although not Jerusalem) in 132, annihilating Roman troops stationed in Judaea and even a unit sent from Egypt. Bar Kokhba ruled Judaea for more than two years. He inaugurated a new calendar, "the First Year of the Redemption of Israel" and issued leases of parcels of land. He probably inspired Jewish insurrection elsewhere in the Empire too.

---

[110] Feldman worked hard to ram his thesis into his sources. He claimed that Pomponius Mela "clearly differentiates Judaea from Palestine," since Pomponius Mela wrote: "here is situated Palestine [presumably only a minor part of Syria], where Syria touches the Arabs…" Louis H. Feldman, *Studies in Hellenistic Judaism* (Leiden: Brill, 1996), 560. Feldman seems to force his thesis onto the evidence with Philo as well. "The one passage that is difficult to explain is the one (*Quod Omnis Probus Liber Sit 12.75*) in which he [Philo] declares that Palestinian-Syria has not failed to produce high moral excellence. He states that a considerable part of the Jews live there, and cites as an example the Essenes." (ibid, 563-4). It is only "difficult to explain" if one presupposes the erasure hypothesis from the outset. Feldman describes evidence that undermines his argument as a "problem" in another instance as well: "the one passage in Josephus which seems to present a problem is the one at the very end of the *Antiquities* (20.259), where he says that his work contains a record of the events "that befell us Jews, Egypt, Syria and in Palestine" (ibid, 564-5). On his point about the "correct" use of the word Palestine, see ibid, 576.

[111] For evidence of the change, see, for instance, D. Barag, "The Borders of Syria-Palaestina on An Inscription from the Raphia Area," *Israel Exploration Journal* 23(1) (1973): 50-52.

In response, Emperor Hadrian summoned his best generals to quell the revolt. This included Julius Severus from Britain and other units from Syria and the Danube. In total, some 12 or 13 legions participated, an enormous troop deployment for a territory the size of Judaea. Hadrian even made two visits to the front lines himself. His units incurred heavy losses, but managed to crush the rebellion, obliterating 50 major outposts, 1,000 villages and killing tens if not hundreds of thousands of Jews. The Romans dispossessed Jews of their land in Jerusalem after their re-conquest in 135 AD. They destroyed a Samaritan (Hebrew offshoot) sanctuary at Mount Gerizim (near Nablus) and sold Jewish slaves in Gaza and Hebron for the price of a horse. The Romans outlawed anyone from practicing Mosaic law or owning scrolls. Pagan shrines were built over Jewish ones. The rabbis were traumatized by the gruesome violence, even claiming that "the gentiles fertilized their vineyards for seven years with the blood of Israel without using manure." Hadrian had ample reason to change the name and "to stamp out the embers" of "Jewish nationhood and statehood," as Bernard Lewis put it.[112]

But there are also some major problems with the erasure hypothesis. It assumes that Palestine was not already the name of a region that included Judaea. If it was, then how could Hadrian have changed the name *to* Palestine? If you go to a protest against the separation barrier in Bil'in, and get sprayed with chemically manufactured horse manure, you can't say you'll change clothes and come back smelling like chemically manufactured horse manure. You have to change out of that, just like Palestine had to emerge forth from Judaea.

---

[112] Mary Smallwood, *The Jews under Roman Rule: From Pompey to Diocletian* (Leiden: Brill, 1976), 446, 448, 450, 463; Elizabeth Speller, *Following Hadrian: A Second-Century Journey through the Roman Empire* (New York: Oxford University Press, 2004), 201; Anthony Everitt, *Hadrian and the Triumph of Rome* (New York: Random House, 2009), 296-305. On the vineyards quote, see ibid, 304.

But Palestine did not emerge forth from Judaea, it had coexisted with it long before it was putatively changed to it. Herodotus (d.425 BC) was the first on record in the Greek world to use the term Palestine. The prevailing theory is that he adopted the term from Aramaic—both because Aramaic was the closest thing the Near East had at that time to a *lingua franca* and because Middle Aramaic, a Semitic language related to Hebrew, had a form of that word—*Pi-li-s-ta'in*—closest to Herodotus's Greek usage. Herodotus used the term multiple times to refer to the entire coast from Egypt to Phoenicia, and potentially the interior as well. In addition to Herodotus, Aristotle claimed the Dead Sea was in Palestine; Philo of Alexandria indicated Palestine bordered Arabia, and was part of Syria; Josephus said his work recorded what "befell us Jews, Egypt, Syria and in Palestine." Pomponius Mela explained that "here is situated Palestine, where Syria touches the Arabs, then Phoenicia, and Antiochia, where Syria borders Cilicia." Others writers including Xenophilus, Polemon of Athens, Agatharchides, Vitruvius, Ovid, Statius and Dio Chrysostom also used the term before 135 CE, and they included Judaea in it. So, Palestine included Judaea a long time before Hadrian said it included Judaea. We have a plausible motive for the change without knowing anything else about Hadrian: he called the place what it was called.[113]

---

[113] On Herodotus's borrowing of Aramaic, see Martin Noth, "Zur Geschichte des Namens Palastina," *Zeitschrift des Deutschen Palastina Vereins* 62 (1939): 125; Noth summarized these conclusions in his idem, *The Old Testament World* (Philadelphia: Fortress Press, 1962), 7-9; on Herodotus, Aristotle, Philo of Alexandria and Josephus, see Francis Schmidt, *How the Temple Thinks: Identity and Social Cohesion in Ancient Judaism* (Sheffield, U.K.: Sheffield Academic Press, 2001), 29, and Feldman, *Studies in Hellenistic Judaism*, 564-5. Then see Pomponius Mela (c. 43), Frank E. Romer (ed.), *Pomponius Mela's Description of the World* (Ann Arbor: University of Michigan Press, 2001), 52; see also De Chorographia 1.11.62-63, cited in Feldman, *Studies in Hellenistic Judaism*, 560. Note that even people who didn't think Palestine included Judaea, such as Pliny the Elder, still thought Palestine extended as far north as Phoenicia and bordered Arabia. A similar point is made by Douglas A. Howard, "It Was Called "Palestine": The Land, History and Palestinian Identity," *Fides et Historia* 35(2) (2003): 61-78.

Interestingly, Hadrian also had a soft spot for Greece and tried to revive Greek customs, traditions and names. He was chosen as a full Archonship in Athens and he was most welcome and respected in Greece. He admired Greek aesthetics, art and philosophy and even changed provincial names to Greek ones elsewhere in the Empire as symbolic acts of restoration. This included the city of Antigonea, called that by the Macedonian king Antigonus Doson, which he changed to Mantinea—its Greek name during the time of Sparta's prominence; the city of Sepphoris, which was renamed Diocaesarea in Hadrian's honor in 130; he renamed Jerusalem *Aelia Capitolina*—to remind Christian Roman dissenters that it was Aelius Hadrianus—i.e. himself—who held power in Jerusalem. It's plausible he renamed Judaea not because he wanted to give BDS a head start, as Malcolm Hoenlein believed, but rather because he loved the Greeks—and he thought the Greeks called the place Palestine.[114]

Also, Roman rulers frequently renamed cities and districts for banal reasons, usually to honor emperors. The first century ruler of the Galilee and Perea, Herod Antipater, rename the city of Sepphoris to Autocratoris in the Roman emperor's honor, but it didn't stick. The Hellenistic city of Samaria was renamed Sebaste—the Greek equivalent of the first Roman emperor Augustus (which did stick); Philip the Tetrarch (d.34) renamed the village of Bethsaida (near the Sea of Galilee) to Julias in honor of the Emperor's daughter; Herod Agrippa II (d.92 or 100) (briefly) renamed the city Caesarea Philippi to Neronias in honor of the Roman emperor Nero (d.68). Official name changes were common in the Roman Empire, and most of them had nothing to do

---

[114] On the Mantinea name change, see K. W. Arafat, *Pausanias' Greece: Ancient Artists and Roman Rulers* (Cambridge: Cambridge University Press, 1996), 185; on Doson, see William Hazlitt, *The Classical Gazetteer: A Dictionary of Ancient Geography, Sacred and Profane* (London: Whittaker, 1851), 215; on the Sepphoris name change, see Smallwood, *The Jews under Roman rule*, 432-3; for more on his efforts to restore earlier Greek icons, such as statues of Zeus, see Smallwood, *The Jews under Roman Rule*, 410; on his successes in and liking of Greece, and his reception there, see Speller, *Hadrian: A Second-Century Journey*, 202; on the Jerusalem name change, see Golan, "Hadrian's Decision," 228-9, 238.

with the Jews. The decision to change the name to Palestine may have been a banal bureaucratic choice. The whole affair might have passed without anyone thinking there was anything vengeful about the change. This seems plausible, especially given the paucity of direct evidence around who made the change, when and under what circumstances.[115]

If the administrative reorganization was indeed banal, then we might have expected both names to have persisted after the change, which is exactly what happened. An inscription in modern Austria from after the reported change described someone as the procurator of Judaea; another from Ephesus, Turkey, identified Sextus Erucius Clarus as governor of Judaea —and those were official inscriptions. Other Greek and Roman unofficial sources, including Galen, Celsus, Dio Cassius, Festus, Eutropius, Martianus Capella, Orosius and the anonymous author of *Epitome de Caesaribus* used the term Judaea, often side by side Palestine, as if they were synonyms—centuries after it had putatively been erased. The 4th century writer Epiphanius, for instance, explicitly claimed "Palaestina" is "Judaea." Could all those writers have been so blasphemous against Rome—reviving the name that Hadrian vengefully erased? 135 AD might not have been as important a moment as everyone seems to think.[116]

So why is the erasure hypothesis widely known among Israel's apologists and even referred to as the beginning of BDS? It supported the theory of an everlasting conspiracy against the Jews. Among Israel's less nuanced propagandists, it was also evidence that the Palestinians were a

---

[115] On Sebaste see Smallwood, *The Jews under Roman Rule*, 77; on, Sepphoris see ibid, 118; on Bethsaida, see ibid, 118; on Caesarea Philippi, see ibid, 273.

[116] On Epiphanius, see Lewis, "The Palestinians and the PLO";
See also Feldman, *Studies in Hellenistic Judaism*, 560-576; Smallwood, *The Jews under Roman Rule*, 552; on Orosius, see Paulus Orosius (d. 420), Alfred, King of England, Joseph Bosworth, E FitzGerald, V B Redstone, *A Literal English Translation of King Alfred's Anglo-Saxon Version of the Compendious History of the World by Orosius* (London: n.p., 1855), 32-33.

modern reincarnation of timeless Jew hatred, a useful retort wherever anyone criticizes Israel or Jews. Regrettably, modern political agendas drove the research agenda of even the most serious scholars of the ancient world. Now let's turn from Roman to Byzantine Palestine.

* * *

Byzantine Palestine (4th-7th centuries). To recap, by the first few centuries before the birth of Christ, as we saw, Greek speakers across the Mediterranean were using the term Palestine. By the time of Hadrian, a century after Christ, both Judaea and Palestine were popular designations, living in harmony for many centuries to come.

But, as all governments do, the Romans and Byzantines chose names for the places they governed. The accepted view, as noted above, is that the Romans created the province of Syria-Palaestina in 135, which lasted until 390. Although the Roman Empire divided in the mid-4th century, the Byzantine successors to Rome preserved the erstwhile Roman districts. (Note that the Byzantine Empire was actually known as the Roman Empire during its time, but historians today use the term Byzantine to differentiate it from the other Roman Empire in the Latin west). In 390, the Byzantines divided the province Syria-Palaestina, creating an administrative district called Palaestina Prima and Palaestina Secunda. In the 6th century, they added a 3rd Palestine, Palaestina Salutaris. Aside from the brief Persian conquest of Jerusalem in the early 7th century—these districts remained until the eve of the Arab conquest in the mid-7th century.

Byzantine Christians called the place Palestine and wrote many works about it. Some of them dealt with Palestine's urban geography, military organization and political configuration. Eusebius of Caesarea (d.339), for instance, mentioned Palestine at least 35 times in his *Church History*. Eusebius Pamphili also used the word Palestine dozens of times in his classic *On the Place-Names in the Holy Scripture* to describe the locations of Biblical cities, mountains and tribes. Dozens of other Byzantine writers between the 4th and 7th centuries wrote about Palestine because that was the name of the province according to the people that ruled it. The Byzantines made Palestine great by political fiat.[117]

We stated in the previous chapter that maps made Palestine seem real to people, and that the first victory for maps came with permanent dwelling places, owing to the walls. Incidentally—and I did not realize this—those dwelling places also had floors. People put maps on those also. The Madaba map, dating from the 6th century, is the earliest known floor map, the earliest Christian map and the earliest map of the Holy Land. It's the kind of map you read about in coffee table atlases—the kind of books used to write this section.

It was also the earliest map of Palestine—that word appearing in the original map. The map depicts an area from Byblos and Damascus in the north to Alexandria and the Red Sea in the south, measuring 7 by 22 meters, one quarter of which you can still see today in Madaba (Jordan). It illustrates contemporary (i.e. 6th century) roads, buildings, bridges, towns and ports,

---

[117] On Eusebius, see his Eusebius, of Caesarea (d. 339), (translated by S.E. Parker) *An Ecclesiastical History to the Twentieth Year of the Reign of Constantine: Being the 394th of the Christian Area* (London: S. Bagster and Sons, 1842). He mentioned Palestine in entries for Azotus (Asdod), Arbela, Askalon, Arkem, Gaza, Emmaous. He also claimed Ailam and Bethphou were located at the borders of Palestine; see also F. M. Abel, *Geographie de la Palestine* (Paris: Librairie Lecoffre, J. Gabalda et Cie, 1938), II, 171-187.

scenes of gazelles, palm trees and fish—and Biblical sites such as Jacob's well and the Israelite tribal territories. It also included the Greek phrase "οροι Αιγυπτου και Παλαιστινης"—on the "border of Egypt and Palestine," probably taken from Eusebius of Caesarea's *On the Place-Names in the Holy Scripture* (see figure 7).[118]

Figure 7. Section of Byzantine floor mosaic map at St. George Church Madaba depicting "οροι Αιγυπτου και Παλαιστινης" (the border of Egypt and Palestine).

* * *

The Latin west. The term Palestine survived from the 3rd-9th centuries in the Latin west, but on the margins. Adomnán (d.704), for instance, used the term Palestine once in its broader sense. It more often appeared as a descriptor of Caesarea, as in "the Caesarea of Palestine"—its capital during the Byzantine period. An anonymous cleric in Ravenna compiled a list of known place in

---

[118] See Kenneth Nebenzahl, *Maps of the Holy Land: Images of Terra Sancta through Two Millennia* (New York: Abbeville Press, 1986), 24-25; Jerry Brotton, *Great Maps* (New York, New York: DK Publishing, 2014), 32-35. Eusebius of Caesarea stated that Bethaffu is "on the way to Egypt, which is the boundary of Palestine." See Eusebius of Caesarea (d. 339), Joan E. Taylor (ed.), G.S.P. Freeman-Grenville (trans.) *The Onomasticon by Eusebius of Caesarea* (Jerusalem: Carta, 2003), 34.

about 700, in which he listed the following cities located in the "Hebrew Jewish homeland in Palestine:" Jerusalem, Bethlehem, Rama, Hebron, Emmaus-Nicopolis, Lod, Nazareth Antipatrion and Bethsaida.[119]

Three versions of Palestine persisted in the Latin west from the Middle Ages until the early modern period. First, many associated Palestine with Gaza, mirroring the Bible's usage of *Peleshet*, or its Latin equivalent, *Philistia*. Writers had poor access to Greek and Latin encyclopedias, chronicles and church histories—and so were unaware of Palestine's enlarged image in the Greek, Roman and Byzantine worlds. Instead, people had access to the Bible, and so the Bible's version of Palestine was quite popular. John Mandeville (fl. 14th century), for instance, claimed that Palestine was the city of Gaza, owing to the Philistines having lived there. The Dominican theologian Felix Fabri (d. 1502) similarly associated Palestine with Gaza in the early 1480s. "I will describe Gaza together with its province of Palestine," he wrote, adding that the term was most commonly used in his era to refer to "the country by the sea." He claimed that the Mountains of Israel bound Palestine on the east, the Mediterranean Sea in the west, the mountains of Ephraim in the north and Gaza in the south. In other words, Palestine's chief city was Gaza, it included the coastal strip and excluded the mountainous interior.[120]

---

[119] Adamnan (d.704), "Arculf's Narrative about the Holy Places, written by Adamnan," in *The Library of the Palestine Pilgrims' Text Society*, Vol. III (London: Committee of the Palestine Exploration Fund, 1897), II, 33; n.a., M Pinder and G Parthey (eds.), *Ravennatis Anonymi Cosmographica et Guidonis Geographica* (Berolini: Nicolai, 1860), 82.

[120] John Mandeville's 14th century Anglo-Norman French travelogue was extremely popular, but it was almost certainly a forgery based on copied material, not actual travel. The text also claimed Palestine was a land between Jerusalem and Ashkelon, part of Syria (as was the Kingdom of Judaea, the Galilee, Little Cilicia); and that Jerusalem was in the land of Judaea]. See John Mandeville (c. 1350s-60s), Alfred W. Pollard (ed.), *The Travels of Sir John Mandeville* (London, Macmillan, 1900), 79, 197; on his identification of Jerusalem as "in the land of Judaea" and also in "the Kingdom of Syria," which "was beside the land of Palestine, beside Ascalon [sic], beside the land of Maritaine [Maronites?]," see ibid, 49; for other ambiguous reference to Palestine, see ibid, 39, 48, 97; then see Felix Fabri (c. 1480-1483), *Library of the Palestine Pilgrims' Text Society 9/10 The Wanderings of Felix Fabri* (New York: AMS Press, 1971 [1887-1897]), II, 449-450. He preferred the term *the Holy Land* to Palestine. Fabri also mentioned other definitions of Palestine, including the "whole of the Holy Land, so that Jerusalem and its Mountains

Other writers seem to have forgotten Palestine altogether. In England, Germany, Belgium and the Netherlands, the terms *the Holy Land* or *the Holy Places* were much more popular than Palestine. The former emphasized the Holy Scriptures, the latter that Rome, too, was holy. Both phrases were accepted and used. Cartographers writing in Latin, Czech, English, Danish, Dutch, French, German, Italian, Polish, Slovenian and Swedish often called the place with the names of the Biblical tribes, such as Gad, Naftali and Dan, or used other geographical terms from the Bible, such as the Galilee, Samaria and Judaea. (In some cases, Philistin or Palestina was used to denote the area of settlement of the Biblical Philistines).[121]

Third, a much larger version of Palestine persisted as well. The 13th century English Franciscan, Bartholomeus of Paris, explained that Palestine was a province of Syria, that Judaea was a country in Palestine and at the center of Judaea was Jerusalem—the center of the world. Sounds a lot like the Palestine we know today. His Latin encyclopedia was translated into French, Spanish, Dutch and English within a century and a half. The wealthy mid-14th century Venetian

---

are called Palestine," as well as "a certain part of the province of Galilee, near the Mountains of Gilboa." He also cited Isidorus (b. 139) of Roman Egypt, who reportedly described Palestine as a wide region, bounded by the Red Sea on the east, Judaea in the south, the land of Tyre in the north, and by the Sea and Egypt in the West, known as Philistia in ancient times. He also noted that the "entire Holy Land is sometimes called Syria, because both Judaea and Palestine are large parts of Syria."

[121] A late 11th/early 12th century Norman crusader, who saw combat in the Near East, did not mention the word Palestine in his account of the first Crusader in 1099. See Rosalind Hill (ed.), *The Deeds of the Franks and other Pilgrims to Jerusalem* (Thomas Nelson and Sons, 1962), ix-xvi; the 14th century English Pilgrim William Wey (d.1476) does not use the term Palestine either. See William Wey (d.1476); George Williams; Bulkeley Bandinel; Roxburghe Club, *The Itineraries of William Wey, Fellow of Eton College To Jerusalem, A.D. 1458 and A.D. 1462; and to Saint James of Compostella, A.D. 1456* (London, J.B. Nichols and Sons, 1857); Johannes Witte de Hese (fl. 14th-15th century) refers to the Holy Places, not Palestine in his *Itinerarius*. See Scott Douglas Westrem, "A Critical Edition of Johannes Witte de Hese's "Itinerarius," The Middle Dutch Text, An English Translation and Commentary, Together with an Introduction to European Accounts of Travel to the East," (Ph.D Dissertation, Northwestern University, 1985), 568-593; most Belgium, German and Dutch pilgrims fail to mention Palestine as well: see Kathryn M. Rudy, *Virtual Pilgrimages in the Convent: Imagining Jerusalem in the Late Middle Ages* (Turnhout, Belgium: Brepols, 2011), 49, 61, 93, 95, 147, 263, 272, 275; on the cartographers, see Catherine Delano-Smith and Elizabeth Morley Ingram, *Maps in Bibles: An Illustrated Catalogue* (Geneve: Librairie Droz, 1991), 63-67, 90-95.

merchant, Marino Sanudo Torsello (c.1300-1321), also used the term Palestine as the standard name of the region in his treatise written in the aftermath of the Muslim conquest of Acre from the Crusaders in 1291. Having said that, the book came to be known as *A Treatise on Expeditions to the Holy Land.*[122]

Others in the Latin west used the term Palestine in both its limited and broad senses. The English chronicler Ranulf Higden (d.1364)'s *Polychronicon* —the "standard work of general history for its time"—surviving in more than 100 manuscripts today claimed Syria included the provinces of Commagena, Palestina, Phonecia, Canaan, Idom and Judaea, but then added on the next page that Palestine included Judaea and it was called the Canaan of Shem, the son of Noah. Many travelers also used the term Palestine ambiguously, but probably in the larger sense, such as the late 13th century Veronese poet, Giacomino da Verona. Still, even he preferred the term the Holy Land to Palestine.[123]

A few things can be said about Palestine in the Latin West from the 8th through 16th centuries: most people preferred to call it the Holy Land, not Palestine; many did not use the term Palestine at all; some believed Palestine referred to Gaza alone, the coastal area or the land inhabited by

---

[122] On Bartholomeus, see Robert Steele (ed.) *Medieval Lore: An Epitome of the Science, Geography, Animal and Plant Folk-lore and Myth of the Middle Age* (London: Elliot Stock, 1893), 1; then see Marino Sanudo; Peter Lock (trans.), *The Book of Secrets of the Faithful of the Cross = Liber Secretorum Fidelium Crucis* (Farnham, Surrey, England; Burlington, Vermont: Ashgate, 2011), 247, 262, 266, 277, 378, 388, 415.

[123] See, for example, Great Britain. Public Record Office, *Rerum Britannicarum Medii aevi Scriptores: Or, Chronicles and Memorials of Great Britain and Ireland during the Middle Ages* (London: Longman, 1858), 101-3; Suzanne Conklin Akbari, *Idols in the East: European Representations of Islam and the Orient, 1100-1450* (Ithica: Cornell University Press, 2009), 116; for Middle Age writers who used the term Palestine, see Giacoma da Verona (c. late 13th cent.) [Nicole Chareyron, *Pilgrims to Jerusalem in the Middle Ages* (New York: Columbia University Press, 2005), 121], who mentioned Palestine along with Assyria and the Land of the Philistines.

the Philistines; others thought Palestine referred to a larger area including Judaea. Why did the latter win out?

It was Europe's fascination with Greek and Latin texts in the early modern period. As more people could earn a living as scholars, teachers, publishers, mapmakers and writers, more Greek and Latin manuscripts got published in European vernaculars. Herodotus's (d. 425 BC) *The Histories* appeared in 55 editions in European vernaculars (plus 13 Latin or Greek editions), making it the 6th most popular text in Europe for three centuries. Josephus's (d. 100 AD) *History of the Antiquities of the Jews* appeared in 14 different editions in either Latin or Greek from 1450-1700. His *History of the Wars of the Jews* appeared 59 times in various European vernaculars, making it the 5th most popular text in Europe for over three centuries. Claudius Ptolemy's (d. 168 AD) *Geography* was reissued a whopping 61 times between 1475 and 1730, most of which were translations to European vernaculars. In Italy, the Latin poet Tibullus's (c. 30 BC) works were published more than a dozen times over roughly the same period. Herodotus, Josephus, Ptolemy and Tibullus had something else in common, besides getting published repeatedly. They used the word Palestine in the Greek or Roman sense, a land "from Egypt to Phoenicia"—for Herodotus, or from "Syria to Arabian Petraea"—for Ptolemy. They also thought Palestine included Judaea, as noted above.[124]

Renaissance Europeans brought many other popular works out of manuscript and into print, including many who called the place Palestine. Constantine VII (d.959)'s *De Administrando*

---

[124] See Henry N. Stevens, *Ptolemy's Geography: A Brief Account of all the Printed Editions Down to 1730* (2nd ed.) (London: Stevens, Son and Stiles, 1908), 37-62; Peter Burke, "A Survey of the Popularity of Ancient Historians, 1450-1700," *History and Theory* 5(2) (1966): 135-152; see also David M. Jacobson, "Palestine and Israel," *Bulletin of the American Schools of Oriental Research* 313 (1999): 65-74; on Tibullus, see worldcat.org.

Imperio was published a half-dozen times from the 16th century to the 18th centuries. Ranulf Higden's *Polychronicon*—which described the region as Palestine as well—was also translated and published a half-dozen times in the late 15th and 16th centuries, primarily in England.[125]

Renaissance Europeans removed the dust from the manuscripts that had given Palestine refuge for centuries, popularizing classical nomenclature. They did it because they could earn a living as scholars, editors, teachers, professors, cartographers, map artists and translators. The boom was also made possible by the printing press, which enabled even the poor to gain access to the printed word. Education expanded and the cost of books decreased. Reading, writing and scholarship proliferated. Europe's emerging middle classes started to read about Greek, Roman and Byzantine Palestine in Cologne, Venice, Florence, Ulm, Bologna, Rome, Amsterdam, Leiden, Arnhem and London with Josephus, Herodotus, Ptolemy, Tibullus, Higden and Constantine VII as their guides.

But what was so special about the ancients? They presented independent accounts of the Biblical era. Herodotus's *The Histories*, often considered the founding work of history in the Greek tradition, narrated the rise of the Persian Empire and the Greco-Persian Wars in the 5th century BC—filling in critical gaps between the Old and the New Testaments. Josephus' *Antiquities of the Jews* included two references to Jesus himself and a reference to John the Baptist, while it narrated the history of the Jews who played such a critical role in scripture. Ptolemy's *Geography* provided detailed descriptions and every longitudinal and latitudinal coordinate of every place name in the Bible (and many not in the Bible). These texts became required reading

---

[125] See worldcat.org.

for Renaissance Bible reformists, enthusiasts, critics and nihilists. Increasingly, Christians started putting other texts in conversation with the Bible, scripture and doctrine. The religious climate of the age gave the ancient Greek and Latin texts newfound purpose.

Some observers explicitly pointed out the discrepancy between how modern Europeans called the place—the Holy Land—and how the ancients did—Palestine. In 1570, The Flemish cartographer, geographer, and map colorist Abraham Ortelius explained the discrepancy: "That which the ancients called Palestine and Phonecia, all the Europeans generally now call the HOLY LAND, under which name they comprehend that whole country which God gaue [sic] unto the Israelites by the name of the Land of Promise." He was almost saying that the HOLY LAND was a mistake, that the more accurate name of the place was Palestine.[126]

In 1587, Jean Zuallart also claimed people preferred to call it the Holy Land rather than Palestine, all the while reviving it. "The land between Dan and Beersheba included the provinces of Syria-Phonecia, and had different names, such as Canaan, Palestine, Judaea, and by us Christians, the Holy Land." But he also delineated the entire coastal area as Palestine, and used the word on occasion. The realization among some European Renaissance writers that Palestine *used* to be the term of choice partially led to its revival.[127]

---

[126] Nabil Matar, "Protestant Restorationism and the Ortelian Mapping of Palestine (with an Afterward on Islam)," 59-82 in *The Calling of the Nations: Exegesis, Ethnography, and Empire in a Biblical-Historical Present* Mark Vessey (ed.) (Toronto; New York: University of Toronto Press, 2011), 59-60.
[127] Jean Zuallart (Giovanni Zuallardo) (d.1634), *Il Devotissimo Viaggio di Gervsalemme* (Rome: Per F. Zanetti, & Gia. Ruffinelli, 1587), 291-293, 305. Zuallart was a judge, mayor, chronicler and traveler from Hainaut in Belgium.

Palestine was making a comeback by the late 16th century. The English wanderlust Fynes Moryson (d.1630), the Franciscan Johannes Dubliulius and the German nobleman and traveler, Martinus à Baumgarten, picked up the term as well. They, in turn, published their travelogues, many of which were issued multiple times in the late 16th and early 17th centuries. Palestine's stock was rising.[128]

By the 17th and 18th centuries, the word appeared in hundreds if not thousands of printed books in at least a dozen European languages. The Catholic Scottish General Patrick Gordon summarized this point nicely in 1704.

> Palestine or Judaea. This country, most memorable in Holy Scripture, and sometimes called *Canaan* from *Canaan*, the Son of *Cham*, sometimes the land of promise, because promis'd to *Abraham* and his seed, and sometimes *Judaea*, from the Nation of the *Jews*, or People of the Tribe of *Juda*, and now bounded on the East and North by part *Syria Propria*; on the West by part of the *Mediterranean* Sea, and on the South by *Arabia Petrea* is termed by the Italians and the Spaniards, *Palestina*; by the French, *Palestine*, by the Germans, *Palestinen* or das *Gelobte land*; by the English, *Palestine*, or the *Holy Land*.[129]

By the 18th century, Christians in Europe adopted the term Palestine, alongside the Holy Land, displacing other terms like The Holy Places and Judaea and Samaria. The transition was subtle and gradual. By the 19th century, few realized its astounding popularity was relatively recent.

---

[128] For other 16th century cartographers of "Palestine," see, for instance, Jakob Ziegler (d. 1549), *Palaestina Emendata ad Observationem Ziegleri*, Bibliothèque Nationale de France, Département Cartes et plans, CPL GE DD-2987 (10122 B); Kristian Nissen, "Jacob Ziegler's Palestine Schondia Manuscript University Library, Oslo, MS. 917-4°" *Imago Mundi* 13 (1956): 47. Other maps, supposedly based on calculations first made by Claudius Ptolemy (d.168) also included the name Palestine. See Giorgio Galignani, et. al., *Palaestina vel Terra Sancta. Descrittione della Palestina o della Terra Sancta* (Venezia: Giovanni Battista & Giorgio Galignani, 1598); Johannes Dubliulius, *Hierosolymitanae Peregrinationis Hodoeporicvm* (Coloniae: Grevenbruch, 1590), 1; Martinus à Baumgarten, Christoph Donauer; Kauffmann, Paul (Nürnberg), *Peregrinatio in Aegyptum, Arabiam, Palaestinam et Syriam* (Noribergae: Pau. Kauffmann, 1594); Salomon Gesner; Elias Thanneberger, *Disp. de Turca altera ex cap. XXXVIII. et XXXIX* (Witteberga: Lehman, 1595); David Chytraeus, *Epistola Continens Hodoeporicon Navigationis ex Constantinopoli in Syriam, Palaestinam et Aegyptum et Montem Sinai, Necnon de bello Persico, et Circumcisione Mahometis filii Imperatoris Turcici* (n.p., 1597); Fynes Moryson, *An Itinerary Written by Fynes Moryson* (Glasgow: James MacLehose and Sons, 1611), I, 224, 462.

[129] Patrick Gordon, *Geography Anatomiz'd: Or, the Geographical Grammar. Being a Short and Exact Analysis of the Whole Body of Modern Geography, after a New and Curious Method* (London: R. Morden, T. Cockerill, and R. Smith, 1704), 290.

* * *

The East. Let's turn to the situation in the Middle East. Christians remained in regions conquered by Muslims and continued to write Church history. While the classical Greek tradition was in some cases lost among monks and priests in the Latin west, it was remembered in the Byzantine and Arab East. Folks like Herodotus and, especially, Thucydides, served as important models of how to write chronicles in the Byzantine East for centuries to come, and this meant that they were familiar with Greek history long after the decline of the Byzantines and the rise of the Muslims. The Christian chroniclers of the East, such the Chronicle of Theophanes (d. 818), Abraham of Tiberias (9th century) Fettelus (c. 1130) and Bar Hebraeus (d. 1286) all wrote about Palestine's history, especially during periods of Greek and Byzantine ascendance.[130]

Within a few centuries after the Arab conquest, though, the formerly Byzantine Greeks were now writing in Arabic. Many knew both languages, though, writing in Arabic using Greek sources. The Aleppan born Makariyus III ibn Za'im (d. 1672), Patriarch of Antakya, for instance, wrote a book called *A History of the Lives of the Saints* relying significantly on earlier Greek writers. He claimed the See of Jerusalem had authority over the land of Palestine, that Beisan and Tiberias constituted the second See of Palestine, and that Petra was the Third See of Palestine. These were the political divisions of the land during the Byzantine period.[131]

---

[130] Harry Turtledove (ed. and trans.), *The Chronicle of Theophanes: An English Translation of Anni Mundi 6095-6305 (A.D. 602-813)* (Philadelphia: University of Pennsylvania Press, 1982), x-xi; on Theophanes's discussions of Palestine, see ibid, 6, 11, 34, 37, 39; then see Rorgo Fretellus (c. 1130), James Rose Macpherson (ed.), *n.t.*, (London: Palestine Pilgrims' Text Society, 1896), 25; then see Bar Hebraeus (d. 1286), Antun Salihani (ed.), *Tarikh Mukhtasar al-Duwal* (Beirut: al-Matba'a al-Kathulikiyya lil-Aba' al-Yasu'iyyin, 1890), 67, 81, 110, 208.

[131] On his description of the jurisdictional boundaries of the five Ecumenical Sees and Three Sees of Palestine, see Makariyus III ibn Za'im, *Majmu'a Mubarak* (British Library, OC ADD 9965), folios 76a, 122b, 123a; 133b and

Muslims. The Muslims created the most powerful empire in the world in the 7th century. They preserved the Byzantine administrative boundaries but changed some of the names. They kept Palaestina Prima as Palestine, or *Filastin* in Arabic, but renamed the others. Then the Crusaders brought an end to Palestine's political status in the late 11th century. They called their state the Kingdom of Jerusalem or the Holy Land. When Salah al-Din recaptured the area from the Crusaders, he did not revive the name Palestine, instead preferring to name districts after the cities in which they were based: Gaza, Lod, Qaqun, Jerusalem, Hebron and Nablus. The Ayyubids followed this pattern of administration. The 14th century Mamluks divided the region into smaller administrative units as well, and they too corresponded to cities: Sham, Aleppo, Tripoli, Hama, Safad, al-Karak and Gaza. The Ottomans also governed from cities. The centers of power during the first few centuries of Ottoman rule were Tiberias, Safed, Gaza, Acre, Nablus, Marj ibn 'Amar, Hawran or Tripoli. In the mid-late 19th century, Jerusalem and Beirut also became administrative centers. Although there were discussions at the Ottoman Palace in Istanbul in the 1880s to consider making Palestine a district within the Empire, the idea was

---

142b; ibn Za'im also told stories about Jesus's life in Palestine and the Persian invasion of Palestine (ibid, folio 50b). He described Palestine as the scene for great wonders, splendid marvels and the well of prophets—cited from Damianos. See ibid, folio 142a. for further mention of Palestine, see ibid, 122a-122b; on his knowledge of Greek, see Habib al-Zayyat, "Rihlat al-Batriyark Makariyus," *al-Mashriq* (1902): 1016; for more on his background, see Georg Graf, *Geschichte Der Christlichen Arabischen Literatur* (Città del Vaticano, Biblioteca apostolica vaticana, 1949), III, 94-110; Nikolaj Serikoff, "Patriarch Macarius Ibn al-Za'im," pp. 236-251in Samuel Noble and Alexander Treiger (eds.), *The Orthodox Church in the Arab World, 700-1700: An Anthology of Sources* (Dekalb, IL: Northern Illinois University Press, 2014); Nabil Matar, "An Arabic Orthodox Account of the Holy Land, C.1590s," pp.28-51 in *Through the Eyes of the Beholder: The Holy Land, 1517-1713*, July A. Hayden and Nabil I. Matar (eds.), (Leiden: Brill, 2013), 32. For a brief biography and a list of his edited and published works, see Makariyus III ibn Za'im (d. 1672) *al-Siniksar al-Antaki: 1647-1672 lil-Makariyus al-Thalith Ibn Za'im* (Juniyah, Lebanon: al-Maktaba al-Bulisiyya, 2010), 7-13; on his Greek borrowings from Symeon the Metaphrast (fl. late 10th cent.), Agapius Landus (fl. 17th cent.) and Damianos, see ibid, 12. Ibn Za'im's son, the Paul of Aleppo (d.1669), also mentioned Palestine in a book about his father's travels, noting that the saints Anthonius the Great (d.356) and Theodosius the Great (d.395) were "the one light of the deserts of Askit, the other wilderness of Palestine." See Paul of Aleppo Archdeacon (d.1669), F C Belfour (ed.), *The Travels of Macarius, Patriarch of Antioch* (London: Printed for the Oriental translation committee, sold by J. Murray, 1836), 213-4.

abandoned out of fear it would encourage foreign interference in Ottoman affairs. From the time of the Crusades until the end of World War I, Palestine served no administrative purpose. That's why Palestine is an anomaly. It survived for nearly a millennium without a state guarantor.[132]

But Palestine did find a home in the Arab literary tradition. The Arabs, much like the Byzantines, preserved the stories of their tradition. They often considered earlier sources more authoritative than later ones, collating them in word for word copies. This ensured the long-term survival of geographical terms like Palestine that were popular during the early days of Islam. The great historian Shelomo Dov Goiten summarized the point well: once a description or genealogy was embraced as part of the historical tradition, "everyone versed in the technique of Arabic historiography knows that it appears again and again in later compilations."[133]

---

[132] On the 14th century Mamluks, see Jo Van Steenbergen, *Order out of Chaos: Patronage, Conflict and Mamluk Socio-political Culture (1341-1382)* (Leiden: Brill, 2006), 38-9; on discussions to make Palestine an administrative district in the Empire, see Johann Büssow, *Hamidian Palestine: Politics and Society in the District of Jerusalem 1872-1908* (Leiden: Brill, 2011), 54; the term Palestine was not used in Ottoman administrative parlance, and scarcely appeared in Ottoman court or state records until the 1830s. 'Abla Sa'id Muhtadi and Muhammad 'Adnan Bakhit [*Sijill Mahkamat al-Quds al-Shar'iyya: Fahrasa Tahliliyya* ('Amman: Markaz al-Watha'iq wa-l-Makhtutat al-Jami'a al-Urduniyya, 2007-), I-IX] found the word Palestine zero times in the Jerusalem Shari'a court records in their 9-volume index covering the 1550s, 1880s and early 20th century. For each entry, they provided a summary of the case and persons and places mentioned in it; Judith Mendelsohn Rood [*Sacred Law in the Holy City: The Khedival Challenge to the Ottomans as Seen from Jerusalem, 1829-1841* (Boston: Brill, 2004), 44-5] found the term once in her study of the Jerusalem court records in the 1830s in an order issued by Ibrahim Pasha to permit repairs to Orthodox monasteries in Bethlehem in the "Land of Palestine" that resulted from earthquake damage. See the Jerusalem Shari'a Court records, vol. 319, p.74 [29 November 1834]. Iris Agmon explained to me via personal correspondence that "I never came across the term *Filastin* in the court records of late Ottoman Jaffa or Haifa;" Beshara Doumani [*Rediscovering Palestine: Merchants and Peasants in Jabal Nablus, 1700-1900* (Berkeley: University of California Press, 1995), ch.1, note 1] wrote that "in official correspondence and court cases registered in the Nablus Islamic court up to 1865 the word [Palestine] appeared only once, and the context precluded a nationalist meaning;" Felicita Tramontana never came across the term in her work on the 17th century Jerusalem court records. I did not come across the word either in scanning the Gaza (held at the ISAM library in Istanbul) or Nazareth court records (held at the Israeli State Archives) from the 1870s either. Likewise, the word Palestine does not appear in Ottoman state records according to the electronic catalogue of the Başbakanlık Osmanlı Arşivi in Istanbul before the 1830s, although it does start to appear by mid-century, discussed in the next chapter.

[133] Shelomo Dov Goitein, *Studies in Islamic History and Institutions* (Leiden: Brill, 1966), 137.

We do the same thing today, actually. Christopher Markiewicz, an Oxford-based historian, explicitly noted he would use the geographical nomenclature of the subjects of his study—15th century Muslims from Bitlis. Presumably he did this because he thought modern place names would have obfuscated the reality he was describing. Muslims might have felt similarly, preserving the language of their sources. Palestine survived as a result.[134]

Stories. Before jumping into the stories, let's briefly look at the genres they could be classified into. Muhammad claimed God revealed the Qur'an to him. It's the holiest book to Muslims. Many thought it was also important to remember everything Muhammad said and did. These "sayings and doings" became known as hadith. They were later compiled into biographies of the prophet, known as *sira*. These biographies snowballed into history—*tarikh*, its own genre by the mid-late 8th century. Biography and history spanned into a new field called merits literature, or *fada'il*. Books of merit identified the merits of places, quoting the Qur'an, *hadith, sira*, and *tarikh*. Many Muslims wrote books of merit about Sham, the Holy Land and Jerusalem. Meanwhile, geography emerged as its own genre, known in Arabic as *surat al-ard, al-masalik wa-l-mamalik*, or *kitab al-buldan*, the "science of countries" or the "atlas of Islam." (The word *geography*, or *jughrafiya*, also entered Arabic from Greek in transliteration, but was scarcely used until the 19th century). Muslims also wrote encyclopedias, travelogues, books of rhetoric, grammar, and much more. Stories about Palestine appeared in all of them.[135]

---

[134] Markiewicz, "The Crisis of Rule in Late Medieval Islam," xvii.
[135] On 8th century *hadith* compilers in the lands of Sham, see Fred Donner, "The Problem of Early Historiography in Syria," *Proceedings of the Second Symposium on the History of Bilād al-Shām during the Early Islamic Period up to 40 A.H./640 A.D.: The Fourth International Conference on the History of Bilad al-Shām* (eds.) Muhammad 'Adnan Bakhit (Amman: University of Jordan, 1987), 2; on the origins of history writing in Arabic, see Chase F. Robinson, *Islamic Historiography* (Cambridge: Cambridge University Press 2004), ch. 1.

Let's take a closer look at some of the earliest. One of the earliest works of history in the Muslim tradition, *The Conquest of Sham*, details the conquest of "the land of Palestine." The famous biographer Ibn Hisham (d.833) wrote that the prophet instructed Usama ibn Zayd ibn Harithah to conquer al-Balqa and other places in Palestine. al-Ya'qubi (d.897/8) surveyed Palestine's borders, urban landscapes and the origins of its name. Ibn al-Faqih (d.902) claimed Palestine's soil was fertile and its landscapes were beautiful. Abu al-Ma'ali (ca.1030s) described Muslim exploits on the battlefield against Palestine's indigenous inhabitants—the Nabataeans. Shihab al-Din Yaqut (d.1229) wrote an encyclopedia of every geographical term known to him and included a section on Palestine. Ibn Khallikan (d.1282) traced the lineages of Muslim names, such as al-Uqhuwani, which originated in a village in Sham in the land of Palestine close to Tiberias. Within a few centuries after the conquest, many stories relating to Palestine circulated around the Muslims world, spanning the entire breadth of the tradition.[136]

Many Muslims also tried to define what Palestine was—as I did in the previous chapter. They did not define it as an idea invented by humans, as I did, but instead as a piece of real estate

---

[136] The *Conquest of Sham* is often credited to Muhammad bin 'Umar al-Waqidi (d.822) [*Futuh al-Sham* (s.n.: Mu'assasat Himada lil-Dirasat al-Jam'iyya wa-l-Nashr wa-l- Tawzi', 2011), 42, 44, 45]; then see Ibn Hisham (d.833), Abdus-Salam M. Harun ed., *Sirat Ibn Hisham: Biography of the Prophet* (Cairo: al-Falah Foundation, 2000), 242, 244; then see Ahmad ibn Abi Ya'qub al-Ya'qubi (d.897/8), *Kitab al-Buldan* (Leiden: Brill, 1891), 328; then see Ibn al-Faqih (d.902) *Mukhtasar Kitab al-Buldan* (Beirut: Dar Ihya al-Turath al-'Arabi, 1988), 153; then see Abu al-Ma'ali (ca.1030s), *Fada'il Bayt al-Maqdis wa-l-Khalil wa-Fada'il al-Sham* (Shafa' 'Amr, Israel: Dar al-Mashriq li-l-Tarjama wa-l-Tiba'a wa-l-Nashr, 1995), 52; for more on the Nabateans of Palestine, see Muhammad bin 'Abd Allah al-Himyari (d.1495), *Kitab al-Rawd al-Mi'tar* (Beirut: s.i., 1975), 355; Muhammad ibn Shihab al-Din al-Suyuti (d.1505) *Ithaf al-Akhissa', bi-Fada'il al-Masjid al-Aqsa* (Cairo: al-Hay'a al-Misriyya al-'Amma lil-Kitab, 1982-4), I, 238, 240; Mujir al-Din al-'Ulaymi (d.1522), *al-Uns al-Jalil bi-Tarikh al-Quds wa-l-Khalil* (Amman: Maktabat al-Muhtasab, 1973), I, 202; 'Abd al-Ghani al-Nabulusi (d.1731), *al-Hadra al-Unsiyya fi al-Rihla al-Qudsiyya* (Saalfeld/Saale: 1918), 25; then see Shihab al-Din Yaqut (d.1229), *Mu'jam al-Buldan* (Beirut: Dar Sadir li-l-Tiba'a wa-l-Nashr, 1955-58), III, 913; then see Ibn Khallikan (d.1282), *Wafayat al-A'yan wa-Anba' Abna' al-Zaman* (Beirut: Dar al-Thaqafa, 1968-1972), II, 488; Ibn al-'Imad (d.1679) *Shadharat al-Dhahab fi Akhbar man Dhahab* (Damascus: Dar al-Tabba', 1991) III, 215; Ahmad ibn Ahmad al-'Ajami (d.1675) *Dhayl Lubb al Lubab* (Manuscript of the Royal Library: National Library of Denmark and Copenhagen University Library, Cod. Arab. 167), folio 10.

defined by its borders or major cities. Some said it was bound by Rafah and Lajjun in the north and south, and by Jaffa and Jericho in the east and west. Others claimed it stretched from al-'Arish to Lajjun or from Jaffa to al-Zu'r or the Balqa, or from the Mediterranean Sea to the cities of Lot. Some preferred merely to list the cities within it—such as Jerusalem, Gaza, Ashkelon, al-'Arish, the Ramla of Palestine and Hebron. Some thought Palestine referred to merely the city of Ramla. Others believed it meant the city of Ramla and its surroundings.[137]

Lots of Muslims also claimed to know the origins of the name Palestine. They did not trace it to the Aegean, but rather to a descendent of Noah named Filastin, based on the Biblical theory that an offspring of Noah named Filastin settled down in that area after the flood and the name Filastin took hold as a result. No corroborating evidence outside of the Bible attests to a

---

[137] For those who defined Palestine as a list of cities, see Ahmad ibn Yusuf al-Qaramani (d.1611) and Muhammad Amin al-Fattal (fl. 18th century)—the former included Jerusalem, Gaza and Ashkelon, the latter added al-'Arish, Gaza, "the Ramla of Palestine," and Hebron. See Ahmad ibn Yusuf al-Qaramani (d.1611), *Kitab Akhbar al-Duwal wa-Athar al-Uwal fi-l-Tarikh* (Baghdad: Matba'at 'Abbas al-Tabrizi, 1865), 368 and Muhammad Amin al-Fattal (fl. 18th century), *Awraq min Rihlat al-Shaykh Muhammad Amin al-Fattal* (Amman: Dar al-Yara' li-l-Nashr wa-l-Tawzi', 2006), 65-6; for the four-point formula, see al-Ya'qubi (d.897/8) *Kitab al-Buldan*, 328; Ibn al-Faqih (d.902), *Mukhtasar Kitab al-Buldan*, 153; Muhammad bin Ahmad al-Muqaddasi (a.k.a. al-Maqdisi) (d. 991), *Ahsan al-Taqasim* (Leiden: Brill, 1904), 37, 136; Abu 'Ubayd al-Bakri (d.1094), *al-Masalik wa-l-Mamalik* (Qartaj: al-Mu'assasa al-Wataniyya li-l-Tarjama wa-l-Tahqiq wa-l-Dirasat, 1992), I, 464; Yaqut, *Mu'jam al-Buldan*, III, 914; Ibn 'Abd al-Haqq (d.1338), *Marasid al-Ittila' 'ala Asma' al-Amkina wa-l-Biqa'* (Lugduni Batavorum: Brill, 1852–64), III, 1042; Ibn al-Wardi (d.1348), *Kharidat al-'Aja'ib wa-Faridat al-Ghara'ib* (Cairo: Mustafa al-Babi al-Halabi wa-Awladuhu, 1923), 30; al-Himyari (d.1495), *Kitab al-Rawd al-Mi'tar*, 268; al-'Ulaymi (d.1522), *al-Uns al-Jalil*, II, 67; Muhammad ibn al-Hasan al-Diyarbakri (d. 1558), *Al-Juz' al-Awwal min Tarikh al-Khamis fi Ahwal Anfas Nafis* (Cairo: al-Matba'a al-Wahbiyya, 1866), I, 87; Sadiq Ahmad Ibrahim Muhammad al-Turk (ed.), Salih bin Muhammad al-Tamartashi (d. 1644-5), "al-Khabar al-Tamm fi Dhikr al-Ard al-Muqaddasa wa-Hududuha wa-Dhikr Ard Filastin wa-Hududuha wa Aradi al-Sham" (M.A. Thesis, Jami'at Najah al-Wataniyya, 1998), 63, 81-2; Muhammad bin Habib (f. 1649), *Durr al-Nizam*, folio 5B, cited in Yosef Sadan, "Shlosha Mekorot Khadashim mi-Sifrut Shivkhay Erets ha-Kodesh be-'Aravit ba-Meot ha-16-17," *Catheda* 11 (1979): 200; 'Abd al-Ghani al-Nabulusi (d.1731) *Rihla ila al-Quds* (Cairo, 1902), 7; for more on its meaning as Ramla, see Zachary Foster, "Was Jerusalem Part of Palestine? The Forgotten City of Ramla, 900–1900," *British Journal of Middle Eastern Studies* 43(4) (2016): 575-589; an 1849 Ottoman map identified a small region to the north west of Ramla as "the land of Palestine," or "Filastin Ülkesi." See Yuval Ben-Bassat and Yossi Ben-Artzi, "Gvul Erets Yisrael-Mitsrayim be-Re'i ha-Mipu'i ha-'Otomani be-Shilhey ha-Me'a ha-19," *Cathedra*, forthcoming.

historical figure named Noah, let alone that he had a grandchild bearing a name similar to Palestine. Instead, the evidence points to an Aegean origin, as discussed above.[138]

Muslims also told stories about people who lived in, traveled to or died in Palestine. Recall that since hadith formed part of the basis of Islamic Law (alongside the Qur'an and the Sunnah, or Muhammad's life's saying and doings), Muslim activists were incentivized to invent hadiths *ex nihilo*. Believers needed to find a way to distinguish trustworthy hadiths from untrustworthy ones. Muslims starting writing not just what the prophet said or did, but also the chain of people who transmitted the information going back to the prophet himself. It became necessary to know where the transmitters resided, traveled to and died so that commentators could assess the likelihood that they transmitted the hadith they claimed to transmit. Thus, Shaddad ibn Aws, 'Ubadah ibn al-Samit, Tamim al-Dari and Raja' ibn Haywah, for instance, each reportedly lived in Palestine (ibn Haywah was actually identified as Palestinian).[139]

---

[138] For variations on the Noah origins of Palestine, see Ibn al-Faqih (d. 902) *Kitab al-Buldan*, 153; Yaqut (d.1229), *Mu'jam al-Buldan*, III, 913-4; al-Bakri (d.1094), *al-Masalik wa-l-Mamalik*, I, 464; Ibn al-Dawadari (d.1335), *Kanz al-Durar wa Jami' al-Ghurar* (Cairo: al-Ma'had al-Almani li-l-Athar, 1960), II, 80; al-Suyuti (d.1505), *Ithaf al-Akhissa'*, II, 133; al-'Ulaymi (d. 1522), *al-Uns al-Jalil*, II, 67; al-Nabulusi (d.1731), *Rihla ila al-Quds*, 7. The story of Noah may date to one of the cataclysmic floods that covered huge swaths of the earth 14,000, 11,500 and 8,000 years ago. See Peter Watson, *The Great Divide: Nature and Human Nature in the Old World and the New* (New York: Harper Collins, 2012), 38-39; Erik Velasquez Garcia, "The Maya Flood Myth and the Decapitation of the Cosmic," *The PARI Journal* 7(1) (2006): 1-10; on the Biblical theory, see Genesis 10:14 and Chronicles 1:12.

[139] on Tamim al-Dari, see Abu Yusuf Ya'qub Fasawi (d.890/1), *Kitab al-Ma'rifa wa-l-Tarikh* (Medina: Maktabat al-Dar, 1989), e.g., I, 393, 434; II, 373, III, 168; 'Ali ibn 'Abd Allah al-Samhudi (d. 1506), *Wafa' al-Wafa bi-Akhbar Dar al-Mustafa* (London: Mu'assasat al-Furqan li-l-Turath al-Islami, 2001), II, 112 and IV, 225; Muhammad al-Minawi (d.1621) *al-Kawakib al-Durriyya fi Tarajim al-Sufiyya* (al-Aqsa Mosque Library Collection of Historical Manuscripts, EAP521/1), folio 87; Mustafa As'ad al-Luqaymi (d.1764), 'Mawanih al-Uns bi-Rihlati ila Wadi al-Quds', in Taysir Khalaf (ed.), *Mawsu'at Rihlat al-'Arab wa-l-Muslimin ila Filastin* (Damascus: Dar al-Kan'an, 2010), 101; for more on Tamim al-Dari, see Yehoshua Frenkel, "Tamim al-Dari and Hebron during the Mamluk Period," pp. 435-446 in *Egypt and Syria in the Fatimid, Ayyubid and Mamluk Eras*, U. Vermeulen, K. D'Hulster and J. Van Steenbergen (eds.), (Leuven, Paris, Walpole, Mass.: Uitgeverij Peeters en Departement Oosterse Studies, 2013); on Shaddad ibn Aws, see, for instance, al-Fattal (fl. 18th cent.), *Awraq min Rihlat al-Shaykh*, 63; Ibn al-'Imad (d.1679), *Shadharat al-Dhahab fi Akhbar man al-Dhahab* (Beirut: al-Maktab al-Tijari li-l-Tiba'a wa-l-Nashr wa-l-Tawzi', 1966), III, 208; Rija' bin Haywa was also defined as Palestinian (*Filastini*). See ibn Hilal al-Muqaddasi (d. 1364) Ahmad Samih al-Khalidi (ed.), *Muthir al-Gharam bi-Fada'il al-Quds wa-l-Sham* (Jaffa: Maktaba al-Tahir Ikhwan, 1946), 216, 343.

Muslims wrote biographies not just of the transmitters, but of all prophets in Islamic history. Some thought the prophet Luqman, for instance, was buried in the Land of Palestine in a village called Sarafand, close to Ramla. Abraham, who is mentioned 69 times in the Quran, was claimed to have traveled westward with Lot and Sara from Kutha in Iraq to Harran, Egypt, Sham and then to Sabu' in the land of Palestine. The Berber or Amalekite giant, Goliath, lived on the coast of the Mediterranean Sea between Egypt and Palestine and ruled in the region of Palestine. I don't think there was any special legal reason to discuss the whereabouts of Luqman, Abraham or Goliath as was the case with the hadith transmitters. It was just part of how you told stories—you talked about whereabouts.[140]

The Qur'an mentions the term "the Holy Land" and so it naturally became the subject of commentary. Some thought the Holy Land referred to the land of Palestine. Others defined it as the Land of Sham, the Land of Palestine and Jordan, Damascus, Palestine and some of Jordan,

---

[140] Commentators reported that thirty prophets were buried in Homs, five hundred in Damascus, and one thousand in Jordan, Palestine and Jerusalem. See, for instance, Abu al-Ma'ali (ca.1030s), *Fada'il Bayt al-Maqdis*, 206; Musa bin Sahal al-Nisaburi al-Ramli (c. 1250-1517?), *Kitab fi Fada'il Bayt al-Maqdis wa-fihi Kitab fi Fada'il al-Sham*, cited in Ghalib Anabsa, *Min Adab Fada'il al-Sham: Nusus Mukhtara min Makhtutat Mamlukiyya wa-'Uthmaniyya* (Kafr Qari': Dar al-Huda 'Amman; Dar al-Fikr; Bayt Birl: Markaz Dirasat al-Adab al-'Arabi, 2007), 33; see also Ibn 'Abd al-Razzaq (d.1721), *Hada'iq al-An'am fi Fada'il al-Sham* (Beirut: Dar al-Diya' li-l-Tiba'a wa-l-Nashr wa-l-Tawzi', 1989), 126; Abu al-Qasim ibn Ahmad al-Zayyani (d.1809), *al-Tarjumana al-Kubra fi Akhbar al-Ma'mur Barran wa-Bahran* (Rabat: Dar Nash al-Ma'rifa, 1991), 276; On Luqman, see Mustafa Bakri al-Siddiqi (d.1749), "Nufhat al-Isda' wa-l-Akram fi Midha al-Anbiya al-Kiram," folios 63-85, in *Majmu'a* (Manuscript Section of the National Library of Israel, JER NLI AP Ar. 572), folio 85a; on Abraham, see Abu al-Ma'ali (ca.1030s), *Fada'il Bayt al-Maqdis*, 332; al-Suyuti (d.1505), *Ithaf al-Akhissa'*, II, 97, 105; 'Abd al-Razzaq (d.1721), *Hada'iq al-In'am*, 41-2; Ahmad Ibn 'Ajiba (d.1809), *al-Bahr al-Madid fi Tafsir al-Qur'an al-Majid* (Cairo: Dar al-Kutub al-'Ilmiyya, 1999), III, 478; IV, 297; Muhammad al-Mazhari (d.1810/11), *al-Tafsir al-Mazhari* (Beirut: Dar al-Kutub al-'Ilmiyya, 2007), IV, 485; Burhan al-Din (d. unknown), *Kitab Jalil fi Fada'il Bayt al-Maqdis wa-l-Masjid al-Khalil* (02854 Atif Efendi Collection, Sulaymaniye Manuscript Library, Istanbul), folio 70a; on Goliath, see al-Diyarbakri (d.1558), *Tarikh al-Khamis*, I, 87; al-Luqaymi (d. 1764), *Mawanih al-Uns*, 146-7; al-Mazhari (d.1810/11), *al-Tafsir al-Mazhari*, I, 338. For slightly different renditions, see al-'Ulaymi (d.1522), *al-Uns al-Jalil*, I, 104; Ahmad bin Muhammad al-Maqqari (d.1631), *Azhar al-Riyad fi Akhbar al-Qadi 'Iyad* (Rabat: Sanduq Ihya' al-Turath al-Islami, 1978), 30; al-Himyari (d.1495), *Kitab al-Rawd al-Mi'tar*, 441; al-Qaramani (d.1611), *Kitab Akhbar al-Duwal*, 58; al-'Ajami (d.1675), *Dayl Lubb al Lubab*, folio 17-18; for other prophets, see, for instance, Abu al-Fida' (d.1331), *Tarikh Abi al-Fida': al-Musamma al-Mukhtasar fi Akhbar al-Bashar* (Beirut: Dar al-Kutub al-'Ilmiyya, 1997), I, 43.

the Damascus of Sham, Jordan and Palestine, and the Land of Jerusalem, Mount Tur and it surroundings. Others said it was surrounded by the land of the Hijaz and that it stretched from the Shura Mountains to Dumat al-Jandal, and from the Euphrates in the east to the Sea in the west and the sands of Egypt and al-'Arish, which led to the Sinai Peninsula.[141]

Palestine came up in passing in stories told about other places too. Muslims wrote stories about Sham, where Palestine often surfaced. They also identified ambiguous Qur'anic places as located in Palestine: a river, the land delivered to Abraham and Lot, the surroundings of Masjid al-Aqsa and "the Eastern and Western regions." There were other somewhat arbitrary designations in which Palestine came up as well, such as in descriptions of "the lands of Islam" or the Eastern Mediterranean. Muslims also described cities, such as Nablus, as the most beautiful city in Palestine. Chroniclers wrote stories about battles, including when governors were forced to flee to various places, such as the Qalansuwa forest in Palestine. They wrote stories about the construction of mosques, such as the Mosque of David in Jerusalem, which was built it in the land of Palestine. Naturally, travelers wrote about the places they passed through on their travel journeys, such as the village of Karak Nuh or Sabastia, both apparently located in Palestine. Palestine was a useful point of reference for chroniclers, travelers, jurisprudents, genealogists

---

[141] See Yaqut (d.1229), *Mu'jam al-Buldan*, III, 914-5; Ibn Hisham (d.1359), *Tahsil al-Uns li-Za'ir al-Quds*, 105; Ibn Rajab (d.1392), 'Adil Ibn Sa'd (ed.), *Fada'il al-Sham (Majmu'a)* (Beirut: Dar al-Kutub al-'Ilmiyya, 2001), 207; al-Diyarbakri (d. 1558), *al-Juz' al-Awwal min Tarikh al-Khamis*, 63; N.a. (fl. 18th century), n.t. (Dar al-Kutub Manuscripts, Bab al-Khalq, Cairo, Egypt, 4628, film #7528], 60; Khalil al-Zahiri (d.1468), *Zubdat Kashf al-Mamalik wa-Bayan al-Turuq wa-l-Masalik* (Paris: al-Matba'a al-Jumhuriyya, 1894), 17; Muhammad bin 'Isa bin Kannan (d. 1740), *al-Mawakib al-Islamiyya fi al-Mamlik al-Shamiyya* (Cairo: Dar al-Ma'arif al-'Ilmiyya, 2001), 223; al-Diyarbakri (d. 1558), *al-Juz' al-Awwal min Tarikh al-Khamis*, 63; 'Abd al-Razzaq (d.1721) *Hada'iq al-In'am*, 42; Ahmad ibn 'Ali al-Mamimi (d.1758), *al-I'lam bi-Fada'il al-Sham* (Jerusalem: Matba'at al-'Asriyya, 19??), 50; see also Haim Gerber, "'Palestine' and Other Territorial Concepts in the 17th Century." *International Journal of Middle East Studies* 30 (1998): 563-572; Douglas Howard, "It Was Called "Palestine": The Land, History and Palestinian Identity," *Fides et Historia* 35(2) (2003), 67.

and encyclopedists. To tell stories, you usually need to use nouns of place. The Muslims were no exception.[142]

In short, Palestine was a popular geographical designation in the early Islamic period. Because Muslims continued to copy and collate the texts of the tradition for centuries to come, Palestine continued to appear in writing in all genres of literature during every period of Islamic history. Just as historians today write about Syria-Palaestina, Transjordan, Phoenicia, Galatia and Mesopotamia even though we don't use these terms in our day-to-day speech, biographers, historians, geographers, travelers, grammarians, genealogists, hadith compilers and merits writers all wrote stories about Palestine from the 9th-18th centuries.

---

[142] On the Eastern Mediterranean, see al-Idrisi (d. 1161), *Nuzhat al-Mushtaq fi Ikhtiraq al-Afaq* (Cairo: Maktabat al-Thaqafa al-Diniyya, 2002), I, 11; al-Maqrizi (d.1442), *al-Mawa'iz wa-al-I'tibar*, I, 44; al-Himyari (d.1495), *Kitab al-Rawd al-Mi'tar*, 163; Mubarik bin 'Umar (fl. 1707), *Wasf Rihla fi Shamal al-Jazira (al-Hijaz), wa-Misr wa-l-Sham* (Columbia University, film #414), 153; Ibn Nasir al-Dar'i (d.1823), *al-Rihla al-Nasriyya* (The University of Jordan Manuscript Library, 387935), 152; on the ambiguous places mentioned in the Qu'ran, such as the river (Qur'an 2:249), see al-Mazhari (d.1810), *al-Tafsir al-Mazhari*, I, 340; on the Eastern and Western regions (Qur'an 7:137), see al-Muqaddasi (d. 991), *Ahsan al-Taqasim* 187; al-Muqaddasi (d. 1364), *Muthir al-Gharam*, 68; al-Suyuti (d.1505), *Ithaf al-Akhissa'*, II, 132; on the land delivered to Abraham and Lot (Qur'an 21:71), see Ibn Faqih (d.902), *Kitab al-Buldan*, 153; Yaqut (d.1220), *Mu'jam al-Buldan*, III, 914-5; on the surroundings of the al-Aqsa Mosque (Qur'an 17:1), see Abu al-Ma'ali (w. 1030s.), *Fada'il Bayt al-Maqdis*, 316; Ibn Hisham (d.1360), *Tahsil al-Uns li-Za'ir al-Quds*, 113; al-Muqaddasi (d. 1364), *Muthir al-Gharam*, 71; al-'Ulaymi (d.1522), *al-Uns al-Jalil*, II, 66; Isma'il Haqqi (d.1724), *Tanwir al-Adhhan min Tafsir Ruh al-Bayan* (Damascus and Beirut: Dar al-Qalam, 1989), II, 329; III, 265; al-Luqaymi (d.1764), *Mawanih al-Uns*, 54; Ahmad ibn 'Ali al-Mamimi (d.1758), *al-I'lam bi-Fada'il al-Sham* (Jerusalem: Matba'at al-'Asriyya, 19??), 52; on the Qalansuwa forest, Ibn Jum'a (fl. 18th century) wrote that the appointed governor of Damascus in 1710 was surrounded and nearly killed by forces loyal to the Ottoman Sultan, and was forced to flee to Hish and Ghaylan, which was reportedly located in the Qalansuwa forest in Palestine." My guess is that Ibn Jum'a must have heard or read about the Qalansuwa forest, looked it up in popular geographical dictionary like Yaqut—as I did—where he would have discovered that it was located in Palestine—as I did. See Muhammad bin Jum'a, "Pashat wa-al-Qada' 1516-1744," pp.1-70 in Salah al-Din Munajjid, *Wulat Dimashq fi al-'Ahd al-'Uthmani* (Damascus: n.p., 1949), 54-5, presumably citing Yaqut, *Mu'jam al-Buldan*, IV, 392; on the Mosque of David in Jerusalem, see Evliya Çelebi (d.1682), *Evliya Tshelebi's Travels in Palestine: 1648-1650* (Jerusalem: Ariel Pub., 1980), 67-8; on the travelers, see 'Abd al-Ghani al-Nabulusi (d. 1731) [cited in 'Abd al-Ghani al-Nabulusi and Ramadan ibn Musa 'Utayfi, *Rihlatan ila Lubnan* (Beirut: Dar al-Nashr Frants Shtaynar, 1979), 73], who passed through the village of Karak Nuh on his way from Damascus to Ba'albek and cited earlier commentators who mentioned Karak could refer to al-Shawbak in the land of Palestine. He also cited Ibn Maktum al-Nahwi and Yaqut (d. 1229) in his discussion of Karak. al-Nabulusi (d.1731) [*Rihla ila al-Quds*, 6-7] cited al-Harawi (d.1089) in his claim that Sibastia, near Nablus was also called *Filastin*. Elsewhere, 'Abd al-Ghani al-Nabulusi (d.1731) [*al-Haqiqa wa-al-Majaz fi Rihlat Bilad al-Sham wa Misr wa-l-Hijaz* (Damascus: Dar al-Ma'arifa, 1998), 305] also cited Yaqut (d. 1229), claiming that Sabastia was a city in Palestine close to Nablus, between it and Jerusalem.

* * *

Retreat. Palestine was preserved in writing even though it retreated in speech, especially from the 15th century onwards. Most chroniclers, biographers, and travelers writing in Arabic from the 15th to the mid-19th century never mention the word Palestine in their chronicles, biographies and travelogues even though they deal extensively with that piece of real estate. This suggests they were probably not terribly familiar with the term.[143]

---

[143] On chroniclers, see Jibra'il ibn al-Qila'i (d.1516), *Zajaliyyat Jibra'il ibn al-Qila'i* (Beirut: Dar al-Lahd Khatir lil-Tiba'a wa-l-Nashr, 1982); Hamza bin Ahmad ibn Asbat (d.1520), *Sidq al-Akhbar: Tarikh ibn Sabat* (Tripoli, Lebanon: Jarrus Bris, 1993); Ahmad al-Khalidi al-Safadi (d. 1624), As'ad Rastum and Fu'ad Afram al-Bustani (eds.) *Lubnan fi 'Ahd Fakhr al-Din al-Ma'ni al-Thani* (Beirut: Université Libanaise 1969); Jirjis Zughayb (d.1729), Bulus Qara'li (ed.) *'Awdat al-Nasara ila Jurud Kasrawan* (Beirut: Jarrus Bars, 1963), 11-30; Muhammad bin Muhammad bin Sharf al-Din al-Khalili (d. 1734), "Kitab Tarikh al-Quds wa-l-Khalil 'Alayhi al-Salam," pp. 129-165 in Anabsi (ed.), *Min Adab Fada'il al-Sham* ('Amman: Dar al-Fikr, 2007); Muhammad al-Makki ibn al-Sayyid ibn al-Khanqah, (fl. 1722) *Tarikh Hims: Yawmiyyat Dimashq* (Damascus: al-Ma'had al-'Ilmi al-Faransi li-l-Dirasat al-'Arabiyya bi-Dimashq, 1987); al-Ab Agustin Zunda (w.1728), *al-Tarikh al-Lubnani*, 1714-1728 (Kaslik, Lebanon: Jami'at al-Ruh al-Quds, 1988); Muhammad bin 'Isa bin Kannan (d.1740), *Hada'iq al-Asmi fi Dhikr Qawanin al-Khulafa' wa-l-Salatin* (Beirut: Dar al-Nafa'is, 1991); Mikha'il Burayk (fl. 1782), *Tarikh al-Sham* (Damascus: Dar al-Qutayba, 1982); Muhammad Murtada al-Husayni al-Zabidi (d. 1791), *Alfiyat al-Sanad* (Beirut: Dar Ibn Hazm, 2006); 'Abbud al-Sabbagh (fl. 18th century), *al-Rawd al-Zahir fi Tarikh al-Zahir* (Irbid: Mu'assasat Hamada lil-Khadamat wa-l-Dirasat al-Jami'iyya, 1999); Ibrahim al-Danafi al-Samiri (fl. 1783), *Zahir al-'Umar wa Hukkam Jabal Nablus*, 1185-1187/1771-1773 (Nablus: Jami'at al-Najah al-Wataniyya, 1986); Ahmad al-Budayri al-Hallaq, *Hawadith Dimashq al-Yawmiyya, 1154-1175H, 1741-1762* (Cairo: al-Jam'iyya al-Misriyya lil-Dirasat al-Tarikhiyya, 1959); Hasan Ibn al-Siddiq (fl. 1771), *Ghara'ib al-Bada'i' wa 'Aja'ib al-Waqa'i'* (Damascus: Dar al-Ma'rifa, 1988); Rufa'il ibn Yusuf Karamah (d. 1800), *Hawadith Lubnan wa-Suriya min Sanat 1745-Sanat 1800* (Beirut: Jarrus Bars, 1980); Haydar Rida al-Rukayni (d.1783), *Jabal 'Amil fi al-Qarn*, 1163-1247H/1749-1832M (Beirut: Dar al-Fikr al-Lubnani, 1997); Niqula ibn Yusuf al-Turki (d.1828), *Dhikr Tamalluk Jumhur al-Faransawiyya: al-Aqtar al-Misriyya wa-l-Bilad al-Shamiyya* (*Histoire de l'Expedition des Français en Égypte*) (Paris: Royale, 1839; Beirut: Dar al-Farabi, 1990); Hananiyya al-Munayyir (d.1823), *al-Durr al-Marsuf fi Tarikh al-Shuf* (n.p.: Dar al-Ra'id al-Lubnani, 1984); N.a. (fl. 1858), Asad Rustum (ed.), *Hurub Ibrahim Basha fi Suriya wa-Anadul* (New Cairo: al-Matba'a al-Suriyya, 1927); Mikha'il al-Dimashqi (c.1843), *Tarikh Hawadith al-Sham, 1782-1841* (Beirut: al-Matba'a al-Khathulikiyya lil-Aba' al-Yasu'iyyin, 1912); See also n.a., Ahmad Ghassan Sabanu (ed.), *Tarikh Hawadith al-Sham wa-l-Lubnan, 1782-1841* (Beirut: Dar Qutayba, 1981); Khalil ibn Ahmad al-Rajabi (d.1827), *Tarikh al-Wazir Muhammad 'Ali Basha* (Cairo: Dar al-Afaq al-'Arabiyya, 1997); Hasan Agha al-'Abd, *Hawadith Bilad al-Sham wa-l-Imbaraturiyya al-'Uthmaniyya 1186-1241/1771-1826* (Damascus: Dar Dimashq, 1986); Ibrahim ibn Hanna al-Awra (written in 1853), *Tarikh Wilayat Sulayman Basha al-'Adil* (Sidon: Matba'at Dayr al-Mukhlis, 1936); for travelers, see Mustafa bin Kamal al-Din al-Bakri al-Siddiqi al-Dimashqi (d.1748/9), *al-Khamra al-Mahisiyya fi al-Rihla al-Qudsiyya*, pp. 71-90 in Ghalib Anabsi, *Min Adab Fada'il al-Sham* (Amman: Dar al-Fikr, 2007); Ilyas Ghasban (fl. 1755), *Rihlat Ilyas Ghasban al-Halabi Ila Ziyarat al-Amakin al-Muqaddasa* (Bibliotheque Orientale Universite St. Joseph Beyrouth Liban, 34/754); 'Abd al-Qadir Abi al-Sa'ud (c. 1840s), *Min Misr ila Islambul* (Dar al-Kutub Manuscripts, Bab al-Khalq, Cairo, #755); 'Awn Kamil Najib, Antonius Shibli (ed.), "Nubdha min Tarikh Lubnan," *al-Mashriq* (1927): 810-820; for biographers, see Najm al-Din Ghazzi (fl. 16th

Ramla and its Surroundings. There was one major exception: Ramla and its surroundings. Lots of people from Ramla called their place of origin Palestine for much of Islamic history. This is because the 7th-century Umayyad Caliph, Sulayman 'Abd al-Malik (d.717) ruled the District of Palestine—and the rest of the Empire—from Ramla. Ramla then serve as the capital of the District of Palestine during the Umayyad (661–750), Abbasid (750-878), Tulunid (878-970), Fatimid (970-1071) and Seljuk (1071-1099) periods. It was also the economic center of the region, lying at the crossroads of key trading routes within the District of Palestine and the route connecting Damascus and Cairo. Although a massive earthquake in 1068 left some 15,000-people dead and the city in total ruins, Ramla recovered during the Crusader (1095–1291) and Ayyubid periods (1187–1260) and remained the most important regional trading hub well into the Mamluk period (1250–1517). The town grew in population even after the 16th century Ottoman conquest.[144]

This helps explain why many inhabitants of Ramla from the 11th century onwards used the term Palestine as the standard name of region. Solomon b. Semah, for instance, an 11th century Jewish merchant of Ramla, wrote to Ephrayim b. Shemarya, of the Jewish community of Fustat in December 1033 after having seen the earthquake damage in the region, that

> The sun had not yet risen, and all of a sudden, in Ramla, and all of the Land of *Palestim*, it aroused the fortress until the Parzi village, and in all of the fortresses of the coast, until the fortress of Haifa, and in all of the towns of the *Negev* and hills until Jerusalem, and in all of its cities until Nablus and all of its

---

century), *al-Kawakib al-Sa'ira* (Beirut: American University Press, 1945-58), I-III; Muhammad Amin b. Fadl Allah al-Muhibbi (d.1699), *Khulasa al-Athar fi A'yan al-Qarn al-Hadi 'Ashar* (Matba'a al-Wahiba, 1867); 'Abd al-Latif al-Husayni (d. 1811), *Tarajim Ahl al-Quds fi al-Qarn al-Thani 'Ashar al-Hijri* (Amman: al-Jami'a al-Urduniyya, 1985); Muhammad Khalil al-Muradi (d.1792) [*Kitab Silk al-Durar fi A'yan al-Qarn al-Thani 'Ashar* (Bulaq: al-Matba'a al-Amiriyya, 1874-83), III, 141] does not use the word Palestine to describe people who lived, worked or died in Jerusalem, Gaza and Nablus either, although he did mention the word Palestine in an ode written by the poet 'Abd al-Nabi al-Nabulusi (d. 1741) for Salih Pasha al-Nabulusi ibn Tuqan.
[144] See Foster, "Was Jerusalem Part of Palestine."

villages until Tiberias, and all of its daughters of the Galilee hills and in all the Land of Tzvi, where people were walking along the roads, the elders will tell you that we saw the hills roaring like dancing rams.[145]

From the 15th century onwards, the evidence begins to mount that Palestine was remembered in Ramla. The scholar Abu al-'Awn Muhammad al-Ghazzi al-Shafi'i al-Faruqi (d.1504) is identified on his tombstone in the city of Ramla as a scholar from the "Palestinian frontiers." This could have been a coincidence, or people in Ramla knew about Palestine and used that term to describe their region. A number of Ramlan Arabs used the word Palestine in their writings from the 17th century onwards—not in citations or collations of early sources, but to describe the people and places of their lives. The 17th century jurist from Ramla, Khayr al-Din al-Ramli (d. 1671), used the word Palestine at least three times in his two-volume fatwa collection in very unconscious ways. He mentioned, in one case, that Palestine's northern border was either "'Uyun al-Tujjar or Acre," a definition of Palestine I've not seen elsewhere, suggesting it was an original thought rather than something he copied. His son, Najm al-Din (fl. 1718), lived his entire life in Ramla and also used the word Palestine very casually multiple times in a collection of religious certificates he wrote for his father. The Arab Orthodox priest, Yusuf Jahshan, born and raised in Ramla, wrote a diary covering politics, agriculture and climate in what he called Palestine. Jahshan mentioned the word Palestine more than a dozen times in 90 small folios, font size 36ish. In the early 20th century, the only poet known as "a poet of Palestine," to the best of my knowledge, was Sulayman al-Taji al-Faruqi (1882–1958)—also from Ramla. Keep in mind that Ramla was an intellectual backwater, and any of these mentions of Palestine are noteworthy in and of themselves even had none of them been from Ramla. It turns out that Solomon b. Semah,

---

[145] The term *Palestim* rarely appeared in Cairo Geniza documents. Perhaps it's rare appearance here had something to do with the fact that Solomon b. Semah was not like most other Jews. He was from Ramla. The terms in the document were *Kofer ha-Parzi* and *Eretz ha-Tzvi*. See TS 18 J 3, f. 9, ed. Gil, *Palestine*, Pt. 2, pp.382-384 (Doc. #209), C.B. 01-26-88 (p).

Abu al-'Awn, Khayr al-Din al-Ramli, Najm al-Din, Yusuf Jahshan and Sulayman al-Taji al-Faruqi were all from Ramla. People in Ramla remembered Palestine, while most others forgot it.[146]

Ramla was not isolated from its surroundings. It was subject to rule from Gaza during the 16th, 17th and 18th centuries. Some families, the Jahshans included, held political sway in both cities. Others from Ramla, such as Khayr al-Din al-Ramli, spent time in Gaza. Merchants moved

---

[146] On Abu al-'Awn Muhammad al-Ghazzi al-Shafi'i al-Faruqi (d.1504), see Foster, "Was Jerusalem Part of Palestine;" Khayr al-Din was well known and respected across the region and wrote a legal opinion dealing with a man from "a village of Palestine" who had a dispute with his wife, where the man reportedly claimed that if he was in the same land a year from that point, his wife would be divorced three times (Islamic law forbids a person from being divorced more than three times). So Khayr al-Din was asked if the villager would be exempt from his marriage obligation if he traveled outside of what was known as Palestine (*musamma Filastin*), such as in 'Uyun al-Tujjar or in Acre? Khayr al-Din said he would be exempt so long as he was in a region that could not be pointed at from his own village or town, i.e., that it was not within eyesight. In the end, Khayr al-Din concluded it was immaterial whether he was in or out of Palestine. Khayr al-Din mentioned the word Palestine unconsciously in at least three other instances. Khayr al-Din al-Ramli, *al-Fatawa al-Khayriyya li-Naf' al-Bariyya* (Istanbul: Matba'a-i 'Uthmaniyya, 1893), I, 86. For two further references to Palestine, see ibid, I, 190 and II, 233, 240; for more details, see Gerber, "Palestine and other Territorial Concepts," 566. (Benjamin of Tudela (d.1173) [(A. Asher, trans. and ed.), *The Itinerary of Rabbi Benjamin of Tudela* (New York: "Hakesheth" Publishing Co., 19??), 64] also identified Acre as the northern border town of Palestine); Najm al-Din wrote a book of religious certificates (*ijazat*) that detailed to whom his father issued *ijazat* and from whom he received them, using the word Palestine frequently. He wrote the following benediction to judges, for instance: "King of the universe, who has shown [good graces] to the poor and weak of the people of White Ramla, who have increased their devotion to the high heavens...and foamed their freewill offerings to the Sultan with the blessing of the dominion of shari'a in the Jerusalem region and the Palestinian land" (*al-diyar al-Qudsiyya wa-l-bilad al-Filastiniyya*). In another instance, he explained that a certain Husayn Pasha was imprisoned in a castle in Damascus even though he was a brave and loyal servant of the Ottoman state as well as a man of outstanding moral character. He implored all those who utter god's name among the ranks of power in the Palestinian land to pray to god for his speedily release from prison. Najm al-Din also described Khayr al-Din as a transmitter of knowledge in Sham and Palestine in a certificate he issued to one of his Damascene students, 'Abd al-Rahman Kamal al-Din. See Khayr al-Din al-Ramli (d.1671), *Diwan Makatabat Khayr al-Din al-Ramli* (1708-1718) (Manuscript Section of the National Library of Israel, JER NLI AP Ar. 344). For the benediction for judges, see ibid, folio 42a; on Husayn Pasha, see ibid, folio 25a; for Kamal al-Din's *ijaza*, see ibid, folio 46a-b.; Yusuf Jahshan, *Waqa'i' Filastin: al-Ramla wa Ghazza* (1765-1769) (Manuscript Section of the National Library of Israel, JER NLI AP Ar. 121) claimed in an untitled diary is untitled that appears in a collection of seven essays that the following things happened in "Palestine:" prices increased (folios 42, 63); Arabs fought battles and wars (folio 77); disquieting rumors spread (folios 66, 77 and 83); livestock and cattle perished (folio 78); a plague befell elders and wicked diseases spread (folio 85); the ruler of Sham died, and it occurred in a city in the land of Palestine (folio 79); the ruler of Persia died (folio 82), and disputes between rulers increased, and great harm was caused to people, an old city was destroyed, and a man was killed in the land of Palestine (folio 64); No good came from that year in the land of Palestine (folio 44); it is colder than it has even been, and some of the crops spoiled, and the fire increased (folio 60). For more on the famines of the 1760s, see Yaron Ayalon, "Famines, Earthquakes, Plagues: Natural Disasters in Ottoman Syria in the Writings of Visitors," *The Journal of Ottoman Studies* 32 (2008): 242-3; on Sulayman al-Taji al-Faruqi, see Foster, "Was Jerusalem Part of Palestine?"

between the two cities a great deal as well. The road connecting Jerusalem and Gaza (and onwards to Egypt) went through Ramla and Gaza. This might explain why a chief Ottoman religious authority, Minkarizade Yahya Efendi (d.1678), once asked Khayr al-Din al-Ramli for his opinion on a legal issue, calling him Khayr al-Din al-Ghazzi, "the Gazan."[147]

No surprise that Salih bin Muhammad al-Tamartashi (d.1644-5), born and raised in Gaza, is the only Muslim before the 19th century to include the word Palestine in the title of his work—*The Merits of the Holy Land and its Borders, the Land of Palestine and its Borders and the Lands of Sham*. The treatise focused on three geographical concepts: Sham, the Holy Land and Palestine, and dealt with the origins of the name Palestine—much as I did—as well as its borders and cities, especially Ramla, Ashkelon and Gaza—much as I am doing here.[148]

The question, then, is not *was* the place called Palestine but *who* called it Palestine *when*, for *what* purposes and in *which* contexts? In the transmitted sciences, such as hadith and merits literature, Palestine appeared often enough since it was collated from earlier sources. But most people didn't use the word Palestine in their day to day speech, save for folks from Ramla and its

---

[147] Jahshan came from a prominent Orthodox Christian family in Ramla whose members also held positions as clerks in Ramla, Lod and Gaza, including Qustandi Jahshan in Ramla, Ishaq Jahshan in Lod. See Ibrahim al-'Awra, *Tarikh Wilayat Sulayman Basha al-'Adil* (Sidon: Matba'at Dayr al-Mukhlis, 1936), 167; on Khayr al-Din's time spent in Ramla, see Mary Ann Fay, "Biography as History: The Exemplary Life of Khayr al-Din al-Ramli," In Mary Ann Fay (ed.), *Autobiography and the Construction of Identity and Community in the Middle East* (Palgrave Macmillan, 2002), 9-18; on Minkarizade Yayha Efendi, see Guy Burak, *The Second Formation of Islamic Law: The Hanafi School in the Early Modern Ottoman Empire* (Cambridge: Cambridge University Press, 2017), 153.
[148] The work is essentially a compilation of *hadith* reports and descriptions culled from earlier texts—such as Suyuti's *Ithaf al-Akhissa'*, as the author himself noted. Still, the work suggests both al-Tamartashi's familiarity with and interest in Palestine. The full Arabic title is *Al-Khabar al-Tamm fi Dhikr al-Ard al-Muqaddasa wa-Hududuha, wa-Dhikr Ard Filastin, wa-Hudududa wa-Aradi al-Sham*. The manuscript was first published and translated into Hebrew in Sadan, "Sheloshah Mekorot Khadashim," 186-206; a second edition appeared in Ghalib Anabsi's 1993 Master's Thesis at Tel Aviv University; a third edition appeared in Sadiq Ahmad Ibrahim Muhammad al-Turk's Master's Thesis at the University of Najah in Nablus. See idem, "al-Khabar al-Tamm fi Dhikr al-Ard al-Muqaddasa wa-Hududuha wa-Dhikr Ard Filastin wa-Hududuha wa Aradi al-Sham" (M.A. Thesis, Jami'at Najah al-Wataniyya, 1998); see also Gerber, ""Palestine" and Other Territorial Concepts," 567.

surroundings. In Damascus and Cairo, the term Palestine may have meant very little to the overwhelming majority of Arabic speakers from the 12th through the 18th centuries.

There shouldn't be anything surprising here. People from San Francisco do not call the place SanFran, even if people from Michigan might. They might say "the city" or SF. The UP is intelligible to people from Michigan but New Yorkers may wonder why I capitalized the word "up," and why Michiganders think a direction refers to a place. "The Land" refers to Cleveland in Cleveland. "el D.F" is meaningful to Mexicans but few Americans. NOLA is meaningful to people in New Orleans, but was not meaningful to me when I first heard it. The Toronto Star wrote in May 2016 that "you've probably referred to yourself as living in "The Six,"" a term I'm assuming is as meaningless to most people as it was to me. We'll never agree on the same nicknames for the places we inhabit. That's part of what makes us human, our incredible ability to invent places, nicknames and define them arbitrarily. In a world with rapid mass communication, we still have a great deal of regional variation in place names. Until recently it must have been a lot worse.[149]

* * *

Identities. We stated in the previous chapter that we identify with Palestine because it seems real to us, and it seems real to us because we have named it, told stories about it and made maps of it. We've already noted above that hadith commentators did describe some Muslims as Palestinian

---

[149] Mark Daniell, "Drake Finally Explains 'The Six' Rapper reveals he rejected 'The Four' as Toronto's nickname," *The Toronto Sun* 20 August 2016 (https://goo.gl/FFdz3f).

for the purposes of hadith verification. But did people themselves identify as Palestinian? Did they care deeply about Palestine so much so that they were willing to die for it?

The Muslim conquerors called the place the District of Palestine from the 7th-11th centuries. They even minted coins with the word Palestine on them in the 7th and 8th centuries (see figure 8). This meant that merchants and even illiterate farmers may have been somewhat familiar with the term. Although, I wonder how much an average person knew what places are written on which coins, let alone think those places are important to their identities because they appear on coins. I think we need more than coins to get us to identify with places.

Figure 8. A 7th century coin minted in Jerusalem by the Caliph with the word *Filastin*.[150]

---

[150] Tony Goodwin, "The Arab-Byzantine Coinage of Jund Filastin - A Potential Historical Source," *Byzantine and Modern Greek Studies* 28 (2004): 5.

Before the late 19th century, most people in the world spent most of their lives close to their hometown. Travel was slow, dangerous, expensive and arduous. In the 18th century, it took a group of pilgrims nearly a year to get from Uzbekistan to Damascus, and another month to get from Damascus to Mecca. A journey from Damascus to Tripoli took six days in the 18th century; Damascus to Aleppo took nearly two weeks; Jaffa to Jerusalem took a day and a half in the mid-1850s; Alexandretta to Aleppo took three days by mule; a good rider could make it from Lajjun to Rafah in two days, but the trip lasted four days or more with a heavy load; from Jenin to Nazareth took six hours in the 1850s – which increased to twelve hours in 2003 thanks to modern technology: Israeli military checkpoints. Even one of the most well-traveled Muslims in history, ibn Hawqal (d. 988), never left the Islamic world. This meant that there were fewer encounters between people from distant lands and fewer opportunities for people to say they were from Palestine rather than from Jaffa or Jerusalem.[151]

Palestine didn't manifest itself in customs, traditions or institutions either. People did not commemorate battles won or lost in Palestine through annual ceremonies, marches or keynote addresses. Famous songs and poems rarely dealt with Palestine. Village elders probably did not share stories with their grandchildren about Palestinian cuisine, Palestinian Arabic or Palestinian

---

[151] On Damascus to Tripoli and Damascus to Aleppo, see James Grehan, *Everyday Life and Consumer Culture in Eighteenth-Century Damascus* (Seattle: University of Washington Press, 2007) 45; then see Abraham Marcus, *The Middle East on the Eve of Modernity: Aleppo in the Eighteenth Century* (New York: Columbia University Press, 1989), 248; on Jaffa to Jerusalem, see Glenda Abramson, "Two Nineteenth-century Travelers to the Holy Land," *Israel Affairs* 8(3) (2002): 71, 78; on Alexandretta to Aleppo, see Gregory M. Wortabet, *Syria and the Syrians; or, Turkey in the Dependencies* (London, J. Madden, 1856), 20; on Lajjun to Rafah, see the sources discussed above on Palestine's four-point borders; on Jenin to Nazareth, see Josias Leslie Porter, *A Handbook for Travelers in Syria and Palestine* (London: J. Murray, 1858), I, 353; on ibn Hawqal (d. 988), see Dharif Ramadan Murad, *Dirasa fi al-Turath al-Jughrafi al-'Arabi, Ibn Hawqal wa-Manhajuhu al-Jughrafi* (Cairo: Maktabat al-Anjlu al-Misriyya, 2004), 29-32. The Middle East was not unique in this respect. A trip from Florence to Rome would take about four days by carriage and cost 350 dinarii, about an entire year's wages for a laborer. "Today it takes about three hours by car or three and a half if you want to avoid the tolls." The hardships, expenses and risks of robbery, disease and loneliness discouraged most people from traveling far before the mid-late 19th century. See Vlogbrothers, "How Young Is History? *youtube.com* 17 January 20017 (goo.gl/RZxFbr).

customs. They did not take their grandchildren to Palestine coffee shops, Palestine post offices, or Palestine mosques, as far as I know. Palestine was not studied in school: the merchant al-Muqaddasi (d.991), for instance, who had more to say about Palestine's geography and economy than virtually anyone else during his era, studied *fiqh*, grammar, literature, philology, theology, hadith and history, but no geography or economics, and nothing specifically about Palestine. There is not much evidence to believe Palestine was talked about at dinner conversations, Sufi lodges, wedding ceremonies or mosque sermons. Palestine was not the word used to describe much of anything in day-to-day speech, let alone be the basis for stories, myths, legends or a dissertation about the history of the usage of the word Palestine itself.[152]

But what about all the stories about Palestine we discussed above? Although the people that wrote them must have known a bit about Palestine, most of them would not have even been from Palestine, so it's unlikely they identified as Palestinian. In any case, their works had a limited circulation. Books were expensive to own. You had to buy the leather-bound manuscript itself and pay a copyist to copy the entire thing word for word. In fact, people even invested their savings in ornate copies of Qur'an and other manuscripts as commodities and symbols of prestige. Peopled dumped savings into books the same way people today dump savings into gold, in part because books were expensive.[153]

---

[152] A. Miquel, "al- Muḳaddasī," Encyclopedia of Islam, 2nd ed.
[153] Şükrü Hanioğlu, *A Brief History of the Late Ottoman Empire* (Princeton: Princeton University Press, 2008), 30-33; R. Aslıhan Aksoy-Sheridan, "Forms of Literacy: Notes on the Life and Cultural Background of a 16th-century Ottoman Sanjak Governor," *New Trends in Ottoman Studies* (2014): 728-740. See Aksoy-Sheridan's footnote 21 for a nice list of studies on book ownership in Ottoman history.

But even if people had money and access, what kinds of books were available to buy or read? One of the only surviving pre-modern library catalogues is the 13th century Ashrafiya Library in Damascus, whose contents reflected the "wider literary interests as they existed in a city such as Damascus." Here are the contents divided by genre:[154]

Theme	Percentage
Poetry	32%
Transmitted Sciences	20%
Adab [Refinement]	16.5%
Philological Sciences	9.5%
Medicine	5%
History	4%
Political Thought	3.5%
Philosophy & Theology	2.5%
Other	6%

Table 1. Contents of the 13th century Ashrafiya Library in Damascus

Another way to slice the same data is to look at the most popular titles. Of the 23 most popular titles, 14 were poetry, 3 *adab*, 2 lexicography, 1 medicine, 1 hadith, 1 pharmacology, and 1 sayings of 'Ali. Most striking about this distribution is the salience of poetry and *adab*, or refinement, especially pre-Islamic poetry. Muslims were interested in the linguistic context in which the Qur'an emerged, as well as their own Arab origins. Moreover, poetry and *adab* often bled into "transmitted sciences," such as hadith. Whatever the precise distribution, history and especially geography were noticeably lacking.

---

[154] See Konrad Hirschler, *Medieval Damascus: Plurality and Diversity in an Arabic Library* (Edinburgh: Edinburgh University Press, 2016), 106, 117. Within "transmitted sciences," Hirschler includes prayer books, hadith, fiqh, Koran, Sufism, sermons, biography, history, poetry, oneiromancy, rituals, sayings attributed to 'Ali, ethics (Islamic), eschatology and afterlife, stories of the prophets, the Prophet Muhammad, biographical dictionaries, principles of religion (*usul al-Din*), jihad, and pre-Islamic revelation.

Most libraries around the Middle East had specialized collections. One historian wrote, describing the contents of the 18th century libraries of Aleppo, that they were "specialized in nature and directed at narrow readerships." Similarly, the contents of libraries in Cairo, Jerusalem or Istanbul as late as the mid-19th or early 20th centuries, were filled with manuscripts on the Qur'an, hadith, Islamic law, grammar, poetry, rhetoric and philology, and even medicine and astronomy, but less on geography. Legal topics were especially popular, and ranged from the foods forbidden to women during pregnancy, appropriate beard length guidelines, prayer attendance requirements and millions of other topics where Palestine didn't matter much. It would have been very difficult to find a travelogue on Palestine or a manuscript about Palestine's art, social classes, architecture or history.[155]

No one was paid to write or think about Palestine, so it was neglected. In fact, few people were paid to write history or geography, and none were paid to write about the history and geography of Palestine. Ibn Hawqal (d.988), who carefully described each province of the Muslim Empire in 978, including Palestine, earned a living as a merchant. Al-Muqaddasi (d.991) wrote one of

---

[155] See Marcus, *The Middle East on the Eve of Modernity*, 238; Hirschler, *Medieval Damascus,* ch.3; Edward Lane, *The Manners & Customs of the Modern Egyptians* (New York: J.M. Dent, Dutton, 1908 [1836]), 214-5; on the private collections, see Hanioğlu, *A Brief History of the Late Ottoman Empire*, 30-33; the library of Ibrahim Pasha, for instance, the 19th century Egyptian governor of Sham, included sections on the Qu'ran, Qur'anic commentary, the oral tradition, jurisprudence, Algebra and Mathematics, the Arabic language, semantics and rhetoric belles-lettres, logic, science of discourse, Sufism, medicine, astronomy the science of war, and the history and biography of the prophet. See n.a., *Catalogue of Ibrahim Pasha's Collection of Manuscripts* (British Library, OR15382), 1-112. When the Khalidiyya Library in Jerusalem first opened in 1900, less than 10% of its published contents dealt with geography or history, the rest dealt primarily with Islamic religious sciences. See n.a., *Barnamij al-Maktaba al-Khalidiyya al-'Umumiyya* (Jerusalem: Matba'at Jurji Habib Hananiyya, 1900), 1-78; on its catalogue, see Nazir Ju'ba, Walid Khalidi, Khadir Ibrahim Salama, *Fihris Makhtutuat al-Maktaba al-Khalidiyya, al-Quds* (London: Mu'assasat al-Furqan lil-Turath al-Islami, 2006). The situation was similar in Istanbul. George Zaydan surveyed the contents of twenty-five libraries in Istanbul in 1909, reporting that of the 44,930 classified volumes, 13% were Qur'anic Commentary, 15% the prophetic tradition, 21% jurisprudence, 10% Sufism, 13% belles-lettres, 16% grammar and about 13% history (Geography was not even listed as a genre). See "Istana al-'Ulya: Makatib," *al-Hilal* 18(2) (1909): 105-6; on the concern with women eating the proper foods, see Michael Chamberlain, *Knowledge and Social Practice in Medieval Damascus, 1190-1350* (Cambridge: Cambridge University Press, 2009), 125; on a beard length, see for instance Grehan, *Everyday Life and Consumer*, 197; on prayer attendance, see ibid, 145.

the most impressive Arabic works of geography in the pre-modern Muslim world, which included lengthy discussions of Palestine, and he came from a family of architects and seems to have earned a living as a merchant as well. Ibn 'Asakir (d.1176), whose *History of Damascus* is one of the longest books ever written in Islamic history (mentioning Palestine hundreds of times), was a deputy judge, preacher and mufti, i.e. he wrote legal opinions. Ibn Kathir (d.1373) wrote a lot about Palestine's history as well, but he was better known as a scholar of hadith, Islamic law, Qur'anic interpretation and biographies of Muslim legal authorities, earning a living as a *khatib*, hadith teacher and ad-hoc jurisprudent for the state, not as a Palestine expert. Al-Din al-'Ulaymi (d.1522) wrote extensively about the geography of Palestine too, but he was a judge and teacher of Islamic law. Al-Tamartashi (d. 1644-5) published the only pre-modern Arabic work that included the word Palestine in the title, as noted above, but also some 80-other works on Islamic jurisprudence, Qur'anic interpretation, belief, Sufism, *nikah*, agriculture, churches, elocution, grammar and more. Istifan al-Duwayhi (d.1704) wrote about Palestine's history also, but he was a priest and most of his two-dozen works were theological or liturgical commentaries. The Sufi Damascene 'Abd al-Ghani al-Nabulusi (d.1731) wrote a few travelogues discussing Palestine but most of his three hundred some works had to do with theology and Sufism. Yusuf Jahshan wrote a diary in the 1760s largely about Palestine, but he made a living as a priest, not a climatologist of Palestine. These were some of the most prolific writers on Palestine, and none were paid write about it.[156]

---

[156] On how historians made their living, see Robinson, *Islamic Historiography*, chapter 1; on Ibn Hawqal, see Murad, *Dirasa fi al-Turath al-Jughrafi al-'Arabi*, 29-32; Guy Le Strange, *Palestine Under the Muslims: A Description of Syria and the Holy Land from A.D. 650 to 1500* (London: Alexander P. Watt, 1890), 5; on al-Muqaddasi, see Miquel, "al- Muḳaddasī," Encyclopedia of Islam, 2nd ed.; on Ibn 'Asakir's coverage of Palestine, see Ali ibn al-Hasan Ibn 'Asakir, *Tarikh Madinat Dimashq Li-Ibn 'Asakir* (Beirut: Dar al-Fikr, 1995-1998), VXXX, 63; on Ibn 'Asakir's biography, see James Lindsay (ed.), *Ibn 'Asakir and Early Islamic History* (Princeton, New Jersey: The Darwin Press, 2001), 6; on Ibn Kathir, see H. Laoust, "Ibn Kathir", Encyclopedia of Islam, 2nd ed.; Younus Y. Mirza, "Ibn Kathir," Encyclopedia of Islam, 3rd ed.; on al-Nabulusi, see Elizabeth Sirriyeh, *Visionary of Ottoman Damascus: The Sufism of Abd al-Ghani al-Nabulusi (1641-1731)* (London: RoutledgeCurzon, 2004); on

It is not a coincidence that Haim Gerber's 1997 study on the concept of "Palestine" during the Ottoman period relied primarily on a 17th century collection of legal opinions written by a Muslim jurisprudent. Gerber also consulted a work of merits literature, which was primarily a compilation of quotes from the transmitted sciences, another legal opinion by the chief Ottoman legal authority, yet another collection of legal opinions by an early 19th century jurisprudent, and some remarks about Palestine in a travelogue. The emphasis on legal or transmitted texts rather than geographical or historical ones is reflective of what was written in the 16th, 17th and 18th centuries in the Arab Middle East. There wasn't much on Palestine.[157]

Muslims could find salaried jobs as judges, imams, prayer leaders, scribes, sermonists, Qur'an and hadith teachers, jurisprudents, copyists, bookbinders, notaries, *waqf* administrators and petition writers. 8th and 9th century mosques served as colleges and acted as charitable foundations, with money from the endowments usually paying the salary of the Imam, or prayer leader. When the Fatimid Caliph al-Hakim founded the House of Knowledge in the 11th century, those invited to lecture were Qur'an readers, jurists, hadith experts, astronomers, mathematicians, grammarians, philologists and physicians, not geographers or historians. The 13th century Ashrafiya Library in Damascus, for instance, employed a single professor who taught Qur'an recitation, his assistants and an administer who managed finances. These kinds of

---

al-Tamartashi's life works, see Muhammad al-Tamartashi, *Turjamat Musannaf al-Matn al-Mubarak Tanwir al-Absar* (Süleymaniye Manuscript Library, Esad Efendi Collection, 02212-01), folios 2-4; (al-Muhibbi mentions he wrote fewer works, most of which are *fiqh* commentaries, cited in al-Tamartashi (d. 1644-5), al-Turk (ed.), "al-Khabar al-Tamm," 55); Istifan al-Duwayhi (d.1704) wrote about Abu Bakr's battles against the Saracens in Palestine, 'Umar ibn al-'As campaign in Palestine, the Crusader King Fulk reign in Palestine and Salah al-Din's re-conquest of Palestine. See Istifan al-Duwayhi (d.1704) *Tarikh al-Azmina* (Beirut: Dar Lahd Khatir, 198?), 12, 13, 115, 133, 165, 224.
[157] Gerber, "Palestine and Other Territorial Concepts."

jobs required an expertise in literacy, the Qu'ran, prayer, Islamic law or religious practice, not knowledge of Palestine's economy or history. People concentrated their scholarly energies on what mattered for the job market. The prestige, social rewards and financial compensation associated with these positions created a feedback loop, further popularizing them at the expense of scholarship on Palestine.[158]

I think people would have been more interested in Palestine—perhaps even identifying with it—had there been more people paid to write about it, tell stories about it, make maps of it and deliver conferences papers about Biblical Researches or intertextual subjectivities in it, as was the case in the 19th and 20th centuries—respectively, of course. Tabari (d.923), for instance, who wrote about Palestine, was quickly translated into Persian, and later Turkish. More than a thousand copies of his universal chronicle were said to have been held in the 12th century Fatimid library of Cairo. Al-'Ulaymi's (d.1522) *History of Jerusalem and Hebron* dealt extensively with Palestine as well and it too was a best-seller during its age, surviving in some three-dozen manuscripts today. Al-Qaramani's (d.1611) geographical dictionary—which included a section on Palestine—can be found in a dozen some copies today. Al-Tamartashi's (d.1644-5) treatise on Palestine has survived in four manuscript copies. This may not seem

---

[158] On 8th-9th century endowments, see George Makdisi, *The Rise of Colleges: Institutions of Learning in Islam and the West* (Edinburgh: Edinburgh University Press, 1981), 28-9; on the establishment of the 11th century House of Knowledge, see Heinz Halm, *The Fatimids and their Traditions of Learning* (New York: I.B. Tauris and The Institute of Ismaili Studies, 2001), 73-74; on the Ashrafiya Library employees, see Konrad Hirschler, *Medieval Damascus*, 23; the Ghaznavids and Saljuks (10th-14th centuries) employed scribes to record revenue sources, oversee income and expenditures and codify tribal custom into imperial law. See Chamberlain, *Knowledge and Social Practice*, 33, 35; on salaried positions as clerks and judges, see Abdurrahman Atçtıl, *Scholars and Sultans in the Early Modern Ottoman Empire* (Cambridge: Cambridge University Press, 2017), 76-8, 99; during the late Ottoman period, professional petition writers, or *arzuhalciler*, set up shops in markets, cafés and other public spaces and wrote petitions to the Ottoman authorities in Istanbul for a fee. See Yuval Ben-Bassat, "The Ottoman Institution of Petitioning when the Sultan No Longer Reigned: A View from Post-1908 Ottoman Palestine," *New Perspectives on Turkey* 56 (2017): 87–103.

significant, but recall that the overwhelming majority of his works were never copied at all and are presumed lost today, even the titles unknown. Al-Duwayhi's (d.1704) *History of the Times*, which also covers Palestine's history, has survived in a whopping twelve manuscripts. What was written about Palestine did circulate, there just wasn't that much of it.[159]

This is not an indictment of theology or law. Both are fascinating topics, and I do not think of myself as any less sensible because I once wanted to be a lawyer and a rabbi. The search for truth, the justice system and the origins of life are noble intellectual pursuits, potentially as noble as Roman administrative nomenclature or the history of the historiography of the historiography of Palestine.

Some Muslim traditions did nevertheless indicate Palestine was an important or special place. One tradition claimed god blessed the area between al-'Arish and the Euphrates, and "Palestine in particular." Whoever first invented this tradition probably worked for the governor of the District of Palestine, or served as a scribe of a court in Palestine, or something that would have given him or her reason to single out Palestine for its sanctity. But traditions like this are hard to

---

[159] On Tabari, see Hirschler, *Medieval Damascus*, 107; Halm, *The Fatimids and their Traditions*, 91; on al-'Ulaymi, see Carol Brockelmann, *Geschichte Der Arabischen Litteratur* (a.k.a. GAL) (Leiden: Brill, 1949), II, 53-4; H. Busse, "Mudjīr al-Dīn al-'Ulaymī." Encyclopedia of Islam, 2nd ed.; additional extant manuscripts not mentioned by either can be found in the Süleymaniye Manuscript library (Esad Efendi 2977; Hamidiye Collection, 888 and 889; Karacelebizade, 02257; Kiliç Ali Paşa, 729; Laleli, 1998 and 1999; Musalla Medrese 132; Yeni Cami 820; Hudai Effendi, 1047; Feyzullah Efendi 1384; Feyzullah Efendi 1384; Selimiye 2/1642; two additional copies are held at the Israeli National Library; six at the British Library; and one at the Center For Islamic Research, Abu Dis; on al-Qaramani, five copies are located in the British Library (see Peter Stocks, Colin F Baker, *Subject-guide to the Arabic Manuscripts in the British Library* (London: The British Library, 2001), 249) and six at the Süleymaniye Manuscript library (Aşir Efendi 00230, Hamidiye 00885, Serez, 01845, Nuruosmaniye, 03042, Nuruosmaniye, 04961, Nuruosmaniye 03155; on the al-Tamartashi manuscripts, see Khidr Ibrahim Salama (ed.), *Fihris Makhtutat al-Maktaba al-Budayriyya* (Jerusalem: Idarat al-Awqaf al-'Amma, Maktabat al-Masjid al-Aqsa, 1987) and Ghalib Anabsi, *Ab'ad fi Adab Fada'il al-Ard al-Muqaddasa* (Huda, Kufr Qar', Israel: Markaz Dirasat al-Adab al-'Arabi, 2006), 368; on Duwayhi, see Roland E. Murphy, "Al-Batriyark Istifanus ad-Duwayhi Ta'rikh al-Azminat," *Journal of the American Oriental Society* 72(4) (1952): 176-177.

find. It's much easier to find Muslim traditions that heap lavish praise onto other places like Jerusalem, the Holy Land or the Land of Sham, or other things altogether like prophets, tribes, rulers, rules or principles.[160]

Muhammad bin Ahmad al-Muqaddasi (d. 991) was one of the few Muslims or Arabs before 1898 to have identified as Palestinian himself. Al-Muqaddasi wrote a work called *The Best Divisions in the Knowledge of the Regions*, a detailed, original study of the geography and economy of the Middle East, much of it based on his own observations during his travels. He passed through the city of Shiraz, Iran and exchanged friendly banter with some builders chiseling into a thick, clay stone. al-Muqaddasi told them they would have an easier time making a hole in the stone if they used a wedge. "I told them of the construction in Palestine," and was asked by one the Shirazi stonecutters:

"Are you Egyptian?"

"No, I am Palestinian," al-Muqaddasi responded.

In a second instance, he wrote that during his sojourns abroad he had been called 36 different names, one of which was Palestinian.[161]

---

[160] al-Himyari (d.1495), *Kitab al-Rawd al-Mi'tar*, 410; an unknown manuscript from the Mamluk period (13th century), cited in *Fada'il al-Sham wa-Fada'il Mudunuha*, in Anabsi, *Min Adab Fada'il al-Sham*, 61; Ibn 'Abd al-Razzaq (d.1721) *Hada'iq al-In'am*, 60.

[161] See Muhammad bin Ahmad al- Muqaddasi (d. 991), Shakir Lu'aybi (ed.), *Ahsan al-Taqasim fi Ma'rifat al-Aqalim* (Beirut: Dar al-Suwaydi li-l-Nashr wa-l-Tawzi', 2003). On Shiraz, see ibid, 362; on the 36 names, see ibid, 68; Other Muslims rarely if ever defined themselves or others as Palestinian before the late 19th century. Al-Ya'qubi (d.897/8) [*Kitab al-Buldan*, 329] for instance, described people with their ethnic, linguistic or tribal affiliations to refer to them, such as "the people of the District of Palestine are a mix of Arabs and non-Arabs, as well as from the tribe of Lakhm, Judham, 'Amila, Kinda, Qays and Kinana." The biographer al-Hasan ibn Muhammad al-Burini (d. 1615) [*Tarajim al-A'yan min Abna' al-Zaman* (Damascus: al-Majma' al-'Ilmi al-'Arabi, 1959-62), 11] explained a guest of his father asked his father about his origins, and Burini's father answered that he was from the "village of Burin, which adjoins the lands of the city of Nablus." In the 1840s, al-Sa'ud (c. 1840-1) [*Min Misr ila Islambul*, folio 25b] traveled to Istanbul and relayed an encounter he had along the way in Anatolia. "The two of them asked us in the Turkish language: where are you from? We informed them that we are from the people of Jerusalem." He identified others by city also—such as Ramla (folio 19, 49), Jaffa (ibid, folio 15, 49) and Jerusalem (18b, 38).

What was so special about al-Muqaddasi, and why was he the only Muslim in history to define himself as Palestinian? During al-Muqaddasi's era, Palestine was an administrative district in the most powerful Empire in the world. Moreover, geographical literature had reached a zenith of popularity in the Muslim world around the same time. al-Muqaddasi was also one of the most well-traveled Muslims for his time. As noted above, travelers often identified not with the smaller towns and villages they were from, since such places are often not known abroad, but rather the larger regions they are from. This combination of circumstances was rare before the 19th century.

* * *

Conclusion. The first records attesting to the word Palestine in history come from the ancient Egyptians, Assyrians, Hebrews, Greeks and Romans. Later, the word was adopted in Arabic, modern European languages, Ottoman Turkish and dozens of other languages. States played a critical role in the rise of Palestine in the Greek, Roman, Byzantine and Arab worlds. Palestine flourished during its period of ascendency in the Muslim world from the 7th-11th centuries, so much so that one well-traveled and well-read merchant, al-Muqaddasi (d. 991), even identified himself as Palestinian and claimed others referred to him as Palestinian as well. But the name Palestine fell out of use in most places in the Middle East after it lost political purpose in the 11th century. Still, it persisted in the city of Ramla and its surroundings owing to its erstwhile political and economic prominence within the District of Palestine.

Still, Palestine didn't figure prominently in most people's lives. Although some Caliphs minted coins bearing the name Palestine, and some Muslims etched the word onto tombstones and many others told stories about it, no one could earn a living doing things related to Palestine. No one was paid to write books, tell stories, recite poems about or make maps of Palestine. No one was paid to teach about Palestine's history or geography. No one could earn a living as an investigator of human rights abuses in Palestine, a surveyor of Palestine's topography or economist of Palestine's economy. No surprise few people cared much about Palestine before the 19th century or identified as Palestinian.

From the 16th century onwards, though, the word Palestine gained in popularity in the Latin west. Scholars published ancient Greek and Latin manuscripts, translated them into modern European vernaculars and circulated them around Europe. Renaissance Europeans discovered that the ancients called the place Palestine, and started calling it Palestine too, alongside the Holy Land. Slowly, Palestine supplanted the Holy Land as the standard name of the region in Europe. By the 19th century, Palestine had become a very popular designation in the West, but not in the Arab world, save for Ramla and its surroundings. This would change in the 19th century. How and why is the subject of the next chapter.

CHAPTER FOUR

The Modern World

This chapter is about the modern history of Palestine and the Palestinians. When, how and why did a group of people now known as the Palestinians come into existence? In the 19th century, more people in the Middle East started to earn a living as bureacrats, teachers, journalists, publishers, missionaries, economists, lawyers, geographers and mapmakers. These people played a critical role in making Palestine important to people, since they taught about its history, wrote reports about its economy, surveyed its geography and made maps of its topography.

The modern world also became flat. What got popular in one part of the globe caught on in other places. Names got standardized. Books about history and geography and maps increasingly resembled one another. School curricula included the same familiar subjects everywhere. And so when Palestine became popular in the West in the 19th century, its popularity rose in the East as well. Muslim and Christian Arabs increasingly used the name Palestine, wrote lots of stories about it and mapped it. By the end of the 19th century, they even started to identify with it.[162]

Third, states penetrated the lives of their subjects in the modern world. State-funded institutions such as schools, missionary enterprises, universities, consular offices and the bureaucracy flourished. States published annual yearbooks and military handbooks, provided ariel tours to

---

[162] On the phrase, "the world is flat," see Thomas Friedman, *The World is Flat* (New York: Penguin Books, 2005).

people so they could write geography books and tested students on the history and geography of the state. States played a critical role in bringing places like Palestine into people's lives.

The exact sequence of events that led people to care about Palestine and identify as Palestinian were mostly happenstance. The governor of Egypt invaded the land of Sham in the 1830s and pemitted foreigners to establish consular offices, travel freely and open schools and missionary stations. This led Europeans and Americans to travel to the Middle East as diplomats, tourists and missionaries. The expansion of commercial steamship travel provided a huge boost to migration, tourism, diplomacy, scholarship and missionary activity. People in Europe, the United States and the Middle East learned one another's languages. Americans published in Arabic and Arabs published in French and English. Missionaries taught about Palestine's history and geography in class. Arabs published books, magazines and newspapers about Palestine and distributed them to towns and villages across the Middle East. By 1898, some people started to identify as Palestinian.

The British conquered the land of Sham in 1917 and 1918 during World War I and established the Government of Palestine in 1920, ratified by the League of Nations as The Mandate for Palestine in 1922. This contributed significantly to the rapid spread of a Palestinian identity: the workforce became more diversified, the world became even flatter, and the state played an even more critical role in people's lives. More people could pursue careers in education, journalism and civil service. The British employed teachers, inspectors, bureaucrats and mapmakers. Thousands of Arabs worked for a government whose name included the word Palestine. More kids got an education and learned to read and write from the 1920s and 1930s onwards, and

Palestine continued to blossom as a result. More people animated Palestine on maps, eulogized Palestine in poems and taught their kids the importance of Palestine's history and geography. Eventually, by the 1920s and 1930s, some thought Palestine was worth dying for. This chapter explains how all of that happened.

* * *

The First Palestinian. The first Arab to use the term Palestinian in modern history was Khalil Baydas. He always seemed to have a cigarette dangling from an ivory holder. Sporting a dark suit and fez, he would cough through clouds of smoke that encircled him. Somehow, it feels about right that the first Arab to use the term Palestinian in modern history loved to smoke tobacco.[163]

In 1898, he translated *A Description of the Holy Land* from Russian to Arabic because "the Arabic geography books on the topic were insufficient" and "the people of Palestine needed a geography book about their country." The book, Baydas claimed, was "a description of the land of Palestine" and it referred to the people of Palestine as Palestinians in multiple places. "The ancient inhabitants of Palestine used limestone to whitewash the walls of their buildings," Baydas wrote, "while the modern Palestinians also whitewash the inside, and occasionally the

---

[163] Palestinians smoke as much tobacco as almost any other group of people in the world. Some 38-39% of adults in the West Bank smoke tobacco, or about 8th in the world. In Gaza, some 26.3% of adults aged 15 or older smoke cigarettes, 36th in the world. Large numbers of Palestinians reside in Lebanon, which ranks 7th in the world and Jordan, which ranks 5th in the world. See Mohammed Jawad, Ali Khader and Christopher Millett, "Differences in Tobacco Smoking Prevalence and Frequency between Adolescent Palestine Refugee and Non-refugee Populations in Jordan, Lebanon, Syria, and the West Bank: Cross-Sectional Analysis of the Global Youth Tobacco Survey," *Conflict and Health* 10:20(2016) (https://goo.gl/tWsaFu); see also see also World Health Organization, "World Health Statistics Data Visualizations dashboard: Tobacco Smoking," WHO, accessed 8 June 2017 (https://goo.gl/rNONYv).

outside, of their homes with it as well." Presumably it got annoying to repeat the word *modern*, and so modern Palestinians became simply Palestinians. "The Palestinian peasant," Baydas noted elsewhere in the book, "waits impatiently for winter to come, for the season's rain to moisten his fossilized fields" after many rainless months following the May summer wheat and barley harvest. The first modern Arab Palestinian peasant was born.[164][165]

Who was Khalil Baydas and how did he learn Russian? In the late 1880s and early 1890s, Baydas studied in one of the best high schools in the region, the Teacher's Training Seminary in Nazareth. It was established by Russian missionaries in the mid-1880s, one of hundreds of foreign schools built in the Ottoman Empire in the 19th century. The school was funded by Russian tax payers and staffed by Russians, Arabs and even a Zionist. The Seminary invited the best graduates of its preparatory schools to attend it. By 1914, more than ten thousand Arab kids had completed their primary education at a Russian primary school, and hundreds had attended high school at the Seminary.[166]

---

[164] Akim Aleksyeevich Olesnitskii, Khalil Baydas (trans.), *Kitab al-Rawda al-Mu'nisa fi wasf al-Ard al-Muqaddasa* (Ba'bda, Lebanon: al-Matba'a al-'Uthmaniyya, 1898), 2.

[165] The Arabic for the modern Palestinians was *Filastiniyyun al-haliyyun*. See Baydas, *Kitab al-Rawda al-Mu'nisa*, 33-5 and 67, respectively.

[166] Previously, I claimed (incorrectly) that the Beiruti Farid Georges Kassab [*Palestine, Hellénisme et Cléricalisme* (Constantinople: Impr. de La Patrie, 1909), 5, 8, 22, 26, 31] was the first Arabic speaker to use the term to explain that "Palestinians" preferred to call themselves Arabs, incidentally enough; on the smoking anecdote, see Gish Amit, "Salvage or Plunder? Israel's "Collection" of Private Palestinian Libraries in West Jerusalem," *Journal of Palestine Studies* 40(4) (2011): 15; on the figures for the Russian schools and graduates, see Şamil Mutlu, *Osmanlı Devleti'nde Misyoner Okulları* (İstanbul: Gökkubbe, 2005), 84-7; Hanna Abu Hanna, *Tala'i' al-Nahda fi Filastin: Khirruju al-Madaris al-Rusiyya, 1862-1914* (Beirut: Mu'assasat al-Dirasat al-Filastiniyya, 2005), 21-2; Lucien J. Frary, "Russian Missions to the Orthodox East: Antonin Kapustin (1817-1894) and his World," *Russian History* (2013): 149; Derek Hopwood, *The Russian Presence in Syria and Palestine 1843-1914: Church and Politics in the Near East* (Oxford: Clarendon, 1969), 150-3; Theofanis George Stavrou, *Russian Interests in Palestine, 1882-1914* (Thessaloniki: Institute for Balkan Studies, 1963), 164; Julius Richter, *A History of the Protestant Missions in the Near East* (New York: F.H. Revell, 1910), 57.

At the Seminary, Baydas was encouraged to take pride in his Arab identity. In class, he wore Arab rather than European dress; he studied Arabic grammar with Ibn al-Muqaffa', Ibn Malik and Ibn 'Aqil; he read Arabic books by Ibrahim al-Hawrani, George Zaydan, Iskandar Shahin, Shakir Shuqayr and George Post—yes, George Post wrote in Arabic. Baydas studied the geography of Palestine and the history of Palestine in class; and yes, his teachers called the place Palestine.[167]

The Seminary emphasized the Russian language and the Bible as well. Baydas woke up at 6:00 a.m. for prayer and 6:30 a.m. for the gospels, then studied Bible, catechism, Greek, Turkish, mathematics, geometry, and song. The school also focused on the Russian language, Russian geography, Russian history and Russian culture, as well as Greek independence from the Ottoman Empire, interestingly enough. Russian maps were posted on the walls of his classrooms; Russian books filled its library; Russian literature was read in the classroom; Russian songs were song; and Russian plays were performed for public viewings.[168]

Incidentally, Khalil Baydas got good at Russian. "I began to devour the Russian books in the school library," Baydas divulged of his early years. "Something which had been only a word,

---

[167] On the study of "Palestine," see Stavrou, *Russian Interests*, 114; on the contents of the library, see Abu Hanna, *Tala'i' al-Nahda fi Filastin*, 31-44, 172-3. The headmaster of the school called the place Palestine, such as when he addressed a crowded audience on the 25th anniversary of the establishment of the Imperial Orthodox Palestine Society to celebrate its achievements in "our country Palestine and in Syria." See Shukri Khalil Suwaydan, *Tarikh al-Jam'iyya al-Imbaraturiyya al-Urthudhuksiyya al-Filastiniyya* (Boston: Matba'a Suriya al-Jadida, 1912), 71-2; the school's Arabic teacher, Bandali al-Juzi [*Mabadi' al-Lugha al-Rusiyya li-Abna' al-'Arab* (Kazan: Jam'iyyat al-Tabshir al-Urthudhuksiyya, 1898), III] also called the place Palestine.

[168] On Russian maps, see Frary, "Russian Missions," 149; on the curriculum, see Hopwood, *The Russian Presence*, 144; Mikha'il Nu'ayma, *Sab'un: Hikaya 'Umr: 1889:1959* (Beirut: Dar Sadir, 1959-1960), 122-3, 142; al-Juzi [*Mabadi' al-Lugha al-Rusiyya*, III] toured its feeder schools around the region, claiming Russian has spread extremely rapidly, "especially in Palestine;" on Bible study, see Iskandar Kazma, *al-Tarikh al-Muqaddas Lil-'Ahad al-Qadim* (Beirut: al-Matba'a al-Adabiyya, 1888); for more on the curriculum, see Hopwood, *The Russian Presence*, 144; Nu'ayma, *Sab'un*, 122-123, 142.

became first a country, then an idea and finally a world—the only world in which I live and breathe." He grew into one of the most impressive intellectuals of his age, translating Dostoyevsky into Arabic and publishing multiple novels and his own magazine.[169]

After graduation at age 16, Baydas was hired to teach in and administer the primary schools he had just graduated from in the 1890s. That made him one of the first Arabs in history to get paid to teach the history and geography of Palestine. Teachers like good teaching materials, which is probably why Baydas chose to translate *A Description of the Holy Land* from Russian to Arabic, as we discussed above. To repeat, Baydas taught "a description of the land of Palestine," to generation of Arab youth from the 1890s onwards.

To recap, a Russian archeologist named Akim Aleksyeevich Olesnitskii wrote a book about the Holy Land or Palestine; The Russian Empire paid Arab and Russian teachers to run a high school in Nazareth; Khalil Baydas received a subvention to study in it; Russians hired Baydas to teach in Russian-funded schools, translate Olesnitskii's book from Russian to Arabic, and teach it to hundreds of Arab kids in the classroom. No one could have earned a living doing any of those things before the 19th century. Had scholars not been able to find funding to pursue their scholarship in late 19th century imperial Russia; had the Russian government not expanded its bureaucracy with investments in overseas education and soft diplomacy; and had they not been able to print hundreds of books for the classroom, Baydas wouldn't have been reading,

---

[169] On the Russian books anecdote, see Hopwood, *The Russian Presence*, 157-8; on his biography, see 'Ajaj Nuwayhid, *Rijal min Filastin* (Beirut: Manshurat Filastin al-Muhtalla, 1981), 22-3; Roger Allen, *Essays in Arabic Literary Biography: 1850-1950* (Wiesbaden, Germany: Harrassowitz, 2010), 72-79.

translating or teaching about Palestine. And without those things he might not have thought of himself as a Palestinian.

The book also juxtaposed modern events with their Biblical equivalents. In one 1893 incident, 37 Russian pilgrims were reportedly killed on the Nazareth-Jerusalem road due to harsh blizzard conditions. After describing the tragic event, the book then quoted a passage from the Book of Job about harsh weather and frost—evidence that harsh winters were nothing knew to Palestine, and that the land's conditions had changed little since Biblical times. Occasionally, Olesnitskii quoted the Bible directly as if he was describing Palestine's modern customs and conditions. Apparently, nothing had changed since Biblical times.[170]

This approach might seem Orientalist in the pejorative or Edward Saidian sense of the word. To be an Orientalist, in the Saidian sense, meant to believe the land had undergone little change for thousands of years and that it remained untainted by modern or foreign influences. (Said accused Orientalists of a lot more than that, but this simplification is sufficient for our purposes). The problem with this point of view, as Said knew, was that it assumed the answer to the question from the outset. Scholars could learn about the people of the Bible simply by observing its modern inhabitants, so the logic went. (Although few if any scholars today believe this particular conclusion, the approach that underlines it is still very popular: start with a conclusion, and look for evidence to support it.)

---

[170] Baydas (trans.), *Kitab al-Rawda al-Mu'nisa*, 22; on Biblical quotations, see for instance, ibid, 60. Baydas might have inspired another graduate of the Russian seminary, Hanna 'Isa Samara, to translate Niqula Tripolski, *A New Guide to the Holy Land* [*Kalam fi Wasf al-Ard al-Muqaddasa: al-Jiz'a al-Awwal, Madinat Bayt Lahm wa-Jiwaruha* (Beirut: al-Matba'a al-Adabiyya, 1902)] from Russian to Arabic only a few years later, the book explicitly published under the auspices of the Imperial Orthodox Palestine Society.

But why did Khalil Baydas translate an Orientalist rather than a progressive? In the late 19th century, no one thought that making this assumption was all that bad—not even Arabs themselves. A hundred years ago the average scholar knew a lot less about the intervening two millennia. Few scholarly studies had been written about the Byzantine, Fatimid, Ayyubid, Mamluk or early Ottoman Middle East. Libraries and primary sources were difficult to access. Books could not be shipped by airplane from Haifa University to Firestone Library in Princeton, New Jersey, and arrive a few days later—at no cost to the researcher. There was no Google Search, Google Scholar, Wikipedia or Worldcat. Most researchers could not obtain grants to fund international travel to access sources. It was uncommon for students to obtain five year fellowships to fund their research. People knew less about history, so they made naïve assumptions and came to the false conclusions.[171]

* * *

The second Arab in modern history to use the term Palestinian was Salim Qubʻayn. Qubʻayn *also* studied at the Russian Seminary in Nazareth, interestingly enough, and he published an

---

[171] For similarly Orientalist views, see the book Khalil Totah was writing at the time of his death called *Palestine Illustrates the Bible*, which was to provide "rich information on how the Palestine of his childhood in many ways mirrored aspects of the Bible." On the book, see Joy Totah Hilden, *A Passion for Learning: The Life Journey of Khalil Totah, a Palestinian* (Xlibris, 2016), ch.2; for other Orientalist views, see ʻIsa Iskandar Maʻluf, *Dawani al-Qutuf fi Tarikh Bani al-Maʻluf* (Baʻbada, Lebanon: al-Matbaʻa al-ʻUthamniyya, 1907-8), 125; Shahin Makariyus, *Hasr al-Litham ʻan Nakbat al-Sham* (Misr: n.p., 1890), 4; Fadlallah Faris Abu Halqa, *Mukhtasar fi al-Jughrafiya* (Beirut: Matbaʻat Jarida, 1890), 25; Afram Dayrani (a.k.a. Dirani), *al-Nahj al-Qawim fi Tarikh Shuʻub al-Sharq al-Qadim* (Beirut: al-Matbaʻa al-Adabiyya, 1903), 30, 37, 42, 60; Negib Azoury, *Le Réveil de la Nation Arabe dans l'Asie Turque: Partie Asiatique de la Question d'Orient et Programme de la Ligue de la Patrie Arabe* (Paris, Plon-Nourrit et cie, 1905), 17-22; Husayn Ruhi, *Mukhtasar Jughrafiyat Filastin* (Jerusalem: L.J.S. Printing Press, 1923), 7, 46-112; Tawfiq Canaan, *Mohammedan Saints and Sanctuaries in Palestine* (London: Luzac & Co., 1927); on Ottoman Orientalist writing on Palestine, see, for instance, See Şirvanlı Ahmet Hamdi Efendi, *Usûl-i Coğrafya-yı Kebir* (Istanbul: Şeyh Yahyanın Matbaası, 1876), 401-2, 410-417.

article titled "A Palestinian Describes Palestinian Towns" in Arabic in 1902. In the article, Qub'ayn compared his observations of Kafr Kanna and Tiberias to those of the famous French scholar Ernest Renan three decades earlier. Qub'ayn agreed with Renan that Tiberias was a thriving city during Biblical times but was as pitiful (circa 1902) as it was a few decades earlier when Renan observed it. "Today, nothing remains of its past greatness," Qub'ayn wrote, noting one exception: Tiberias's new Jewish settlements. They were teeming with vineyards, parks and trees. "It's as if they inherited the productivity of the Israelites who first came to this land." Qub'ayn added that Tiberias's "non-Jewish residents" continued to fish, just as Renan described it. Incredibly, Qub'ayn was in complete agreement with Renan. The second Palestinian in modern history described Tiberias's Arab or Palestinian residents as simply "non-Jews," and seemed to think their lifestyle choices remained unchanged for centuries. Nothing about them was even worthy of specification, aside from the fact that they were not Jewish.[172]

Was it possible that the second Arab to use the term Palestinian was an Orientalist *and* a Zionist? We already noted that Orientalist views of Palestine were common in the Middle East. It's not well known, but sympathy for Zionism existed on the margins. Some Christians and Muslims thought it was sensible that Jews might want to establish a presence in Palestine for historical reasons. Yusuf Diya Pasha al-Khalidi, for instance, wrote in an 1898 letter to Zadok Kahn, the chief rabbi of France, "who can challenge the rights of the Jews on Palestine? Good lord, historically it really is your country." Al-Khalidi connected the Biblical Israelites to the modern

---

[172] Salim Afandi Qub'ayn, "Buldan Filastiniyya Yusiffuha Filastini," *al-Jami'a* 3:6 (1902): 404-6. For biographical information on Qub'ayn, see Abu Hanna, *Tala'i' al-Nahda fi Filastin*, 147-8; then see Edward Said, *Orientalism* (New York: Vintage Books, 1979), 8. This was the same Renan attacked by Edward Said as an "Orthodox Orientalist authority." Said would have presumably accused Qub'ayn for believing in an Orient based "more or less exclusively upon a sovereign Western consciousness," whatever that is supposed to mean.

Zionists, thinking it reasonable that Jews would desire to return, even if he opposed Jewish immigration on the grounds that the land was already inhabited. Other Arabs made peace with the Zionists based on either their shared belief in scientific progress or their shared support for decentralization of the Ottoman Empire, including the prominent political activist Rafiq al-'Azm. In short, Salim Quba'yn was an Orientalist, in the Saidian sense, and he probably did harbor sympathies for Zionism, at least in 1902.[173]

But how did the term spread? The popularity of the magazine *al-Jami'a*—where Qub'ayn published the piece—can offer a preliminary point of departure. Although exact circulation figures are not available, similar publications in the land of Sham boasted between 1,000-1,500 subscribers. The magazine, based in Alexandria, Egypt, reportedly doubled sales by 1902 but still could not keep up with demand. "We were forced to reject many subscription requests," its editor, Farah Antun, lamented. Scalability was a problem then as it is now. "Had we tried to publish responses to all of the questions and letters we received, it would have filled the pages of this entire issue." Antun was probably exaggerating his success, but the publishing industry was growing at that time in Egypt. It's possible that hundreds or even thousands of Arabic speakers in Egypt, and smaller numbers in the lands of Sham, read that Qub'ayn was a Palestinian. It's

---

[173] On Yusuf al-Khalidi's letter, which has been re-quoted by the historian Benny Morris, political scientist Alan Dowty, radio personality Chuck Morse and others. See Neville J. Mandel, *The Arabs and Zionism Before World War I* (Berkeley University of California Press 1980), 47-8; for further evidence that Arabs, such as 'Isa al-'Isa, were not initially hostile to Zionism, see Emanuel Beška, *From Ambivalence to Hostility: The Arabic Newspaper Filasṭīn and Zionism, 1911–1914* (Bratislava: Slovak Academic Press, 2016); Samuel Dolbee and Shay Hazkani, ""Impossible is not Ottoman": Menashe Meirovitch, 'Isa al-'Isa, and Imperial Citizenship in Palestine," *International Journal of Middle Eastern Studies* 47 (2015): 241–262; the prominent political activist Rafiq al-'Azm also published a statement supporting Zionism in 1913 in his capacity as head of the Decentralization party in the Ottoman Empire. See Abigail Jacobson, "Jews Writing in Arabic Chapter in Late Ottoman Palestine The Period of Young Turk Rule," pp.165-182 in *Late Ottoman Palestine: The Period of Young Turk Rule*, Yuval Ben-Bassat and Eyal Ginio (eds.) (London: I.B. Tauris, 2011), 176; Ilyas Zakka, another prominent Arab publisher, accepted subventions from the Zionists. on Ilyas Zakka's biography, see Ya'qub Yehoshua, *Tarikh al-Sihafa al-'Arabiyya fi Filastin fil-'Ahd al-'Uthmani, 1908-1918* (Jerusalem: Matba'at al-Ma'arif, 1974), 51-4.

also possible they skipped that article. Perhaps it sparked dinner table conversations, or perhaps not. We don't really know.[174]

What we can be more certain about is that the Russian seminary acted as a breeding ground for a modern Palestinian identity. Iliya Zakka, a third graduate of the Russian seminary, once praised an Egyptian journalist in 1911 for acknowledging that Palestinians had made important literary contributions but criticized the Egyptian journalist for failing to mention the Palestinians by name. (Interestingly, Zakka was also sympathetic to Zionism). Shukri Khalil Suwaydan, a forth graduate of the seminary, used the term Palestinian in 1912 in his own book about the history of the Imperial Orthodox Palestine Society. The Russian Seminary produced almost as many people calling themselves Palestinian before World War I than most other schools combined.[175]

The Palestinian identity that had formed at the Seminary snowballed as the Qub'ayn article inspired a copycat. A few months later, Najib Nassar published an article in the same magazine with the exact same title: "A Palestinian Describes Palestinian Towns." Nassar similarly compared his own observations to Ernest Renan's, reviewing the geographical positions, ancient inhabitants and modern conditions of Wadi Musa. At one time, he claimed the town boasted

---

[174] *al-Jinan* (Beirut, 1870-1879) boasted 1,500 subscribers. See Fruma Zachs and Sharon Halevi, "From Difa' al-Nisa' to Mas'alat al-Nisa' in Greater Syria: Readers and Writers Debate Women and their Rights, 1858-1900," *International Journal of Middle East Studies* 41(4) (2009), 619); Yusuf al-Dibs's bi-weekly paper, *al-Najah*, printed some 1,000 copies; See Fouad Zouki-Haklany, "Yusuf al-Dibs (1833-1907): Archeveque De Beyrouth, Historien at Homme de Culture," *Journal of Eastern Christian Studies* 61(3-4) (2009): 251; on the letters to *al-Jami'a*, see "Ra'a 'Alim Misr wa-'Alim Suri," *al-Jami'a* 3: 7(1902): 477; on high demand, see "Musa'adat al-Qira' li-Jami'atihim," *al-Jami'a* 3:9(1902): 648.

[175] On Ilya Zakka, see *al-Nafir*, 14 June 1910. I found this article in the personal files of David Yellin, located at the Central Zionist Archives (CZA) in Jerusalem. I would like to thank Haim Gerber for pointing that out to me. For more on him, see Salim Tamari, "Issa al Issa's Unorthodox Orthodoxy: Banned in Jerusalem, Permitted in Jaffa," *Jerusalem Quarterly* 59 (2014): 27. Shukri Khalil Suwaydan worked in the offices of the Imperial Orthodox Palestine Society in Damascus as a secretary after he graduated, and then wrote a history of the Society for the benefit of "Syrians and Palestinians," in his words. See idem, Tarikh *al-Jam'iyya al-Imbaraturiyya al-Urthudhuksiyya al-Filastiniyya*, 33; on Suwaydan's biography, see Abu Hanna, *Tala'i' al-Nahda fi Filastin*, 144.

palaces, temples, stone sculpers and a stadium that could comfortably seat 4,000 people. But "today, nothing remains save for Bedouin tribes who have set up permanent camps in the area." Much like Renan and Qub'ayn, Nassar believed in the land's ancient grandeur and modern desolation—a similarly Orientalist view (in the Saidian sense) that nomads are uncivilized.[176]

In short, the Seminary was special because students were instructed to take pride in their Arab heritage, they learned about the history and geography of the land of Palestine and studied the Biblical scriptures themselves, which took place in the land the teachers were calling Palestine. They were also separated from their families at a young age and placed side by side other Jaffans, Jerusalemites and Nazarenes in dormitories. This is how I would have imagined a Palestinian identity would have come into existence. It was a perfect sandstorm and after the dust had settled the Palestinian people were born.

* * *

The Americans. It seemed odd that so many of the earliest people to use the term Palestinian studied in Russian schools. What was so special about the Russians? I think the reason is that the Russian Seminary was located in Nazareth, and thus attracted students from the area called Palestine, which is why they started calling themselves Palestinians. Graduates of similar schools

---

[176] Najib Nassar, "Buldan Filastiniyya Yusifuha Filastini," *al-Jami'a* 3(9) (1902): 612-5. Interestingly, Najib Nassar was described as Lebanese in a later issue. See Najib Nassar, "Bayt al-Maqdis," *al-Jami'a* 4 (1903): 160. When Nassar founded his own newspaper *al-Karmil* a few years later in 1908—he took a liking to the term. He wrote in 1911, for instance, that "we, your Palestinian brothers, share with you all your difficulties, so why don't you, at least, feel with us a little the disasters raining on us and on our country," cited in Issam Nassar, "Reflections on Writing the History of Palestinian Identity," *Palestine-Israel Journal* 8(4)/9(1) (2001-2002). In a separate article, he explained that "young Palestinians" in Istanbul supported holding an anti-Zionist congress. See Mandel, *The Arabs and Zionism*, 173. He also published a "General Summons to Palestinians" on 7 July 1914 *al-Karmil*. See 'Abd al-Wahhab al-Kayyali, *Palestine: A Modern History* (London: Croom Helm, 1978), 35.

like 'Ayn al-Waraqa, al-Ghazir or the Syrian Protestant College came from other parts of Syria, and tended to embrace the term Syrian. The Russian school was not all that special, and graduates from many other missionary and state schools were introduced to Palestine the same way.

Many of those other schools were founded by Americans. Although American missionaries first reached Ottoman Beirut and Lebanon in the 1820s, their activities were limited to distributing Bibles, preaching in private and paying recruits handsome salaries to teach them local languages and translate Protestant polemics into Arabic. At first, they were not influential and their followers were deemed heretics. Some of them were even excommunicated, such as As'ad Shidyaq, who was subjected to what the Maronite Patriarch called "torture commensurate with the totality of his ruinous evil." He was brutally murdered, described by an American sympathizer as "the first martyr of the Protestant Mission in Syria."[177]

From the 1830s onwards, the American Protestant mission in Syria expanded. They recruited more native helpers and built more schools, growing from 40 students in the 1830s to 240 by the early 1840s. They went from heretics to industry leaders in a few decades. They did it by teaching not just catechism, theology and prayer—but also foreign languages, mathematics, geography and history. By the 1870s, American missionaries had published a small library of

---

[177] On As'ad Shidyaq's handsome salary of hundred piastes per month, see Ussama Makdisi, *Artillery of Heaven American Missionaries and the Failed Conversion of the Middle East* (Ithaca, N.Y.: Cornell University Press, 2008), 105; on the torture, see ibid, 127; on his martyrdom, see Richter, *A History of Protestant Missions*, 189; for more on the American mission, see Abdul Latif Tibawi, *American Interests in Syria: 1800-1901: A Study of Educational, Literary and Religious Work* (Oxford: Clarendon Press, 1966); Adnan Abu Ghazaleh, *American Missions in Syria: A Study of American Missionary Contribution to Arab Nationalism in 19th Century Syria* (Brattleboro: Amana Books, 1990); Christine Beth Lindner, "Negotiating the Field: American Protestant Missionaries in Ottoman Syria, 1823 to 1860," (Ph.D Dissertation, University of Edenborough, 2009).

textbooks and operated dozens of schools, including the SPC, the most prestigious school in the region, today known as the American University of Beirut (AUB).[178]

Let's zoom in on how the American missionaries popularized the name Palestine and made the place seem real to people. They taught extensively about the history and geography of the Bible in class, including the history and geography of Palestine. In 1833, they introduced their first lesson on the "History of the Land of Palestine" into the classroom:

1) When did the Jews come to and conquer the Land of Palestine?
2) How would you characterize Israelite rule?
3) When was David appointed king?
4) Who succeeded him after his death?
5) Who ruled the kingdom after that?
6) What is known about the history of the land of Palestine regarding the destruction of Jerusalem?[179]

To summarize the situation with an emphasis on its peculiarities: the first modern Arabic lesson about the land of Palestine dealt primarily with the ancient Israelites; it was probably written by a Maronite convert to Protestantism from Mount Lebanon—Ahmad Faris al-Shidyaq; it was printed in Malta under American patronage and imported into a land controlled by the Albanian ruler of Egypt who had wrest the country away from its erstwhile Ottoman Turkish heirs in Istanbul.

---

[178] On the American commission report, see Harvey Newcomb, *Cyclopedia of Missions* (New York: C. Scribner, 1854), 737; on the expansion of the mission, see Makdisi, *Artillery of Heaven*, 156; Butrus Labki, "Tatawwar Mu'assasat al-Ta'lim fi Lubnan khilal al-Qarn al-Akhir min al-Hukm al-'Uthmani," pp. 463-492 in *al-Haya al-Fikriyya fi al-Wilayat al-'Arabiyya ithna al-'Ahd al-'Uthmani*, 'Abd al-Jalil al-Tamami (ed.) (Zaghwa, Tunisia: Markaz al-Dirasat wa-l-Buhuth al-'Uthmaniyya wa-l-Muriskiyya wa-l-Tawthiq wa-l-Ma'lumat, 1990).

[179] On the history lesson, see n.a., *Kitab Tawarikh al-Mukhtasar Yunbi 'an Mamlik wa Bilad 'Adida* (Malta: n.p., 1833), 19-22. Palestine is the standard name of the region in the book, and is used in other lessons on the Arabs and Phoenicia (ibid, 16, 38). The Americans published other textbooks dealing with Palestine as well, including n.a., *Kitab al-Khulasa al-Safiyya fi Usul al-Jughrafiyya* (Beirut: n.p., 1883[1858]), 69-85.

The Americans also used maps of Palestine to teach its history and geography. First, they hung maps of Palestine in their offices where their native tutors taught them Arabic. Their first world atlas, published in the 1830s, included a dozen some maps of Europe and the Middle East. They printed another atlas probably in the 1850s that included one of the most beautiful 19th century maps of Palestine (see figure 9). American missionaries like Simeon Calhoun and George E. Post also published maps of the region in their textbooks as well. For the first time, an entire generation of Arab youth saw the *exact* same map of Palestine. The era of standardization had begun.[180]

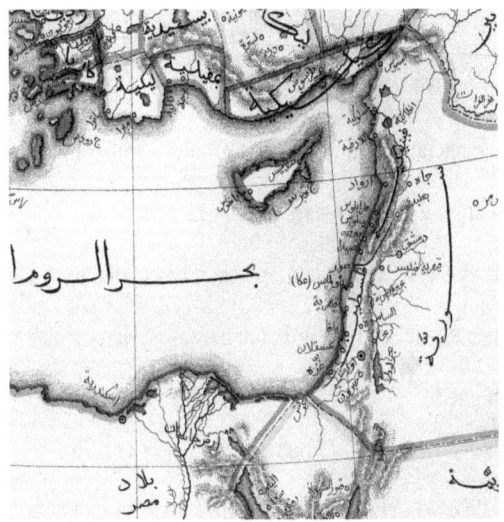

Figure 9. A map of Palestine, or *Filastin*, used in American missionary schools in the mid-19th century.[181]

---

[180] On the map of Palestine hung in the offices, see Isaac Bird, "Missionary Journal from January 1824 Comprehending a tour to Jerusalem etc.," Folder 23, Box 2: Journal 1824 Jan-May, MS 82, pg. 74, Isaac Bird Papers, Sterling Library, Yale University New Haven, CT; I am indebted to Christine B. Lindner for sharing this reference with me; for the first printing, see F. de Brocktorff, *Atlas, Ay Majmu' Kharitat Rasm al-Ard* (Malta: American Press, 1835); on the later edition, see Edward Aiken, *Atlas, Ay Majmu' Kharitat* (New York: Appleton, 1850s?); the atlas is mentioned by Tibawi [*American Interests*, 65] as well. Christine B. Lindner suspects that Edward Aiken died in 1858 or at least left the mission field, and thus the map probably dates to sometime before then.

[181] I zoomed in on the Palestine section of the map. For the original, see Zachary J. Foster, "The Most Beautiful 19th Century Arabic Maps of Syria and Palestine," *midafternoonmap.com*, 29 August 2015 (goo.gl/Nv4R9S).

Palestine was no longer just another fly on the lexical wall of geography; it was a big fly on the wall which circulated beyond the confines of school classrooms. In one case, the missionary Jonas King distributed pamphlets to parents, friends and community members in what he called "Syria and Palestine" explaining why he could not be Catholic. The letter was widely read and elicited responses from concerned priests and local notables.[182]

Let's get to know a couple of missionaries who introduced Palestine's history and geography to a generation of Arab youth. Cornelius Van Dyck (d.1895) fascinated people with his ability to recite from memory Arabic poetry, proverbs, history and science. He wrote and taught in Arabic, even translating parts of the Bible into Arabic with the help of Butrus al-Bustani, his erstwhile roommate and lifelong friend and mentor. Once, a group of armed Druze abruptly approached Van Dyck on a sojourn around Lebanon and mistook him for a native Christian, Dyck's protests notwithstanding. "A pretty story," but "we know that no foreigner ever spoke Arabic as you do." Van Dyck may have been "American by birth, but he was Syrian by his own merit," as his student biographer explained.[183]

---

[182] Jonas King asked As'ad Shidyaq to translate his farewell pamphlet to his friends "in Palestine and Syria," or *Filastin wa Suriya*, in Shidyaq's translation. The letter was also translated into Armenian by another early convert, the Armenian Bishop, Dionysius Carabet (ak.a. Garabed Dionysius). Both the Armenian Patriarch Church in Istanbul and the Maronite Archbishop of Beirut, Butrus Abu Kara, Shidyaq's erstwhile ecclesiastic patron responded. On the original translation delivered to the Maronites, see *Wada' Yunus Kin ila Ahbabihi fi Filastin wa Suriya* (April 1825), Archives of the Maronite Patriarchate (Bkirki, Lebanon) Drawer Yusuf Hbeich, 24/15(2) (Bkerké Archives); Christine B. Lindner pointed out that another copy can be found in the library of the Near East Theological Seminary (NEST); for an English translation, see Jonas King, *The Oriental Church and the Latin* (New York: John A. Gray & Green, 1865); see also Tibawi, *American Interests*, 33, 35-6; Gregory M. Wortabet, *Syria and the Syrians; or, Turkey in the Dependencies* (London, J. Madden, 1856), 53; Makdisi, *Artillery of Heaven*, 103-5; on the Armenian response, see Harrison Gray Otis Dwight, *Christianity Revived in the East; or, A Narrative of the Work of God among the Armenians of Turkey* (New York: Baker and Scribner, 1850), 11-12.

[183] When he first reached the Middle East, Van Dyck spent his first forty days in Beirut in quarantine memorizing Arabic words. A learned Muslim Shaykh of Al Azhar University reportedly told Van Dyck's daughter that "your father taught me, by his published writings, that it is possible to write good Arabic, correct in grammar and in idiom, in a style so simple and so clear as to be easily understood by an intelligent reader, whether learned or unlearned."

Van Dyck used his own geography textbook to teach about Palestine. Students studied from that book for decades—it was reprinted in 1860, 1870 and 1886. The book discussed the mountains, rivers, lakes and ancient history of Palestine, focused on the Bible, the children of Israel, and its ancient past. Interestingly, we find many similar descriptions of Palestine's geography published in Arabic in the subsequent decades.[184]

George E. Post, another American educator, wrote multiple books in Arabic dealing with Palestine, including his *Botanical Geography of Syria and Palestine* and *A Dictionary of the Bible* in which he surveyed the Biblical history, topography, geology, botany and demography of Palestine. Post's work was read at the Russian Seminary in Nazareth, as noted above, discussed in the most popular Arabic magazines of the era, including *al-Muqtataf* and *al-Hilal*, and was

---

See Stephen B. Penrose, *That They May Have Life: The Story of the American University of Beirut, 1866-1941* (Beirut: American University of Beirut, 1941), 36–7. In addition to Arabic, Van Dyck also knew Latin, Greek, Syriac and was even offered a professorship to teach Hebrew in New York, which he declined. Van Dyck also defended the native teachers of the Syrian Protestant College when they faced discrimination by its white American leadership. See "al-Duktur Van Dyck," *al-Hilal* 4(1895-6): 3-8; Iskandar Niqula al-Barudi, *Hayat Kurniliyus Van Dayk* (Ba'abda, Lebanon: al-Matba'a al-'Uthmaniyya, 1900), jim-8; Jurji Zaydan, *Kitab Tarikh Adab al-Lugha al-'Arabiyya* (Cairo: Matba'at al-Hilal, 1911), IV, 218-9; Lutfi M. Sa'di, George Sarton and W. T. Van Dyck, "Al-Hakîm Cornelius Van Alen Van Dyck (1818-1895)," *ISIS* 27(1) (1937): 24-45; Tibawi, *American Interests*, 115.

[184] Van Dyck wrote that the Land of Sham "used to be divided into two parts, Syria and Palestine, but the name Syria was applied to both after they were incorporated into the Roman Empire." Cornelius Van Dyck, *Kitab al-Mir'a al-Wadiyya fi al-Kura al-Ardiyya* (Beirut: n.p., 1852), 96, 105. Nu'man Qasatli [*al-Rawda al-Ghanna' fi Dimashq al-Fahya'* (Beirut, 1879; rpt., Dar al-Ra'id al-'Arabi, 1980), 3-4] wrote similarly in his history of Damascus that "the earliest people called it Syria and divided it into two parts, Syria and Palestine." Shahin Makariyus [*Hasr al-Litham 'an Nakbat al-Sham* (Misr: n.p., 1890), 4] noted in 1890 that ancient scholars divided this land into two parts: Syria and Palestine. Palestine was "the part where the Israelites settled and ruled over most of it during the times of Moses and his successor, Yehoshua Bin Nun. The land was known by these two names, i.e. *Suriya* and *Filastin*, until the Romans controlled it." Fadl Allah Abu Halqa [*Mukhtasar fi al-Jughrafiya* (Beirut: Matba'at Jarida, 1890), 25] likewise explained in his geography book that "today, the northern part of *Bar al-Sham* is called Syria and its southern part, Palestine." For biographical details on Abu Halqa, see Toufoul Abou-Hodeib, *A Taste for Home: The Modern Middle Class in Ottoman Beirut* (Stanford: Stanford University Press, 2017), chapter 3. Christine B. Lindner believes this book might have been co-written with Butrus al-Bustani (recall that Van Dyck lived in the same bedroom with al-Bustani—his lifelong friend and mentor). For more on the book, see Tibawi, *American Interests*, 56-7; on his relationship with students, see "The Dawn in Syria," *The Christian Register* 98(9) (1919): 205.

cited extensively by the earliest Arabic book published on the politics of the Palestine issue in 1919—John S. Salah's *Palestine and its Renewal*. Another American missionary, Simeon Calhoun, wrote and taught about Palestine and the Bible in Arabic in the 1860s and 1870s. The American Harvey Porter also published in Arabic on the civilizations of the ancient Near East, covering Palestine too. American missionaries learned Arabic, taught and published in Arabic and offered a premier education, bringing the name Palestine, maps of it and stories about its history and geography to a generation of Arab youth.[185]

The results were predictable enough. Students read about Palestine's history, studied with maps of its sacred geography and heard it mentioned at lunch. Graduates of American schools became

---

[185] George E. Post mastered Arabic by attaching Arabic words to his office walls so he would see them "whichever way he turned." He impressed folks with his signature Tripoli dialect and mastery of classical Arabic. He launched the Syrian Protestant Medical College in 1867 which he led for 41 years, earning a reputation for resilience in the classroom. One of his favorite expressions was *istasfaret* ("You are zero") an Arabic term he invented and shouted out whenever his students answer questions incorrectly in class. On his office decorations, see Jurji Zaydan, "Duktur Jurj Bust [George Post]" *al-Hilal* 18:4(1910): 223; on his biography, see Ya'qub Sarruf, "al-Duktur Jurj Bust," pp.77-80 and "The Bust of Dr. George Edward Post," pp. 146-150 in *al-Mu'assisun al-Ruwwad Lil-Jam'ia al-Amirkiyya fi Bayrut* – The Founding Fathers of the American University of Beirut, Ghada Yusuf Khoury (ed.) (Beirut: American University of Beirut, 1992); Jurji Zaydan, *Mashahir al-Sharq fi al-Qarn al-Tasi' 'Ashar* (Cairo: Matba'at al-Hilal, 1911), II, 271-2; Lutfi M Sa'di, "The Life and Works of George Edward Post," *ISIS* 28 (1938): 385-417; on *istasfaret*, see Sarruf, "al-Duktur Jurj Bust," 78; For his survey of the Bible, see George E. Post, *Qamus al-Kitab al-Muqaddas* (Beirut: al-Matba'a al-Amrikiyya, 1901), 170-184. For its reviews, see Jurji Zaydan, *Mashahir al-Sharq fi al-Qarn al-Tasi' 'Ashar* (Cairo: Matba'at al-Hilal, 1911), II, 271-2; "Qamus Kitab al-Muqaddas," *al-Hilal* 4 (1895-6): 758-9; George E. Post also published his *Nabat Suriya wa-Filastin wa-al-Qatr al-Misri wa-Bawadiha* (Beirut, n.p., 1884)], also publicized in the local press and used at the Syrian Protestant College. See George E. Post, "al-Mujallad al-Awwal min Kitab Nabat Suriya wa-Filastin wa-al-Qatr al-Misri wa-Bawadiha," *al-Muqtataf* 8(1883): 565; "Aqalim Suriya wa-Filastin al-Nabatiyya," *al-Muqtataf* 8(1883): 417; Salah [*Filastin wa-Tajdid*, 15, 29-30, 118] also cites him; Simeon Calhoun [*Kitab Ittifaq al-Bashirin wa-l-Dalil al-Mustarshidin* (Beirut: n.p., 1876), 5, 8, 21, 98; and idem, *Kitab Murshid al-Talibin ila al-Kitab al-Muqaddas al-Thamin*, (Beirut: n.p., 1869), 16, 19, 46-7, 217, 565] wrote at least three textbooks for use in the classroom: an 1869 history book about the New and Old Testaments, an 1876 book on the Gospels, and a geography book on "Turkey, Asia Minor, Syria and Palestine full of apt quotes in poetry and prose from the old Arab geographers and travelers" that "the people delight in it and quote it with admiration " (the latter is now lost). For details, see Henry Harris Jessup, *Fifty-three Years in Syria* (New York, Chicago, Fleming H. Revell Company, 1910), 107; on Calhoun's biography, see Peter J. Wosh, *Spreading the Word: The Bible Business in Nineteenth-Century America* (Ithaca: Cornell University Press, 1994), 164-74; John Haskell Hewitt, *Williams College and Foreign Missions: Biographical Sketches of Williams College Men* (Boston: Pilgrim Press, 1914), 167-9; Jessup, *Fifty-three years in Syria*, 23, 97-114; Harvey Porter [*al-Nahj al-Qawim fi al-Tarikh al-Qadim* (Beirut: n.p., 1884)] mentions Palestine dozens of times. On his biography, see "The Classes," *Amherst Graduates' Quarterly* 12(1922): 183-6; "Literature: They Know Turkey," *The Cristian Register* 14 (30 January 1919): 110.

prominent writers, publishers and intellectuals. Many used the word in their day to day speech and described the land as Palestine in their works. Many wrote extensively about Palestine's history and geography in the last few decades of the 19th century.[186]

Ya'qub Sarruf and Faris Nimr, both graduates of and later teachers in the American schools, bear special mention. They founded and edited the most popular Arabic magazine of its era, *al-Muqtataf*, distributed it widely around the Arab world and published dozens of articles about Palestine in it from the 1870s onwards. They frequently review of British, French, German and American activities in Palestine, as they called it, and books, maps, reports, surveys, findings and archeological researches about Palestine. Although it's difficult to know how many people read these articles on Palestine, at least one reader sent a letter to the magazine requesting the complete reference to a book on Palestine mentioned in passing but not properly cited. If you were one of the many thousands of *al-Muqtataf* readers, and if you actually read the magazine, you knew a lot about Palestine's ancient and modern history, its prospects for economic development as well as its geology and topography.[187]

---

[186] On graduates who wrote about Palestine, see, for instance, Khalil Sarkis, *Kitab Urshalim, ayy al-Quds al-Sharif* (Beirut: Matba'at al-Ma'arif, 1874), 2, 24, 39, 167-8, 173, 176, 185; on his background, see Ami Ayalon, "Private Publishing in the Nahda" *International Journal of Middle East Studies* 40(4) (2008): 564-6; See also George Zaydan's popular magazine, *al-Hilal*: "al-Athar al-Misriyya wa-Isti'bad al-Isra'iliyyin," *al-Hilal* 4 (1895-6): 637-9; "al-Hilal fi Suriya wa Filastin wa-l-'Iraq," *al-Hilal* 6(1898): 784; "Filastin: Tarikhuha, wa-Atharuha," *al-Hilal* 22 (1913): 43-48; on Zaydan's biography, see Thomas Philipp, "The Role of Jurjī Zaidān in the Intellectual Development of the Arab Nahda from the Beginning of the British Occupation of Egypt to the Outbreak of World War I," (Ph.D Dissertation, UCLA, 1971), 13-76; See also Amin Shumayyil's study of the Eastern Question. Idem, *Kitab al-Wafi fi al-Mas'ala al-Sharqiyya wa-Muta'alliqatuha* (Alexandria: Maba'at al-Ahram, 1879), 518, 526-7, 69, 71-2, 21, 23, 25, 51; on Shumayyil's biography, see Yusuf Assaf, *Dalil Misr* (Cairo: al-Matba'a al-'Umumiyya, 1890), 340-3.

[187] On its popularity, see Ami Ayalon, "Modern Texts and Their Readers in Late Ottoman Palestine," *Middle Eastern Studies* 38(2002): 17-40; on the letter from the reader, see ("al-Jawab Unwanuhu: Biblical Researches in Palestine, John Murry," *al-Muqtataf* (16)(1892): 640; they reported about the British interest in building a Palestine Channel from the Dead Sea to Red Sea ["Tar'at Filastin," *al-Muqtataf* 8(1883): 165] and about a Germans survey of East Jordan in Palestine ["al-Alman fi Filastin" *al-Muqtataf* 26 (1901): 186]; they quoted from the reports of British Console in Jerusalem, Mr. Dickson, on Commerce in Palestine ["Tijarat Filastin," *al-Muqtataf* 16(1892): 787; "Tijarat Filastin," *al-Muqtataf* 27 (1902): 510-11]; they reviewed a Palestine Exploration Fund (PEF) map [*al-Muqtataf*, "Kharitat Filastin," 1878 (3): 154], Edward Hull's *Survey of Western Palestine* ["Julujiyyat Filastin," *al-*

French. French missionaries also made Palestine seem real to people. Although French missionaries had reached the lands of Sham as early as the 17th century, they did not expand rapidly until the mid-late 19th century. By World War I, French Jesuits had enrolled some 100,000 students in total and established 300-500 schools around the region—mostly in what is today Syria and Lebanon. At their flagship institution, the Ghazir Seminary, which later became the University of Saint-Joseph, they taught manners, theology, arithmetic, Latin, Greek, Italian, Arabic, French and Turkish, as well as history, literature and geography. Although it's unclear if Palestine was ever a focus, French missionaries clearly called the place Palestine, based on its popularity in the Francophone world, and they did teach Biblical history and geography, which dealt with Palestine as well.[188]

Having learned about Palestine in class as kids, many graduates of French missionary schools published about Palestine. Rashid al-Shartuni translated Pierre Martin's work on Syria from

---

Muqtataf 8(1883): 446]; Mousier Birluti's *In the Wilderness and Palestine* ["La Taghayyur fi Filastin," *Al-Muqtataf* 19(1895): 236]; they translated selections from *Cook's Tourist's Handbook for Palestine and Syria* ["Jun Kuk," *al-Muqtataf* 23 (1899): 244-7] and Baedeker's *Handbook for Travelers to Syria and Palestine* ["Isti'mar al-Suriyyin bayn al-'Ahdayn," *al-Muqtataf* 50(6)(1917): 542]; they reviewed Salvatori Mitutshi's work on the geology of Palestine ["Filastin Qabl 'Asar al-Tarikh," *al-Muqtataf* 1911(38): 127-131]; Flinders Petrie's findings on Palestine ["Khuruj Bnay Isra'il wa-'Addaduhum," *al-Muqtataf* 31(1906): 537-41]; Conder's *Survey of Eastern Palestine* ["Takhtit Sharqi Filastin," *al-Muqtataf* 6(1881): 272] and Stuart McAlister excavations in Palestine ["athar Filastin" *al-Muqtataf* 33(1908): 678-680; "Madafin Murisha," *al-Muqtataf* 35 (1909):767-770; "Rujma fi Filastin" *al-Muqtataf* 25(1900): 274-5); "al-Naqb 'an Athar Filastin *al-Muqtataf* 31(1906): 614]; for further discussions on Palestine, see "Khara'ib al-Sham," *al-Muqtataf* (1899): 893-7; al-Asrab fi Filastin," *al-Muqtataf* 30 (1905): 1035-6; "Musa wa-Far'un wa-bnu Isra'il," *al-Muqtataf* 11 (1886-7): 709; "Athar Filastin," *al-Muqtataf* 42 (1913): 282-87; "al-Jins al-Shami al-Abyad," *al-Muqtataf* 13 (1888): 269-70.

[188] On the French school estimates, see Mutlu, *Osmanlı Devleti'nde Misyoner Okulları*, 155-163, 170-192, n.a., *Les Jesuites en Syrie, 1831-1931:Université Saint-Joseph* (Paris: Éditions Dillen 1931), V, 11; Rafael Herzstein, "Les Phases de l'Évolution de l'Université Saint-Joseph à Beyrouth: Les Premières Décennies (1875–1914)," *Historical Studies in Education* 24(1) (2012): 22; Mathew Burrows, "Mission Civilisatrice': French Cultural Policy in the Middle East, 1860-1914," *The Historical Journal* 29:1(1986): 109-135; Rafael Herzstein, "Saint-Joseph University of Beirut: An Enclave of the French-Speaking Communities in the Levant, 1875–1914," *Itinerario* 32(2) (2008): 70; *al-Muqtabas* estimated some 90,000 students were studying French in the Ottoman Empire in 1908. See "Madaris Ajnabiyya," *al-Muqtabas* 2 (1908): 672.

French to Arabic in 1899. Afram al-Dirani included a chapter on the geography of Palestine in a book he translated in 1903. And Louis Cheikho wrote extensively about Palestine as well in his renowned scholarly journal, *al-Mashriq* from the late 19th century onwards.[189]

Germans. German missionaries also made Palestine seem real to people. Although much smaller than the French enterprise, it may have been more important for Palestine's sake since its centerpiece was the Syrian Orphanage *in Jerusalem*. Its school opened in 1860 with only 9 students, but managed to expand to 40 students by the end of the year. Their enrollment figures continued to grow with 70 by 1876 and 200 by 1898. By the early 20th century, 1200 students had studied Biblical and Church history, German, Arabic, math, song, Biblical geography, biology, and art at the Orphanage. Students also went on tours to holy places in and around Jerusalem and hailed from around the Land of Sham, as well as Anatolia and Armenia. Tawfiq Canaan and Stephan Hanna Stephan both graduated from the Syrian Orphanage and both matured into fine Orientalists, in the Saidian sense of the word, much like Qub'ayn and Nassar had. Much like them, Canaan and Stephan were also early adopters of the term Palestinian and outspoken activists for the Palestine cause in the 1920s and 1930s.[190]

---

[189] See Pierre Martin, Rashid al-Khuri al-Shartuni (trans.), *Tarikh Lubnan* (Beirut: Matba'at al-Aba' al-Yisu'iyyin, 1889), 10, 20, 137, 162, 177, 194, 286, 297, 306-7, 339, 402, 410, 415, 420, 447, 487, 499, 500; chapter 8: 13, 20, 33, 50, 53, 73, 117; on Shartuni's biography, see Robert Bell Campbell, "The Arabic Journal, al-Mashriq: Its Beginnings and First Twenty-five Years under the Editorship of Père Louis Cheikho, S.J." (Ph.D Dissertation, University of Michigan, 1978), 107; Abdulrazzak Patel, *The Arab Nahḍah: The Making of the Intellectual and Humanist Movement* (Edinburgh: Edinburgh University Press, 2013), 114-7, 209; then see Afram Dirani (a.k.a Dayrani) *al-Nahj al-Qawim fi Tarikh Shu'ub al-Sharq al-Qadim* (Beirut: al-Matba'a al-Adabiyya, 1903), 61-83; For Cheikho reviewed Arcangelo Ghisleri's *Testo Atlante di Geografia Sacra*, for instance, an atlas of sacred geography; he reported about Dr. Frederick Jones Bliss's various archeological discoveries in Palestine ("'Adiyyat Suriyya," *al-Mashriq* 4 (1904): 180; he also reviewed l'Abbe Th. Vazeuz's *Abrege de Geographie: De la Palestine et de la Syrie* ("Matbu'at Sharqiyya Jadida," *al-Mashriq* (Beirut: 1899): 140-1) and Adriaan Reelant's *Palestine Illustrated* (Palaestina Illustrata) ("Shahadat 'Arabiyya fi Mazarat al-Filastiniyya," *al-Mashriq* 5(11)(1902): 487).

[190] See Roland Löffler, "The Metamorphosis of a Pietistic Missionary and Educational Institution into a Social Services Enterprise: The Case of the Syrian Orphanage (1860–1945)" pp. 151-174 in *New Faith in Ancient Lands Western Missions in the Middle East in the Nineteenth and Early Twentieth Centuries*, Heleen Murre-van den Berg (ed.) (Leiden, Boston: Brill, 2006), 157; on discussions of Palestine and the Palestinians in their works, see Stephan

British. British missionaries brought Palestine to Arab youth as well. They founded dozens of schools in Jerusalem, Haifa, Nablus, Nazareth and elsewhere in the 19th and early 20th centuries. Under the auspices of the Christian Missionary Society (CMS), they counted some 45 schools by the mid-1880s. One of them, the St. George's School in Jerusalem, grew rapidly from 15 in 1899 to 43 in 1900 and 72 in 1902. The school branded itself as modern and secular, teaching history, math, science, English and French. They also taught geography with maps like this one:

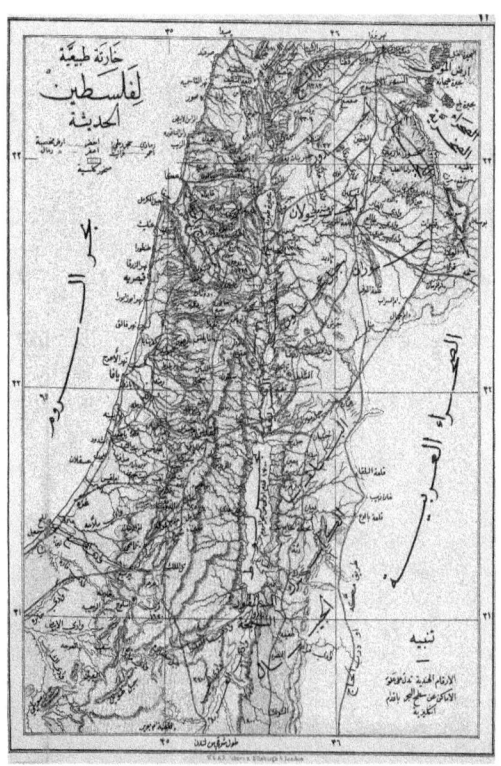

Hanna Stephan, *Modern Palestinian Parallels to the Song of Songs* (Jerusalem: Palestine Oriental Society, 1923); Tawfiq Canaan, *The Palestinian Arab House: Its Architecture and Folklore* (Jerusalem: Syrian Orphanage Press, 1933), 23, 44, 75, 82, 90; Tawfiq Canaan, *Mohammedan Saints and Sanctuaries in Palestine* (London: Luzac & Co., 1927), v, vi, 4, 93, 152, 165, 171, 173, 186, 226.

Figure 10. "A Natural Map of Modern Palestine," in an atlas likely used in missionary schools.[191]

Incidentally, many of the earliest self-described Palestinians and its most prominent protagonists in the 1920s and 1930s graduated from St. George or other CMS schools around the region, including Wasif Jawhariyya, Saliba Juzi, Sharif Nashashibi, Fu'ad Nashashibi, Najib Bawarshi, Khalil al-Sakakini, Imil Ghuri, Wasfi 'Anabtawi, Nabih Amin Faris, 'Umar al-Salih al-Barghouthi, Ahmad Samih al-Khalidi, Bulus Shihada, and Ibrahim Tuqan, while Izzat Tannous and Musa Nasir graduated from the CMS school in Nablus.[192]

Maronites. Why did so many Christian Arabs send their kids to foreign schools rather than their own Maronite or Orthodox Churches? The Maronite churches of the east had been drawn closer to their European (Catholic) co-religionists as early as the 16th century, when the Pope established the Maronite College in Rome in 1584. Over the next two centuries, some 280 Maronites from Aleppo, Hasroun, 'Aqura, Basloukit, Ehden and elsewhere traveled to Rome to study at the College. Most left home as small children and spent the better part of a decade in Europe. They learned Latin, Syriac, Italian, Arabic, philosophy, and theology. Yusuf Istifan (d.

---

[191] "Kharita Tabi'iyya li-Filastin al-Haditha," in n.a., *Atlas al-Kitab al-Muqaddas* (Edinburgh and London- W. & A.K. Johnston, n.d.), 12.

[192] On the expansion of the British schools, see Inger Marie Okkenhaug, *The Quality of Heroic living, of High Endeavour and Adventure: Anglican Mission, Women, and Education in Palestine, 1888-1948* (Leiden: Brill, 2002), 3; on the enrollment numbers, see Inger Marie Okkenhaug and Ingvild Flaskerud (eds.), *Gender, Religion and Change in the Middle East: Two Hundred Years of History* (Oxford, England; New York, N.Y.: Berg, 2005), 48-9; on the curriculum, see 'Umar al-Salih al-Barguthi, *al-Marahil* (Beirut: al-Mu'assasa al-'Arabiyya lil-Dirasat wa-l-Nashr, 2001), 103-105; on the map, see n.a. *Atlas al-Kitab al-Muqaddas*; for the list of students, see Abu Hanna, *Tala'i' al-Nahda fi Filastin*, 17; Izzat Tannous, *The Palestinians: A Detailed Documented Eyewitness History of Palestine Under the Mandate* (New York : I.G.T. Co., 1988), 8-13; on Khalil al-Sakakini's early usage of the term, see his 1918-1921 diary: Khalil al-Sakakini, Akram Musallam (ed.), *Yawmiyyat Khalil al-Sakakini: Yawmiyyat, Rasa'il, Ta'amalat, 1919-1922* (Ramallah: Markaz Khalil al-Sakakini al-Thaqafi: Mu'assasat al-Dirasat al-Muqaddasiyya, 2010), 41) and his 1925 collection of his essays about Palestinian politics, Zionism and the British Mandate (Khalil al-Sakakini, *Filastin Ba'd al-Harb al-Kubra* (Matba'at Bayt al-Maqdis, 1925), 16, 34, 35, 38); on Barghouthi's early usage of the term in 1923 see, 'Umar al-Salih al-Barghuthi and Khalil Totah, *Tarikh Filastin* (Jerusalem: Matba'at Bayt al-Maqdis, 1923), 36, 230.

1793), who graduated from the Maronite College in Rome, started his own college—'Ayn Waraqa in 1789 in Lebanon which he intended to replace the college in Rome as the training ground for Maronite clergy. The school taught religion, logic, philosophy, theology, Biblical exegesis, rhetoric, preaching, Arabic, Syriac, Italian, Latin and Greek.[193]

Many of 'Ayn Waraqa's graduates later became prominent intellectuals, including Nicholas Murad, Yusuf Dibs and Butrus al-Bustani. They also called the place Palestine and wrote about its people, history and geography. Bustani, for instance, wrote about Palestine frequently in his own journal, *al-Jinan*, during the 1870s, in one case citing Adriaan Reelant's classic *The Land of Palestine Illustrated* (in Latin). Dibs wrote a book called *A History of Syria* in the 1890s which included extensive discussions of Palestine as well. From Murad's writing, it seems he called the place Palestine too.[194]

---

[193] On the Maronite College in Rome, see Gemayel Nasser, *Les Échanges Culturels entre les Maronites et l'Europe* (Beirut: Impr. Gemayel, 1984), 95-137; Khater Akram Fouad, *Embracing the Divine: Passion and Politics in the Christian Middle East* (Syracuse, N.Y: Syracuse University Press, 2011), 184-5; Istifan declared in a letter from Bkirki sent on 29 June 1772 that every village, land and town "in Phonecia, Palestine or Syria," the home of the Maronites, had a devoted member of the confraternity. This description sounded more Italian or Latin than Arab, at least for the 1770s, as few Arabs called Lebanon Phoenicia or Palestine *Filastin* in the 1770s. But Istifan spent many years in Italy, where the terms Phoenicia and Palestine were more popular. Having said this, Istifan rarely mentions Palestine in his correspondences with other Maronite priests and his counterparts in Rome. Istifan knew about Palestine even though he usually called the region the East (*al-Mashraq, al-Sharq* or the *Land of Sham*); for his biography, which is equally a compendium of documents and letters found in the Bkirke archives that he himself wrote, see Bulus 'Abbud al-Ghustawi (Paul Abboud Gostaoui), *Basa'ir al-Zaman fi Tarikh al-'Allama al-Batriyark Yusuf Istifan* (Beirut: Matba'at Sabra, 1911); for a shorter biography, see Yusuf Dibs, *Tarikh al-Mawarina: al-Jami' al-Mufassal fi Tarikh al-Mawarina* (Beirut: n.p., 1979 [Beirut: al-Matba'a al-'Umumiyya al-Kathulikiyya, 1905], 446-58; on the letter mentioning Palestine, see Bernard Heyberger, *Hindiyya, Mystic and Criminal, 1720-1798: A Political and Religious Crisis* (Cambridge: James Clarke & Co., 2013), 125, footnote 28; on 'Ayn al-Waraqa, see al-Ghustawi, *Basa'ir al-Zaman*, 219-233; Dibs, *Tarikh al-Mawarina*, 516-7; Tibawi, *American Interests in Syria*, 66; Maqdisi, *Artillery of Heaven*, 77-9; Jurji Zaydan, *Tarajim Mashahir al-Sharq* (Beirut: Dar Maktabat al-Hayat, 1969), II, 303-4.

[194] On Murad's usage of the term Palestine, see Nicolas Murad, *Notice Historique sur l'Origine de la Nation Maronite; Nabdha Tarikhiya fi Asl al-Umma al-Maruniyya*. (Paris- Librairie d'Adrien Le Clere, 1844), 16; on Murad's biography, see Yusuf Hamid Mu'awwad and Antuwan al-Qawwal (eds.), Niqula Murad, *Nubdha Tarikhiyya fi Asl al-Umma al-Maruniyya* (Beiut: n.p., 2007), 19-47; on Yusuf Dibs's stories about Palestine, see *Kitab Tarikh Suriya* (Beirut: al-Matba'a al-'Umumiyya, 1893) e.g., I, 3, 97, 151-8, 170, 203, 257, 264-6, 284, 301, 311]; for his biography, see Zouki-Haklany, "Yusuf al-Dibs (1833-1907)"; on al-Bustani's discussion of Reelant, see Butrus al-Bustani, *A'mal al-Jam'iyya al-Suriyya* (Beirit: n.p., 1852), 65; for further stories about Palestine, see "al-Isra'iliyyun," *al-Jinan* 3 (1872): 328; "Qanat Filastinal-Bahriyya" *al-Jinan* 14(1888): 493; "Finiqiyya," *al-Jinan*

Greek Orthodox. Most Christian Arabs in the lands of Sham were Orthodox, though, not Maronites. By the early 20th century, the Greek Orthodox Church of Jerusalem operated some 65 boy schools and 13 girl schools in Jerusalem, Jaffa, Salt, Haifa, Karak, Ramallah, Jifna, Birzeit, Tayibe, Fuheis, Ajlun, Beit Jala Irbid, Nablus, Beit Sahur, Kafr Kanna and elsewhere. But their Arab Orthodox congregants flocked to the foreign schools, in part, because the church's Greek clergy did not allow Arabs to enter the ranks of priesthood—or the classes that prepared students for it. Even the lower classes were dominated by Greeks: an Orthodox classroom in 1912 might have 4 times as many Greek students as Arab students. So Arab Christians went elsewhere for an education and found it at the French, American, Russian, British and German missionary schools. The Greeks also administred all Church affairs, including its extensive land holdings. This pushed many late 19th and early 20th century Arabs to abandon the Orthodox church altogether.[195]

As early as the 1850s, the Church tried to improve education for its Arab congregants. The Greek Patriarch Cyril commissioned the Damascene priest Jurji al-Khuri Sbiridun Sarruf in 1855 to translate two elementary school textbooks from Greek to Arabic on the Old and New

---

(1) 1870: 373-6; "Khitab fi Tarikh wa-l-Jughrafiya" *al-Jinan* (4) (1873): 10; "al-Huyam fi Futuh al-Sham," *al-Jinan* (5) (1874): 173-9; 606.

[195] On the locations of the Orthodox schools, see *Filastin* 12 June 1912. For a detailed treatment of the disputes between the Greek clergy and the Arab laity, see Khalil Ibrahim Qazaqiya, *Tarikh al-Kanisa al-Rasuliyya* (Cairo: Matbaʻat al-Muqtataf wa-l-Muqattam, 1924), 175-252; Bracy, *Building Palestine*, 30-45; Konstantinos Papastathis and Ruth Kark, "Orthodox Communal Politics in Palestine after the Young Turk Revolution (1908-1910)," *Jerusalem Quarterly* 56/57 (2013/2014): 118-139; Salim Tamari, "Issa al Issa's Unorthodox Orthodoxy: Banned in Jerusalem, Permitted in Jaffa," *Jerusalem Quarterly* 59 (2014): 20, 26; Laura Robson, *Colonialism and Christianity in Mandate Palestine* (Austin: University of Texas Press, 2011), ch. 3; on the enrollment figures for the main Arabic school in Jerusalem, see *Filastin* 2 October 1912; see also Theodore Edward Dowling, *The Orthodox Greek Patriarch of Jerusalem* (London: 1913), 86; on the Greek Orthodox Russian rivalry, see Hopwood, *The Russian Presence*, 37-40, 51-2, 101, 113.

Testaments. In 1860, Mikha'il bin Mitraki wrote a teaching manual in Arabic, an *Ancient and Modern History*, which dealt extensively with Palestine as well. Tawfiq Farah wrote a geography book in 1913 for use in the Orthodox schools that surveyed Ottoman political geography, as it was necessary for students to gain a better understanding of "Palestine and Syria."[196]

In 1904, Sbiridun Sarruf published *The Geography of Palestine* bilingually in Greek and Arabic. It was geared towards third-grade students of the Greek Orthodox schools and explained that Palestine was the land settled by the twelve tribes of Israel; it was home to prophets like Joshua and Saul who spoke before it's mountains; to Jacob's well and Solomon's pools; and to the Phoenicians, ancient Assyrians and Israelites. Palestine stretched from the Galilee in the north to the southern Judaean mountains in the south, and to the mountains on the Eastern side of the Jordan River on the East. To emphasize the oddities of history once again, the first Arabic geography book of Palestine was translated from Greek, focused on the Israelites and was indirectly boycotted by many of the earliest people to call themselves Palestinians.[197]

---

[196] The first textbook surveyed the Old and New Testaments in question and answer format. see Jurji al-Khuri Sbiridun Sarruf (trans.), *Mukhtasar Tarikh Kanayisi Sharif Ta'limi* (Jerusalem: Matba'at al-Qabr al-Muqaddas al-Batrikiyya, 1855); the second textbook covered the exact same material in greater detail with citations to scripture, aimed at teaching older students the nuances of the Biblical narrative. See Jurji al-Khuri Sbiridun Sarruf (trans.), *Kitab Tarikh Kanayisi Sharif Mukhtasar* (Jerusalem: Matba'at al-Qabr al-Muqaddas al-Batrikiyya, 1855). The original Greek title, ΙΕΡΑ ΙΣΤΟPΙΑ (the History of the Bible) appears at the bottom of the text along with corresponding page numbers. For a rich biographical portrait of Sbiridun, see "Wahbat Allah Isbiridun Sarrruf," *al-Athar* 2 (1912/3): 420-431; Mikha'il bin Mitraki [*Majmu'a Ta'limiyya Masihiyya* [1860] (Manuscript Section of the National Library of Israel, JER NLI AP Ar. 113)] dealt with Palestine in his chapters on the Philistines, Romans, Byzantines and the Crusaders. [On the Philistines, see ibid, folios 31-8; on Roman and Byzantine Palestine, see ibid, folios 64, 87, 92-3, 198]; then see Tawfiq Farah, *Kitab al-Jughrafiya* (Jerusalem: Matba'at al-Qabr al-Muqqadas, al-Mutakhassa bi-Dayr al-Rum al-'Amir, 1913), 3.

[197] See "Wahbat Allah Isbiridun Sarrruf," *al-Athar* 2 (1912/3): 430, where al-Athar's editor 'Isa Iskandar Ma'luf noted that Sbiridun Sarruf translated the text from Greek to Arabic; on the translation, see Jurji al-Khuri Sbiridun Sarruf (trans.), *Jughrafiyat Filastin: Li-Isti'mal Madaris al-Qabr al-Muqaddas al-'Amma* (Jerusalem: Matba'at al-Qabr al-Muqqadas, al-Mutakhassa bi-dayr al-Run al-'Amir, 1904); on mountains, see ibid, 9; on water, see ibid, 22; on history, see ibid, 22-52, 58-60; on borders, see ibid, 4, 8-9, 25, 43; on the Biblical and Greek names, see ibid 4, 6, 8, 9, 10, 48, 49.

The Ottomans. The Ottomans also expanded public education—and also taught about Palestine in class. They published a map of the Ottoman Empire in 1804 that was used in Ottoman classrooms in Istanbul and elsewhere for decades.

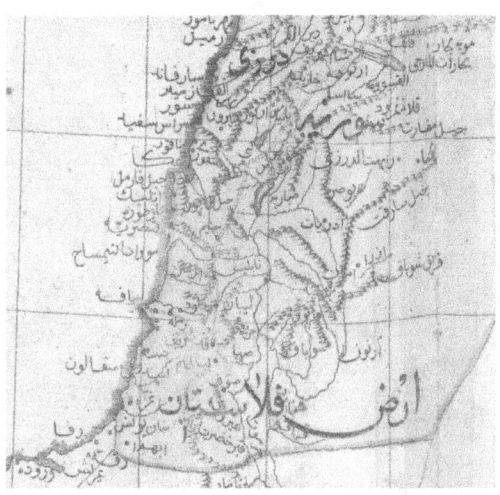

Figure 11. The first Ottoman printed map of Palestine (1804).[198]

They continued to make maps of Palestine throughout the 19th and early 20th centuries. The Ottomans opened rüşdiye preparatory schools in Jerusalem, Hebron and Gaza which together educated about 223 students a year in the late 19th century. The schools taught French, geography, history, hand crafts and more. In geography class, pupils learned to read maps—including maps of Palestine. They also learned to identify the borders of the Ottoman state and its natural and political units. History class covered Adam, Eve, creation and proceeded with the Israelite prophets and every Muslim state to have ever existed in Ottoman lands: the four righteous caliphs, Umayyads, Abbasids, Aghlabids, Fatimids, Ayyubids, Ghaznavids, Seljuqs,

---

[198] See Mahmud Raif Efendi, William Faden, *Cedid Atlas Tercemesi* (Istanbul: Tabʻhane-i Humayun, 1803-1804). For an analysis of the maps, see Zachary Foster, "The First Printed Ottoman Map of Palestine, 1804," midafternoonmap.com, 9 June 2015 (https://goo.gl/TLujdD).

Khwarazmians, Genghis Khan, Timurs and most importantly—the Ottomans, which were studied in great depth Sultan by Sultan.[199]

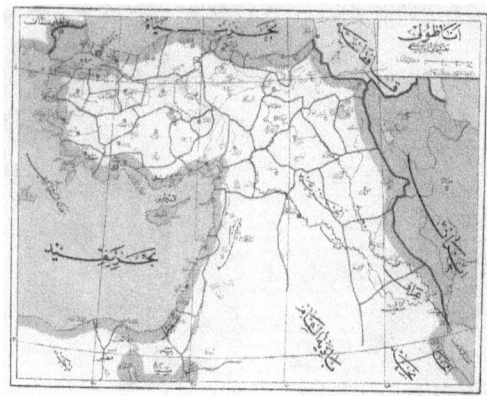

Figure 12. Ottoman map of "Anatolia-Administrative Divisions."[200]

Ottoman efforts to expand education had less to do with saving souls, as was the case among missionaries, and more with training pupils to become loyal bureaucrats. The Ottomans hired thousands of civil servants to work in the ministries of education, finance, war, interior and foreign ministry. By the 1880s, Ottoman bureaucrats had written hundreds of documents dealing with Palestine, mostly about foreigners or Zionists. By the empire's collapse in 1918, tens of thousands of documents had been written on Palestine. The state also published annual years

---

[199] On the first Ottoman map of Palestine, see Mahmud Raif Efendi; Iákōvos Argyrópoulos *Ucaletü'l-coğrafiyye* (Istanbul: Darü't-tıbaat'il-Âmire, 1804); on its use in Ottoman classrooms, see Johann Strauss, "Nineteenth-Century Ottoman Americana," pp. 259-281 in Frontiers of the Ottoman Imagination: Studies in Honour of Rhoads Murphey, Marios Hadjianastasis (ed.) (Leiden: Brill, 2015), 261-3; George Larpent (ed.), *Turkey; Its History and Progress from the Journals and Correspondences of Sir James Porter* (London: Hurst & Blackett, 1854), II, 162; on Palestine in Ottoman literature, see Şırvanlı Ahmet Hamdi Efendi, *Usul-i coğrafya-yı Kebir* (Şeyh Yahya Efendi'nin Matbaası, 1875), 356; Rafet Mehmet, *Seyahat Name-i Arz-i Filistin: Prins Viktur Napuli Imanu'il ve ile maalumat-i Tarihiye ve Cuğrafiye, huruf-i hica Tertibi üzere*, (n.p.: Suriye Vilayeti Matbae?, 1887?), 10-11; on the enrollment figures and school curriculum, see Uğur Ünal, *II. Meşrutiyet öncesi Osmanlı Rüşdiyeleri: (1897-1907)* (Ankara: Türk Tarih Kurumu, 2015), 82-87, 208-209; on maps of Palestine in Ottoman schools, see Mekatib-i Ibtida'iye, *Juğrafiya-i Osmani* (Matbaa-i 'Amire, 1913/1914), 58; for further discussions of Palestine in Ottoman education and military literature, see, for instance, the work of the geographer and teacher Ali Cevad, *Memâlik-i Osmaniyenin Tarih ve Coğrafya Lûgati* (Istanbul: Mahmud Bey Matbaasi, 1897-1898), 569-572.
[200] Cited in Mekatib-i Ibtida'iye, *Juğrafiya-i Osmani* (Matbaa-i 'Amire, 1913/1914), 98.

discussing Palestine's history and geography, and even published a book called *The Palestine Handbook*, which was a geographical, historical and demographic survey of Palestine. It contained some of the most beautiful maps of Palestine printed during its age. The Ottoman state made Palestine seem real to lots of people.[201]

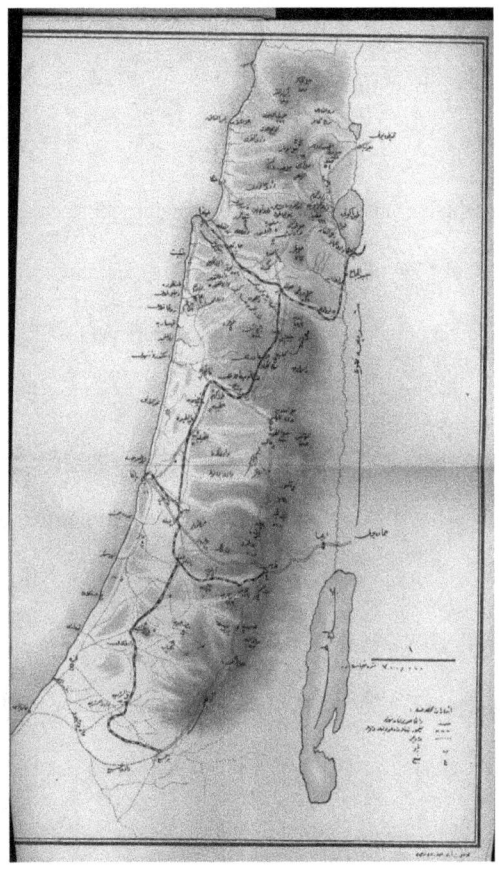

Figure 13. Published in *The Palestine Handbook*, 1915.[202]

---

[201] On the Ottomans commissioning maps of Palestine, see BOA HR TO 446/62 (1864.10.24); on the handbook of the land of Palestine, see *Filastin Risalesi*, discussed by Salim Tamari, "Shifting Ottoman Conceptions of Palestine Part 1: Filistin Risalesi and the two Jamals," *Jerusalem Quarterly* 47(29): 28-38; on Palestine in Ottoman yearbooks, see for instance, n.a., *Bayrut Vilayeti Salnamesi* (Vilayet Matbaası, 1915), 17, 20, 24.
[202] n.a., *Filistin Risalesi* (n.p., 1915/1916), after text.

Graduates of Ottoman schools also published about Palestine as well. Ruhi al-Khalidi, for instance, who graduated from ruşdiye schools in Jerusalem and Tripoli and later the Mektebe-i Mülkiye school in Istanbul, discussed Palestine in his 1897 *An Introduction to the Eastern Question*, and his still unpublished manuscript, *Zionism*, the first book length treatment of Zionism in Arabic, as well in op-eds he wrote as a correspondent of the newspaper *Filastin*. He was also an early adopter of the term, Palestinian.[203]

Egypt. Educational opportunities also expanded in Egypt during the same time period. Egypt's Mehmet Ali sent hundreds of Egyptian students to France to learn military science, industrial engineering, medicine, law, politics, agriculture, and geography. One of those students, Rifaʻa al-Tahtawi, returned to Egypt perplexed that there was "not a single book of geography in the Arabic language," in his words. Tahtawi was being hyperbolic, but he was right that the genre *geography* didn't really exist: plenty of travelogues had been written, as well as encyclopedias of places and peoples, atlases of Islam and biographical dictionaries, but no Arabic works with the word *jughrafiya* in their titles. So, in 1838, he translated Malte Brun's best-seller, the *Summary of Universal Geography* from French into Arabic and he wrote another text, *The Geography of Sham* in Arabic, which surprisingly still languishes in microfilm in the Dar al-Kutub manuscript collection in Cairo. For specialists of 18th century Western thought, imagine if a one of

---

[203] Ruhi al-Khalidi, *al-Muqaddima fi al-Masʼala al-Sharqiyya* (Jerusalem: *Matbaʻat Madrasat al-Aytam al-Islamiyya*, n.d.), page after *kaf* in the preface; for detailed treatment of his unpublished manuscript, see Jonathan Marc Gribetz, *Defining Neighbors: Religion, Race, and the Early Zionist-Arab Encounter* (Princeton: Princeton University Press, 2016), ch.2; Beŝka, *From Ambivalence to Hostility*, 41, 47, 71, 77, 92, 113, 126, 137; Ruhi al-Khalidi also wrote an article titled "The Palestinian Race" for the paper *Filastin*, arguing that Zionists were attempting to create an exclusionary society in Palestine. See *Filastin* 4 June 1913, cited in Michael Bracy, "Building Palestine: 'Isa al-'Isa, Filastin, and the Textual Construction of National Identity, 1911–1931" (Ph.D. Dissertation, University of Arkansas, 2005), 94.

Immanuel Kant's works only existed in manuscript form in its original German, and was only available in one library in the world.[204]

Both works were primarily about things other than Palestine, but Tahtawi nevertheless defined Palestine in both. He listed the following places as part of Palestine in his Malte Brun translation: the Hawran, Golan, Jarash, Ajloun, al-Balqa, Karak, Safed, Lake Tiberias, Samaria, Caesarea, Haifa, Acre, Judaea, Gaza, Hebron, Jerusalem, Jaffa, Bethlehem and Jericho. In his own original work, though, he claimed Palestine was bordered "in the south by the Land of the Arabs, to the north by the District of Acre, to west by the Mediterranean Sea and to the east by the Mountains behind the Jordan River," and included Gaza, Hebron, Jerusalem and Jaffa. Tahtawi's definition of Palestine has its roots as much in the Arab tradition as the European.[205]

Tahtawi absorbed European material and infused it with the Muslim tradition. His periods of focus, range of sources, literary techniques and geographical lexicon in *The Geography of Sham* were eclectic. He devoted a chapter to Palestine, even though his book was about Sham. He covered Jesus and ancient Greek history but also the conquest of Salah al-Din and Ottoman politics. He dealt with geography, demography, agriculture and economy (very European), but he

---

[204] On Tahtawi's translation, see Rifa'a Rafi' al-Tahtawi, *al-Jughrafiya al-'Umumiyya* (Bulaq: Dar al-Tiba'a al-Khidyawiyya, 1838); on his own work, see Rifa'a Rafi' al-Tahtawi, *Jughrafiyat Bilad al-Sham* (date unknown) (Dar al-Kutub Manuscripts, Bab al-Khalq, Cairo, MS#42); on Tahtawi's quote, see Rifa'a Rafi' al-Tahtawi, *Kitab al-Ta'ribat al-Shafiyya li-Murid al-Jughrafiya* (Bulaq: Dar al-Tiba'a al-Khidyawiyya, 1838), 148-152. The classic work on the Egyptian missions to Europe is 'Umar Tusun, *Al-Ba'atat al-'Ilmiyya: Fi 'Ahd Muhammad 'Ali Tumma fi 'Ahday 'Abbas al-Awwal wa-Sa'id* (Alexandria: Matba'at Salah al-Din, 1934). See also Ibrahim Abu-Lughod, *Arab Rediscovery of Europe: A Study in Cultural Encounters* (Princeton, N.J.: Princeton University Press, 1963), 35.
[205] In both his Malte-Brun translation and his own work, he didn't list these places in a single sentence, as I did, but discussed their population sizes, exact locations, attractions, industries, characteristics and histories. On his own work, see Tahtawi, *Kitab al-Ta'ribat al-Shafiyya*, 148; On his own definition of Palestine, see al-Tahtawi, *Jughrafiyat Bilad al-Sham*, folio 34. In his own work, he cited from his translation of Maltre Brun, as well another French geographer, J. G. Masselin, throughout the text. See J. G. Masselin, *Dictionnaire Universel des Géographies Physique, Historique et Politique, du Monde Ancien, du Moyen âge et des Temps Modernes, Comparées* (Paris: Impr. de A. Delalain, 1827).

didn't bother with footnotes or references (very Arab). He mentioned some of his sources briefly in the text, including Josephus (d. c.100), the Muslim historian Abu al-Fida' (d.1331), the English traveler Henry Maundrell (d.1696) and the French geographers, Conrad Malte Brun and J. G. Masselin. Tahtawi marked a moment of transition.[206]

* * *

Egypt Again Let's take a step back. How did Russians, Americans and Germans all get rights to build schools in the Ottoman Empire? Traditionally, the Ottomans had mostly forbid foreigners from establishing permanent residence in the Empire. But this changed dramatically when an earstwhile local governor decided to carve out his own fiefdom from imperial lands. He was Albanian, and he conquered Egypt in the early 19th century from the Empire. His name was Mehmet Ali Pasha, as noted above. In addition to sending students to study in France, he also sent his son to conquer the lands of Sham in 1830.

Mehmet Ali Pasha did not share the same Ottoman hostility to a foreign presence. Americans were permitted to move to Beirut, Tripoli and Mount Lebanon, and they started importing books from Malta, where they had founded a printing press, something the Ottomans had also forbidden. Mehmet Ali also allowed the British Empire to establish a consular office in Jerusalem in 1838, which opened the floodgates. Soon enough, even once the Ottomans retook the land of Sham in 1840, they were soon compelled to allow every major Western power to open a consular office in the city: Prussia in 1843, Sardinia in 1843, France in 1843, Austria in

---

[206] On Islamic history and Salah al-Din, see Tahtawi, *Jughrafiyat Bilad al-Sham*, folio 8-9; on Greek history and Jesus, see ibid, folios 2-7, 28; on demography, agriculture and economy, see ibid, folio 35-6.

1847, Spain in 1854, the United States in 1856 and Russia in 1857. The consular offices used the word Palestine in correspondences with Ottoman officials, and so Palestine started to appear more and more often in internal Ottoman government documents from the 1850s onwards.[207]

Travel. The growth of the commercial steamship industry made possible the mass movement of peoples across seas and oceans beginning in the mid-19th century. French, Russian and Austrian companies began to offer regular steamship travel from European ports to Jaffa by the mid-late 19th century. As a result, the number of tourists to the Holy Land increased from a few thousand annually in the 1840s to as many as 40,000 a year by World War I. Tourists and pilgrims sang Psalms by ruins in the Galilee, prayed by sacred shrines in Nazareth, and wept were Jesus rose to heaven in Jerusalem. Palestine was accessible yet exotic, comfortable enough yet still pristinely Oriental, it was the land of the Israelites and the home of the Bible. My Italian grandmother in-law has left Europe twice in her life, both times to the Holy Land. I don't think that's a coincidence. Or maybe it is, actually, not entirely sure.[208]

---

[207] The Ottomans loathed his betrayal of the Empire; Europeans praised his reforms; while the people of Sham revolted against his policies of mass conscription. On missionaries having free reign, one American commission wrote in 1836 that "Lebanon is completely open. Missionaries can go where they please."; one Ottoman document summarized and translated a note sent to them by the British Console in Jerusalem. See Başbakanlık Osmanlı Arşivi (BOA) H.R.TO. 231.38.2.3 (9 October 1858). See also BOA H.R.TO 220.47.5.8 (23 September 1854).

[208] On the Russian company, see W. E. Mosse, "Russia and the Levant 1856-1862; Grand Duke Constantine Nikolaevich and the Russian Steam Navigation Company," *Journal of Modern History* 26 (1954): 39-48; Abdul Latif Tibawi, "Russian Cultural Penetration of Syria—Palestine in the Nineteenth century (Part I)" *Journal of the Royal Central Asian Society* (1966): 175-6; Frary, "Russian Missions to the Orthodox East," 139; Philip R. Davies, *The Palestine Exploration Fund Annual XI: Tourists, Travelers and Hotels in Nineteenth-Century Jerusalem* (Leeds: Maney Publishing, 2013), 21, n.51.; on French ships, see Khalil Sarkis, *Rihlat Mudir al-Lisan* (Beirut: al-Matba'a al-Adabiyya, [1893] 1911), II, 5-9; Wortabet, *Syria and the Syrians*, 7; on the Austrian company, see *Filastin* 8 November 1911; Rudolf Agstner, "The Austrian Lloyd Steam Navigation Company," pp. 136-157 in *Austrian Presence in the Holy Land in the 19th and Early 20th Century*, Marian Wrba (ed.) (Tel Aviv: Austrian Embassy, 1996), 148; For tourism estimates in Palestine see Zachary Foster, "Why are Modern Famines so Deadly? The First World War in Syria and Palestine," forthcoming.

The travelers wrote a lot about their travels. Some 5,000 volumes on Palestine had appeared in Western languages and another 1,000 in Russian by the mid-19th century. The Russian Andrej Murav'ëv's 1836 travelogue to the Holy Land was so popular that the book even earned a nickname, the "Murav'ëv phenomenon." William Thomson's 1859 travelogue in "Southern Palestine and Jerusalem" sold more copies than any book in the United States with the sole exception of the Bible. Gregory Wortabet summarized the situation nicely in 1856. "More has been written about the history of Syria (including Palestine) than any country in the world." This was an era of Biblemania. You could actually go and visit the land of the Bible![209]

The Biblical archeologists played a key role in this story, because they claimed to be able to prove or disprove Biblical history. In 1838, the American Edward Robinson wandered the lands of Sham for two months, "Bible in hand," of course, "following out all the topographical hints which its record supplied." His magnum opus—*Biblical Researches in Palestine*—was an instant success. The book quickly earned universal praise. As one modern scholar described it, "any study of the field" of Biblical archeology "must begin with Robinson, for all later archeological

---

[209] On Palestine literature, see Peter Thomsen, *Die Palästina-Literatur 1895-1904* (Leipzig: J.C. Hinrich, 1911); Reinhold Röhricht, *Bibliotheca Geographica Palaestinae. Chronologisches Verzeichnis der von 333 bis 1878 verfassten Literatur über das Heilige Land mit dem Versuch einer Kartographie* (Berlin: H. Reuther, 1890); Titus Tobler, *Bibliographica geographica Palaestinae Zunächst kritische uebersicht gedruckter und ungedruckter beschreibungen der reisen ins Heilige Land* (Leipzig, S. Hirzel, 1867). For the 5,000 figure, see Yehoshua Ben-Arieh, "Nineteenth century Historical Geographies of the Holy Land," *Journal of Historical Geography* 15(1) (1989): 70; on Russian travel literature, see Thefanis Stavrou and Peter R. Weisensel, *Russian Travelers to the Christian East from the Twelfth to the Twentieth Century* (Columbus, Ohio: Slavica Publishers, 1986); on the Murav'ëv phenomenon, see Simona Merlo, "Travels of Russians to the Holy Land in the 19th Century," *Quest: Issues in Contemporary Judaism*, Journal of Fondazione CDEC", n.6 (December 2013), text between note 30 and 31, and note 44; on Thomson's book, see Joseph L. Grabill, *Protestant Diplomacy and the Near East: Missionary Influence on North American Policy, 1810–1927* (Minneapolis: University of Minnesota Press, 1971), 38–39; Richter, *A History of the Protestant Missions*, 198; Heleen Murre-van den Berg, "William Mcclure Thompson's The Land and the Book (1859): Pilgrimage and Mission in Palestine," in *New Faiths in Ancient Lands: Western Missions in the Middle East in the Nineteenth and Early Twentieth Centuries*, Murre-van den Berg (ed.) (Leiden; Boston: Brill, 2006), 43; [Najib Nassar, for instance, cited Thomson's *The Land and the Book*. See Najib Nassar, "Buldan Filastiniyya Yusiffuha Filastini," *al-Jami'a* 3(9) (1902): 612-615]; on Wortabet, see Wortabet, *Syria and the Syrians*, xiv.

research in Palestine is in some way indebted to him"— discoveries and errors alike. Another Biblical archeologist, Claude Conder, completed a comprehensive survey of what he called Eastern and Western Palestine between 1881-1889. The book was an etymological dictionary of every place name in the region and it too became a required reference work for all Bible enthusiasts. Conder identified many erstwhile unknown Biblical sites through their modern Arabic reincarnations. The book even led Arabs to start calling the place Eastern and Western Palestine, terms totally unknown in Arabic before the 1880s. The Bible dominated how everyone talked, wrote or thought about Palestine—East and West. I cannot emphasize that point enough.[210]

Pilgrims wandered the streets of Nazareth and Jerusalem carrying their Beadeker, Murray or Cook Palestine guide books "in one hand and a Bible in the other." But that got annoying, so

---

[210] On Robinson's journey, see Robert Alexander Stewart Macalister, *A Century of Excavation in Palestine* (London: Religious Tract Society, 1925), 22; Robinson published an early edition of his work in 1842, and then another in 1856. On the latter, Edward Robinson and Eli Smith, *Biblical Researches in Palestine, and in the Adjacent Regions. A Journal of Travels in the Year 1838* (Boston, Crocker and Brewster, 1856); for those who cited or were influenced by Robinson, see Antun Bulad, *Rashid Suriyya* (Beirut, 1868), 133; Henry Lammens, *Tasrih al-Absar fi ma yahtawi Lubnan min al-'Athar* (Beirut: Matba'a al-Kathulikiyya lil-Aba' al-Yisu'iyyin, 1902), II, 117, 136, 180, 202, 203, 230; As'ad Mansur, *Murshid al-Tullab ila Jughrafiyat al-Kitab* (n.p., 1905), dal; 'Arif al-'Arif, *Tarikh al-Haram al-Qudsi* (Jerusalem: Matba'at Dar al-Aytam al-Islamiyya al-Sana'iyya, 1947), 114; on his importance for later Biblical archeologists, see Thomas W. Davis, *Shifting Sands: The Rise and Fall of Biblical Archaeology* (Oxford; New York: Oxford University Press, 2004), 4; then see Claude Reignier Conder, *The Survey of Western Palestine* (London: Committee of the Palestine Exploration Fund, 1881-1888); *The Survey of Eastern Palestine; Memoirs of the Topography, Orography, Hydrography, Archaeology* (London: The Committee of the Palestine Exploration Fund, 1889). For Arabs who cited Condor, see "Takhtit Sharqi Filastin," *al-Muqtataf* 6(1881): 272; "al-Lurd Kitshnir 'Alim Arshiyuluji," *al-Jami'a* 5 (1901): 423-4; John S. Salah, *Filastin wa-Tajdid Hayatuhu* (New York: The Syrian American Press, 1919), 13; As'ad Mansur [*Tarikh al-Nasira* (Cairo: Matba'at al-Hilal, 1924), before page 1] explained that one of his most important source for his History of Nazareth was Conder's Survey of Western Palestine. Mansur (ibid, 33) also cited Claude R Conder's *Tent Work in Palestine* (London: Bentley, 1878). For those who described Palestine as divided into two parts (usually East and West), see "Aqalim Suriya wa-Filastin al-Nabatiyya," *al-Muqtataf* 8 (1883): 417; Louis Cheikho, "Khara'ib al-Sham," *al-Mashriq* (1899): 894; Dayrani, *al-Nahj al-Qawim*, 63; Azoury, *Le Réveil de la Nation Arabe*, 8, 11; "Hawa' Filastin," *al-Muqtataf* 53 (1918): 244; "A Map of Palestine," in Khalil Totah and Habib Khuri, *Jughrafiyat Filastin* (Jerusalem: Matba'at Bayt al-Maqdis, 1923), before page 1; Yusuf Sufayr, *Jughrafiyat Lubnan al-Kabir wa-Hukumat Suriya wa-Filastin* (Beirut: Mataba' Kuzma, 1924), 84; Sahil al-Sayyid, *Al-Murshid al-'Arabi, Filastin* (Jerusalem: al-Matba'a al-'Asriyya, 1936), 10; Maktabat Bayt al-Maqdis, *al-Mukhtasar al-Jughrafi* (Jerusalem: al-Taba'a al-'Asriyya, 1945), 97.

Cook printed direct quotations of the Bible alongside their modern descriptions. His *Handbook for Palestine and Syria*, published in 1876, was re-issued a dozen times in the following decades and could probably still sell copies today, although I would recommend removing some of the more ambitious proposed day trips—Palestine to Beirut, Palestine to Baghdad, and Palestine to Damascus. Nazareth to Damascus is a mere 4 hours drive, but, as Google Maps warns, the route has "restricted usage or private roads." People wanted to see the land of the Bible itself—and they wanted to know it had remained unchanged (if not deteriorated) since the times of Jesus— and that's what they learned in their guidebooks.[211]

Admittedly, the side by side comparisons must have seemed odd to some readers who probably wondered why the two texts differed at all. "The most reliable guide to the Holy Land" was the Bible itself, as Avraam SergeeviÄ Norov explained. "I consider myself lucky," he wrote, "that I had only the Bible with me for the greater part of my travel." As one journalist reported, "it was possible to buy Russian guide-books to Jerusalem in the shops, but very few pilgrims brought them. They used their Bibles."[212]

The pilgrims had a mostly unknown influence on the locals. It's extremely difficult to find anecdotes from coversations had between guides and pilgrims, hotel owners and patrons, shop owners and tourists. But if "the principle source of the wealth of Joppa [Jaffa] is derived from the annual passage of pilgrims through the town to visit the holy places," as one traveler pointed out,

---

[211] On tourists carrying their Beadeker or Murray guidebooks in hand, see John Fulton, *The Beautiful Land, Palestine: Historical Geographical and Pictorial* (Chicago, IL: John W. Iliff & Co, 1893), v; then see n.a., *Cook's Tourists' Handbook for Palestine and Syria* (London: Thomas Cook & Son, 1876), preface. It was reprinted in 1876, 1888-1889, 1907 and 1921-2. The day trips were included in the 1888 edition.

[212] On Norov, see Svetlana Kirillina, "Imagining the Arab-Ottoman World in Modern Russia- Narratives of Russian Pilgrims to the Holy Land of Christianity (16th-18th Centuries)," *Oriental Archive* 80(2) (2012): 138; then see Stephen Graham, *With the Russian Pilgrims to Jerusalem* (London: Macmillan & Co.: London, 1913), 16.

there must have been a huge amout of street chatter. "Welcome to my shob! Because you are a very good friend, I will make you special offer!" These conversations must have taken place, we just don't know anything about them.[213]

Migration. Beginning in the late 19th century, the opposite thing happened. Not foreigners coming into the Ottoman Empire, but locals leaving it. Some 300,000 Ottoman subjects left the Empire for the New World—primarily the United States, Argentina and Brazil. The migrants found themselves in more heterogeneous communities in their adopted countries. In Chile, for instance, migrants established Ottoman and Syrian Ottoman associations, and in one case wanted to present a joint gift to the Republic of Chile in honor of its 100-year anniversary in the early 20th century. Reportedly, they disagreed over who the gift was from: the Palestinians? Ottomans? Turks? or Ottoman Syrians? *Filastin*'s editors said they should go with "Ottomans" since it united "Turks, Palestinians and Syrians." Something similar happened in São Paulo, Brazil in 1910, when Ottoman emigres thought their community was weakened because it was internally indecisive about its identity—split between self-identified "Turks," "Arabs" and "Syrians." International migration had an underappreciated effect on people's identities.[214]

* * *

---

[213] On the quote, see Fulton, *The Beautiful Land, Palestine*, 50; see also Salah, *Filastin wa-Tajdid*, 96-7; Davies, *The Palestine Exploration*, 247-8.
[214] On the 300,000 figure, see Akram Fouad Khater, "Becoming "Syrian" in America: A Global Geography of Ethnicity and Nation," *Diaspora: A Journal of Transnational Studies* 14(2/3) (2005): 302; on the gift to Chile, see "Man Nahnu wa ma Nusammi?" (Who Are We and How Should We be Called?), *Filastin* 12 October 1912. The article reportedly first appeared in the Argentinian newspaper, *al-Zaman* and was reprinted in *Filastin*. On Brazil, see María del Mar Logroño Narbona, "The Development of Nationalist Identities in French Syria and Lebanon: A Transnational Dialogue with Arab Immigrants to Argentina and Brazil, 1915—1929" (Ph.D Dissertation, University of California, Santa Barbara, 2007), 151.

Technology. I haven't emphasized technology much but it started to play a more significant role on identities like Palestinian from the early modern period onwards. That's when printed texts became affordable to regular people. Periodicals and newspapers were first introduced in Strasbourg in the 1600s, Amsterdam in the 1620s, Cairo in the 1830s and Beirut in the late 1850s. But Arabic newspapers started to regularly appear in Jerusalem, Jaffa and Haifa only in 1908, after the constitutional revolution in Istanbul eased press censorship. Newspapers were a much more cost-effective form of publishing and conveyed information ill-suited to other genres of literature like travelogues, textbooks, theological treatises and chronicles. They could announce time-sensitive information like train schedules, parliamentary candidate platforms and public performances. The speed of publication changed the nature of what was published. Newspapers acquired subscribers—and the subscription business model exploded. (Previously, you could not "subscribe" to authors). Newspapers could engage in conversation with their readers—accepting questions and publishing responses to them. They made readers feel like part of the conversation. They made it possible for tens of thousands of people who had never met one another to participate in the same conversation. The internet revolution is doing something similar today, at an order of magnitude larger. Newspapers hastened the spread of new identities, including Palestinian.[215]

After the Ottomans eased press censorship in 1908, entrepreneurs flocked to the authorities to exercise their constitutional rights. Ilyas Bawwad in Safed tried to establish a newspaper called *Filastin* in December 1908, but was told he had to choose a different name because *Filastin* was

---

[215] Even once newspapers were founded in Jerusalem, Jaffa and Haifa, many people still preferred to import journals and newspapers from abroad, such as *al-Ahram, al-Muqattam, al-Muqtataf, al-Muqtabas, Lisan al-Hal, al-Bashir, al-Mashriq, al-Hilal*. See Yehoshua, *Tarikh al-Sihafa al-'Arabiyya*, 100; Khalil Baydas noted that "there was no literary movement in Palestine during those days [late Ottoman period]. It was dwarfed by Beirut." See ibid, 95.

already taken by the Hebronite Yusuf Siddiqi, granted a license to publish his newspaper, *Filastin*, in Jerusalem four months earlier. Little is known about either Bawwad and Siddiqi, and neither seem to have ever published a newspaper called *Filastin*.[216]

"Look at a classic study of over 50 product categories," explained Adam Grant in his TED talk on the surprising habits of original thinkers. "Comparing the first movers, who created the market, with the improvers, who introduced something different and better." The first movers had a failure rate of 47%, compared with only 8% for the improvers.[217]

As first movers, Bawwad and Siddiqi failed. It was the 'Isa cousins of Jaffa who made *Filastin* famous. They founded a newspaper by that name in 1911 and it became the most popular newspaper in District of Jerusalem, and later the Mandate for Palestine for decades. Dozens of other publications appeared in Jerusalem, Jaffa and Haifa between 1908 and 1914. Only a handful printed more than a few issues and even the most successful accumulated less than 1,600 subscribers. (These figures might seem modest, but consider that some 2% of the population was literate in 1914, or about 12,000 people. I think any newspaper today would be thrilled if more than 10% of the literate population subscribed to it). The paper circulated once or twice a week and was sent to small towns and villages around Jerusalem, Bethlehem, Ramallah, Haifa, Jaffa, Gaza, Nablus, Safed and Tiberias.[218]

---

[216] On Yusuf Siddiqi, see BOA D.H. MKT 1280/23 (8 August 1908); on Ilyas Bawwab, see BOA DH.ID 124-1/31 (10 December 1908).
[217] Adam Grant, "The Surprising Habits of Original Thinkers," TED Talk, youtube.com 26 April 2016 (https://goo.gl/Mcmii1)
[218] *al-Quds* (Jerusalem, 1908-1914) had 300 subscribers and printed around 1,500 copies; *al-Karmil* (Haifa, 1911-1914) claimed 1,000 subscribers; *al-Akhbar* circulated 600 copies; the Jewish paper *Ha-Herut* (Jerusalem) reported 1,500-2,000 subscribers. The 'Isa cousins' *Filastin* (Jaffa, 1911-1914) captured the largest Arabic market share, boasting 1,100-1,600 subscribers. See Yehoshua, *Tarikh al-Sihafa al-'Arabiyya*, 44; Michelle Campos, *Ottoman Brothers: Muslims, Christians, and Jews in Early Twentieth-Century Palestine* (Stanford, CA: Stanford University

The words Palestine and the Palestinians now appeared printed on paper on coffee tables in the homes of hundreds or even thousands of Arabic speakers on a weekly basis. That was something new in 1911 and 1912. The al-'Isa cousins used the term "Palestinian" a dozen some times from 1911-1914; Najib Nassar, as we discussed above, frequently wrote about Palestinians in his Haifa-based paper, *al-Karmil*; as did Farah Antun in his Alexandria-based *al-Jami'a*, as did Ilya Zakka in his Haifa and Jerusalem-based paper, *al-Nafir*. Newspaper editors gave the term Palestinian the impetus it needed to gain wider acceptance.[219]

Demand for newspapers was high, even if people weren't ready to pay them. A reader sent an op-ed to *Filastin* in 1912 describing his love for the paper, but complained he could not afford the subscription fee. The editor of *al-Quds* Jurji Hanania lamented in 1913 that readers tend to share their copy of the paper with fifty others. Najib Nassar, who published *al-Karmil* in Haifa, was surprised when he was received with honor in a small "Palestinian" town—his words—since

---

Press, 2011), 282; Ami Ayalon, *Reading Palestine: Printing and Literacy, 1900–1948* (Austin: University of Texas Press, 2004), 170, n.69; Beška, *From Ambivalence to Hostility*, 18-23; on *al-Karmil*, see *al-Karmil* 20 February 1914, cited in Emanuel Beška, "Political Opposition to Zionism in Palestine and Greater Syria: 1910-1911 as a Turning Point," *Jerusalem Quarterly* 59 (2014): 55; on the 2% literacy figure, see Yehoshua, *Tarikh al-Sihafa*, 24 and Ayalon, "Modern Texts and their Readers," 17. This was modest even compared to neighboring countries like Egypt, which had 4-6% literacy rate at that time. See Donald M. Reid, *The Odyssey of Farah Antun: A Syrian Christian's Quest for Secularism* (Minneapolis: Bibliotheca Islamica, 1975), 45.

[219] *Filastin* (27 November 1912) called on its Palestinian compatriots (*muwatininna al-filastiniyyin*) in Argentina to buy productive land in Argentina; *Filastin* (7 February 1912) also republished a glowing review of itself originally printed in the Homs based newspaper *al-Ikha'* which read as follows: "Its editor is Yusuf Affandi al-'Isa from Jaffa. He is the most capable writer we know of in Palestine. *Filastin* is the only newspaper that Palestinians should subscribe to and be proud of." *Filastin* (2 November 1912) also published a letter from a writer who signed his name "A Palestinian" in 1912, criticizing the Ottoman government for their failure to enforce the three-month limit placed on residency permits granted to Zionist newcomers in Palestine; *Filastin* (9 September 1911) distinguished between "Syrians and Palestinians" in a 1911 review of Bulus Afandi Karulidus's book on the origins of the Orthodox in Palestine and Syria; for further mentions of the term the Palestinian people (*al-umma al-Filastiniyya*), see "Rasa'il lil-Mushtarik," *Filastin* 7 May 1914, cited in Rashid Khalidi, *Palestinian Identity: The Construction of Modern National Consciousness* (New York: Columbia University Press, 1997), 155; Bracy, "Building Palestine," 98.

it had only one subscriber. Apparently, more than fifty people from the town had read the paper at the subscriber's house.[220]

Newspapers reached smaller towns and villages also. A *Filastin* subscriber from al-Bireh complained in 1911 "we were hoping to receive the paper every week but instead we received three or four issues at the beginning of the month." Villagers closer to Jaffa were even luckier. *Filastin* distributed a free copy in 1914 to every village elder in the area. Mufti Husayni, from a village in the Gaza district, sent a petition to the Ottoman Sultan in July 1911, complaining of drought, high prices and economic destitution in Gaza. His proof to the Sultan was an investigative report published in *Filastin* itself on destitution in Gaza. Lots of people were reading *Filastin* and learning they were Palestinian.[221]

* * *

Institutionalization. It was not just newspapers that made Palestine seem real. Palestine also began to appear in brick and mortar, public lecture, marble placard and in public initiatives. People shopped at Yusuf Sa'id's the Palestinian Educational Bookshop in Jerusalem. Public

---

[220] On Hanania, see Yehoshua. *Tarikh al-Sihafa*, 20-1; on Najib Nassar, see *al-Karmil* 20 February 1914, cited in Beška, "Political Opposition," 55; Aida al-Najjar, *The Arabic Press and Nationalism in Palestine*, 1920-1948, (Ph.D. Dissertation, Syracuse University, 1975), ch. 2; on public readings, see Hilma Granqvist, *Marriage Conditions in a Palestinian Villages* (Helsingfores: Societas Scientiarium Fennica, 1931), 99; Ayalon, *Reading Palestine*, 3-4, 159; Campos, *Ottoman Brothers*, ch. 4; on the anonymous letter to *Filastin*, see *Filastin* 7 February 1912; on coffee house recitations, see Jessup, *Fifty-three Years*, 119.

[221] On the al-Bireh complaint, see *Filastin* 10 November 1911. On *Filastin*'s distribution for free, see Yusuf al-'Isa, *al-Akthariyya wa-l-Aqaliyya* Filastin, 30 January 1914, cited in Bracy, "Building Palestine," 7; Yehoshua, *Tarikh al-Sihafa*, 18-9; Ami Ayalon, *The Press in the Arab Middle East: A History* (New York: Oxford University Press, 1995), 157-8; on mufti Husayn, see BOA DH.MTV 52-1/49 (17 July 1911). He included a copy of *Filastin* from 11 March 1911. It's important not to exaggerate the point, though. The term Palestinian appeared infrequently in Arabic sources from the late 19th and early 20th century. It's much easier to find related adjectives like Ottoman, Muslim, Christian, Arab or Syrian. It was a new identity in the early 20th century, and took many years before it was widely used.

lectures were delivered about Palestine. The Deutchse Palastina Bank opened in 1899, the Anglo-Palestine Company in 1902 and the Bank Commerciale de Palestine in 1911. Albert Antebi propose the establishment of the Palestinian Patriotic Company in 1913 whose delegates would purchase imperial lands before Zionists could. Najib Nassar proposed the establishment of a Palestine Congress in 1914 to counter the 11th World Zionist Congress and to coordinate anti-Zionist efforts. Palestine was already started to get institutionalized in the Middle East in the 1900s and 1910s.[222]

Figure 14. Photo from inside the Jaffa Gate in Jerusalem's old city with Deutsche Palästina Bank sign visible (circa early 1900s).

---

[222] On the Palestine bookshop, see *Filastin* 12 October 1912; on public lectures, Kazma celebrated the 25th anniversary of the establishment of the Imperial Orthodox Palestine Society "in our country Palestine and in Syria" in 1907. See Suwaydan, *Tarikh al-Jam'iyya*, 71-2; for more on the festivities, see Mansur, *Tarikh Nasra*, 103; on Palestine banks, see Gad G. Gilbar, "The Growing Economic Involvement of Palestine with the West," in *Palestine in the Late Ottoman Period: Political, Social, and Economic Transformation*, David Kushner (ed.) (Jerusalem: Yad Izhak Ben-Zvi, 1986), 206; Antebi proposed establishing the *al-Sharika al-Wataniyya al-Filastiniyya*. See his "Nad'a lil-Fi'al," *Filastin* 12 July 1913 and 2 August 1913, cited in Mandel, *The Arabs and Zionism*, 173-4; Yehoshua Porath, *The Emergence of the Palestinian National Movement 1918-1929* (London: Cass, 1974), 28; Bracy, 'Building Palestine,' 91; on Nassar's proposal, see Ilan Pappé, "The 'Politics of Notables' to the 'Politics of Nationalism': The Husayni Family, 1840-1922," pp. 163-207 in *Middle Eastern Politics and Ideas: A History from Within* M. Maoz and I. Pappé (eds.) (London and New York: I.B. Tauris, 1997), 200, 206, n. 100.

Arab writers used the term Palestine in print because you had to use the term to discuss current events. The Palestine Imperial Orthodox Society was called the Palestine Imperial Orthodox Society, and to write about it, you had to use the word Palestine. Committees, commissions and journals came into existence in the United States, United Kingdom, Russia, France and Germany all bearing the name Palestine. Condor conducted a survey of what he called East and West Palestine, not East and West Sham or East and West Jerusalem; Zionists moved to what they called Palestine, not Sham or Jerusalem; British consular officials wrote reports of the economy in Palestine, not Jerusalem or Sham; Arthur Ruppin gave speeches about the activities of the Palestine Office, and so that's how Arabs wrote about Condor's surveys, Zionist immigration, and the economy. People used the term Palestine to avoid confusion.[223]

* * *

Muslims and Christians. When I set out to study the origins of the Palestinians, I asked Meir Litvak, a professor of Middle East history at Tel Aviv University, if he thought I'd find very many references to the Palestinians before 1914. He said whatever you'd find, it would all be from Christians. Daniel Pipes agreed. "No Muslim of Palestine called himself a Palestinian before 1920," Pipes claimed.

---

[223] On a "Palestine Committee in Paris" (*al-lajna al-Filastiniyya al-Parisiyya*), see "al-Yahud fi Filastin wa-musta'maratuhum," *al-Mashriq* 1899(2): 1093-4; on a Palestine Commission (*al-Kumisyun al-Filastini*) established by the Russian Czar to protect the interests of Russian pilgrims in Palestine, see Suwaydan, *Tarikh al-Jam'iyya*, 75; on the German Palestine Journal (*al-Majalla al-Filastiniyya al-Almaniyya*) and the Palestine Journal (*al-Majalla al-Filasitniyya*), see Lammens, *Tasrih al-Absar*, I, 119, 135, 143; II, 102; 235, 240; "Shadharat," *al-Mashriq* 6 (1903): 863; on Zionist immigration to Palestine, see, for instance, "Hayat Umma Ba'd Mawtuhu," *al-Manar* 4 (1902): 802-4; *al-Nafir* 15 July 1909; *Filastin* 20 November 1912; *Filastin* 22 July 1912; Khalidi, *Palestinian Identity*, ch. 6; on Ruppin's 1913 speech, and its reception in the Arabic press, see Beŝka, *From Ambivalence to Hostility*, 126.

They were onto something, even if their biases precluded them from understanding why. I was only able to find a handful of Muslims who used the term Palestinian before 1914. In an op-ed, the Muslim Raghib al-Khalidi commended *Filastin*'s editors for having criticized village elders for accepting bribes during the 1912 Ottoman parliamentary elections. He described it as an "insult to the Palestinian people." The Muslim Muhammad Musa al-Maghribi reportedly wrote that his paper *al-Munadi* would only cover news relevant to "the Palestinians." In a 1914 article by the editor of *al-Iqdam*, the Muslim Muhammad al-Shanti warned "Palestinian youth" of the dangers of Zionism. That's at least three Muslims I am aware of who reportedly used the term before 1914, compared to more than a dozen Christians.[224]

So how could it be that Christians accounted for a mere 10% of the population of the area that would be incorporated into the Government of Palestine in 1920, but most of the known references to the word "Palestinian" in the early 1900s? The simple, if false answer, espoused by Bernard Lewis and Daniel Pipes, is that Palestine was irrelevant if not "abhorrent" or "repugnant" to Muslims. This was a point of propaganda, invented because it strengthened Zionism's claim to the land.[225]

But there is no evidence to support the point. Muslims were underrepresented among journalists because they could get more stable and higher paying jobs as bureaucrats. The publishing

---

[224] On Raghib al-Khalidi, see *Filastin* 8 May 1912; al-Maghribi wrote in a 14 March 1913 issue of *al-Munadi* that "we have limited the scope of *Munadi* to the affairs of this *liwa'*, in particular; you will not find any news that is not of concern to the Palestinians (*al-Filastiniyyin*), or news which is not relevant to their country (*biladihim*)." The paper was reportedly written entirely by Muhammad Musa al-Maghribi, while the concessionaire was Sa'id Jar Allah. See Yehoshua, *Tarikh al-Sihafa*, 54-6. For more on the paper, see Khalidi, *Palestinian Identity*, 56; on Muhammad al-Shanti, see ibid, 58-9.

[225] Pipes claimed that Palestine "embodied a purely Jewish and Christian concept, one utterly foreign to Moslems, even repugnant to them." See Daniel Pipes, "The Year the Arabs Discovered Palestine," *The Jerusalem Post* 13 September 2000.

industy was still high risk, and civil service paid better—potentially even 1200 Ottoman lira a month, a small fortune in those days. Also, why would you ever become a journalist if you could become a spy?[226]

Meanwhile, Christians had long been sidelined from politics, a practice the Ottomans inherited from their Mamluk, Ayyubid, Fatimid and Abbasid predecessors. The Ottomans tolerated religious minorities but did not incorporate them in large numbers into the political or military leadership of the state, at least until quite late in the 19th century whence many had already pursued careers outside the bureaucracy. The result was that while Muslims found jobs in the civil service, diplomacy, judiciary and military, Christians pursued commerce, education, translation, journalism and publishing. As a result, most of the Arab translators, journalists and publishers in the Ottoman Empire were Christian, not Muslim.

There was another reason Christians were more likely to publish in the popular press and Muslims were more likely to write government memos and legal opinions in court. Ottoman losses on the battlefield in the 18th and 19th centuries meant capitulations to European powers, who established hundreds of missionary schools in the Empire, discussed above. The state forbid missionaries from teaching Muslims. Most Muslim parents preferred not to send their kids to Christian schools anyways. The result was that Christians in the Ottoman Empire had better and earlier access to higher education than Muslims. Orthodox and Maronite Christians were, on average, earlier to study science, math, foreign languages and geography than were Muslims. Christians in the lands of Sham were therefore earlier to publish newspapers and books.

---

[226] See Zachary J. Foster, "The 1915 Locust Attack in Syria and Palestine and its Role in the Famine During the First World War," *Middle Eastern Studies* 51(3) (2015): 380.

People will only identify with a place if it plays an important role in their life. And a place will only play an important role in people's lives if they name it, make maps of it, tell stories about it, or establish institutions and associations in it or for it. That's what happened to Palestine in the mid-late 19th century, and that's why people began to call themselves Palestinians in the early 20th century.

* * *

Independence In 1648, the Holy Roman Empire, Spain, France, Sweden and the Dutch Republic signed the Peace of Westphalia in which each state agreed to respect one another's sovereignty. That was the birth of the system of states we all know and hate today. The Ottoman Empire joined that system. Palestine was not part of that system because it was part of the Ottoman Empire.

Nevertheless, Europeans wrote and spoke of Palestine a lot, and the Ottomans paid attention attention to some of it. A pamphlet from the mid-19th century titled "Circular of a Project for the Erection of Palestine into an Independent state," which can be found in the Ottoman Archives in Istanbul, stated that "we Christians" of all sects propose that "the Sublime Porte would grant the Cessation of Palestine, or that Portion of Syria commonly denominated "The Holy Land," to all Christians." The independent government would be erected under the "auspices of the Christian Princes of Europe and Asia, into an independent Territory." Meanwhile, an entire movement of Christians in Europe known as Restorationists supported moving Jews to Palestine because of their eschatological belief that the return of Jesus on earth would only come about after the Jews had all returned to Palestine. Presumably, the Ottomans had other ideas for what to do with Palestine—including not turn it into a Christian Principality.[227]

The Westphalian system expanded and the Ottoman Empire shrunk. The Italian city-states unified in the 1850s, Otto von Bismarck centralized the German confederates in the 1870s and Muhammad Ali brought Egypt into that system in 1805. Independence movements in Greece (1820s-1830s), Russian occupation in the Caucuses (1810s-1860s) and the Balkans Wars (1910s) inspired ambitious upstarts around the Ottoman Empire. The later events were collectively known as part of "the Eastern Question," or the belief that Ottoman Empire was inevitably going to collapse and European governments had to prevent a single power (other than themselves) from annexing the spoils (such as Palestine), to maintain the balance of power.

As time passed, though, activists around the world no longer saw themselves as joining the Westphalia system, they saw themselves as gaining independence. Talk of independence, not surprisingly, reached every corner of the Ottoman Empire. This included the Ottoman province of Syria. It was a fringe idea that very few people even knew existed let alone embraced. At first, the part of the Empire that some Arabs thought ought to be independent was ambiguously refered to as the land of the Arabs or Syria, not Palestine.[228]

---

[227] On the pamphlet, see BOA H.R. SYS 1778/1 (01/31/1841). For a brief history of Christians who supported the movement of Jews to Palestine, see Donald M. Lewis, "A Very Short History of Christian Zionism," pp. 108-122 in *A Land Full of God: Christian Perspectives on the Holy Land* Mae Elise Cannon (ed.) (Eugene: Cascade Books, 2017).

[228] On attaching "Syria" to "Egpyt," see Haqqi al-'Azm, *Haqa'iq 'an al-Intikhabat al-Niyabiyya fi al-'Iraq wa-Filastin wa-Suriya* (Cairo: Matba'at al-Akhbar, 1912), 87; see also Hasan Kayalı, *Arabs and Young Turks: Ottomanism, Arabism, and Islamism in the Ottoman Empire, 1908–1918* (Berkeley: University of California Press, 1997), 68-70.

The fringe talks of independence eventually included Palestine as well. In 1912, the Ottomans investigated claims that a resident of Gaza snuck into Egypt as a spy to help the British wrest Palestine and Syria away from the Ottomans. The 'Abd al-Hadi family in Nablus was rumored to have approached British officials in Egypt to push for the British occupation of Palestine. (The newspaper *Filastin* claimed it was a lie that an association in Nablus was negotiating with the British about annexing Palestine to Egypt). *Filastin* reported further rumors in December 1912 that Muslim notables from Nablus had gone to Egypt at the request of the British to discuss a plan that would have annexed Palestine to Egypt. Reportedly, the Greek Orthodox Church of Jerusalem also accused some Arab leaders of aiming to establish "the independence of Palestine." The Jerusalemite Ihsan Turjaman confided on the first page of his 1915 wartime diary that, after the war, Palestine would either be attached to Egypt or gain independence. Rumors had also spread around the Arab world that the Zionists wanted an independent kingdom in Palestine.[229]

---

[229] On the Gazan Arabs, see a report of the special Egypt commission, BOA A.}MTZ.(05) 9-C/300-1 (3 April 1912); on the 'Abd al-Hadi rumors, see Campos, *Ottoman Brothers*, 237; on *Filastin*'s claim it was a lie, see *Filastin* 16 October 1912; on the Nablus notables, see *Filastin* 25 December 1912, citing the journal *The Near East*; on the accusations of the Orthodox Church, see Khalil al-Sakakini, *al-Nahda al-Urthudhuksiyya fi Filastin* (n.p.: n.p., 1913), 12; on Ihsan Turjaman, see Salim Tamari (ed.), *'Am al-Jarad, al-Harb al-Udhma ma-Mahu al-Madi al-'Uthmani min Filastin* (Beirut: Mu'assasat al-Dirasat al-Filastiniyya, 2008), 75-6; on this possibility in 1923, see 'Umar al-Salih al-Barghuthi and Khalil Totah, *Tarikh Filastin* (Jerusalem: Matba'at Bayt al-Maqdis,1923), 13; on the Zionist rumors, Rashid Rida, for instance, wrote that "the Jews are returning in great numbers to their ancient Kingdom, Palestine...the goal is raise enough money to buy Palestine from the Sultan." See Hayat Umma Ba'd Mawtuhu," *al-Manar* 4 (1902): 802-4; Farid Georges Kassab [*Le Nouvel Empire Arabe* (Paris: V. Giard & E. Brière, 1906), 10-11] and Negib Azoury [*Le Réveil de la Nation Arabe dans l'Asie Turque: Partie Asiatique de la Question d'Orient et Programme de la Ligue de la Patrie Arabe* (Paris, Plon-Nourrit et cie, 1905), ch. 1] debated whether the Jews wanted restore a Jewish monarchy in Palestine in 1905 and 1906. (Azoury believed the Jews desired such a restoration, Kassab thought they didn't); Mustafa Affandi Tamar (*Filastin* 22 July 1912) argued that the British were interested in strengthening the Jewish presence in "Palestine and the Syrian country" as well as establishing an independent state there in order to safeguard their position in Egypt, but he thought the formation of a new government in Palestine would only lead to bloodshed.

The State. The British resolved the question during the Great War with the capture of Jerusalem in December 1917 and the rest of the Eastern Mediterranean in the following year. In April 1918, the who's who of Jerusalem organized a banquet at an orphanage school, inviting prominent community members and British military officials. Speakers presented in front of a *This is Arab Palestine* map engraved into marble stone. The organizers sung a song, with audience participation, about what they described as their beloved homeland, *Palestine*. They repeated the word Palestine in each verse and stanza of the song. 'Abd al-Latif al-Husayni spoke about the connection of the Arab nation to Palestine. Hassan Abu al-Sa'ud declared that the Zionists "want to deprive us of our rights that we have in our precious Palestine," encouraging the audience to hold steadfast. "The sweat and blood of our forefathers established the Arab nation in Palestine...Long live our nation and Arab Palestine! Love live the Arab nation! Love live Arab Palestine!" As soon as people start talking about blood and sweat you know that things are getting serious. The April 1918 banquet might have been the first instance in which Arabs gathered publicly to declare their shared love and devotion to their homeland of Palestine.[230]

In the same year, 1918, Woodrow Wilson made his 14 Points Speech and the British and French issued an Anglo-French Declaration. Wilson declared that non-Turkish nationalities now under Turkish rule should be "assured an undoubted security of life and an absolutely unmolested opportunity of autonomous development." The Anglo-French Declaration claimed that Britain and France would assist in the "establishment of government and administration deriving their authority from the initiative and free desire of the native population." The former was widely

---

[230] This information is based on an intelligence report of a Zionist spy who attended the ceremony. See CZA C4/L4/768.

reported in the Arabic press and both were widely cited by Arabs in Palestine, Syria and Egypt as support for their claims of independence in the coming years.[231]

The British ignored both statements. Instead, they obtained approval to rule Palestine not from the people living in it but by the recently founded League of Nations in 1922. In fact, the people of the country were consulted by the American King-Crane Commission in 1919 and rejected a British Mandate, but the British ignored its findings. Instead, they honored their commitment to the 1917 Belfour Declaration to facilitate the establishment of a national home for the Jews in Palestine. The conflict over Palestine intensified. It was the conflict—and the bloodshed—that ironically sealed Palestine's fate in the book of life. Over the coming decades, from the 1920s-1940s, many thousands of people died fighting for Palestine. That gauarnteed Palestine's survival.

Palestine's newfound political status meant that organized political activity was directed towards it. Arabs formed a slew of associations and political parties the late 1910s, 1920s and 1930s to fight the anti-democratic terms of the British Government of Palestine: at first, the Literary Club, the Arab Club and the Muslim-Christian Associations, which met half a dozen times in the 1920s in annual congress called the Palestinian National Congresses. During the third National

---

[231] On the French-Anglo Declaration, see Porath, *The Emergence of the Palestinian National Movement 1918-1929*, 42; on Wilson's warm reception in Egypt, see Erez Manela, *The Wilsonian Moment: Self-Determination and the International Origins of Anticolonial Nationalism* (Oxford: Oxford University Press, 2007), ch.3; on Aleppo, see Keith David Watenpaugh, *Being Modern in the Middle East: Revolution, Nationalism, Colonialism, and the Arab Middle Class* (Princeton: Princeton University Press, 2006), 149-50; on Arab Palestinian protest notes submitted to the British authorities referencing these declarations, see Akram Zu'aytir, *Watha'iq al-Haraka al-Wataniyya al-Filastiniyya, 1918-1939: Min Awraq Akram Zu'aytir* (Beirut: Institute for Palestine Studies, 1979), 7, 11, 15-16, 67, 118, 144, 201, 226; for mention of these declarations in the press, see *al-Karmil* 21 December 1920, Zionist report on the Arabic Press, CZA S22/389; *Bayt al-Muqqadis* 16 November 1920 and 9 March 1921, Zionist reports on the Arabic Press, CZA S22/389; *Mir'at al-Sharq*, 22 October 1919.

Congress, for instance, one resolution passed in 1920 calling on the British to establish "a native Government, to be responsible towards a Legislative Assembly representative of, and elected by, the Arabic speaking population living in Palestine up to the beginning of the war." The 1930s saw the rise of the political partiies—the Istiqlal Party, founded in 1932, the National Defense Party in 1934, the Palestine Arab Party in 1935 and smaller parties including the Youth Congress Party, the Reform Party and the National Bloc. Then, the Arab Higher Committee was formed in 1936 which united rival political factions. The associations and parties all opposed Jewish immigration, but differed in their willingness to accommodate or even assist the British. All of this is to say that Palestine was now the focus of attention, which led more and more people to see themselves as Palestinians.[232]

The British called its own regime, the Government of Palestine. Initially, it printed a monthly newspaper titled *The Official Gazette of the Government of Palestine*. It distributed millions of identity cards, passports, pamphlets, stamps, bills, coins, certificates of education and other documents bearing the word Palestine. The British established the Museum of Palestinian Antiquities, the Palestine Education Department, the Palestine Law Institute, the Palestine Broadcasting Service, the Palestine Forest Service, the Palestine Railways, and the Palestine Surveys Department, whose director published a beautiful road map of Palestine (see figure 15). The British brought Palestine into the lives of everyone, by political fiat, public airways, minted

---

[232] for the best treatment of Arab politics in Palestine from the 1920s-1940s, see Porath, *The Emergence of the Palestinian National Movement 1918-1929* and Yehoshua Porath, *The Palestinian Arab National Movement, from Riots to Rebellion, 1929-1939* (London: Cass, 1977); see also Muhammad Y. Muslih, *The Origins of Palestinian Nationalism* (New York: Columbia University Press, 1988); Ann Mosely Lesch, *Arab Politics in Palestine, 1917-1939: The Frustration of a Nationalist Movement* (Ithaca: Cornell University Press, 1979); on the Istiqlal Party, see Weldon C. Matthews, *Confronting an Empire, Constructing a Nation: Arab Nationalists and Popular Politics in Mandate Palestine* (I. B. Tauris, 2006); on the 1920 protest note, see Robert L Jarman (ed.), *Political Diaries of the Arab World* (Slough: Archive Editions, 1990), 38.

coins, printed texts and brink and mortar. States in the modern world have had this incredible ability to control how we think about spaces, places and regions. The British were no exception with Palestine.[233]

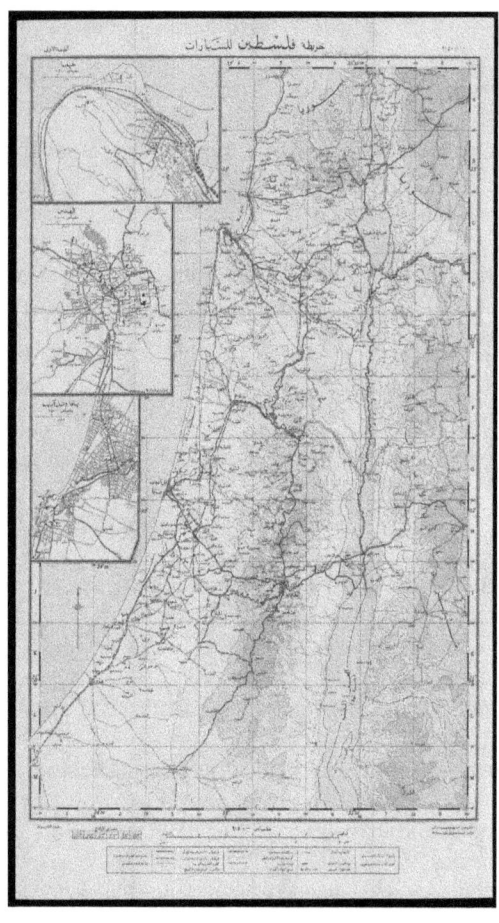

---

[233] For more details about the museum and its holdings, see n.a., *Dalil Mathaf al-Athar al-Qadima al-Filastini* (Da'irat al-Athar al-Qadima bi-l-Quds, 1924); the law school was called *al-Ma'had al-Huquq al-Filastini*. For a selection of the Palestinian radio broadcasts, see, for instance, al-Qism al-'Arabi fi Dar al-Idha'a al-Filastiniyya, *Hadith al-Idha'a* (Jerusalem: al-Matba'a al-Tijariyya, 1942); for a book length treatment on the subject, see Andrea L Stanton, *This is Jerusalem Calling: State Radio in Mandate Palestine* (Austin: University of Texas Press, 2014); on the Palestine Forest Services, see Roza El-Eini, *Mandated Landscape: British Imperial Rule in Palestine 1929-1948* (Routledge, 2015); for more on Arab government employees, see Bernard Wasserstein, "'Clipping the Claws of the Colonisers': Arab Officials in the Government of Palestine, 1917-48," *Middle Eastern Studies* 13(2) (1977): 171-194

Figure 15. "A Map of Palestine for Cars."[234]

All kinds of new associations, companies and commissions came into existence as a result, making Palestine seem so natural a place. The Palestine Boy Scouts Association formed in the early 1920s, the Arab Palestine Sport Federation in 1931 and the Palestine Arab Medical Association in 1944. Companies embraced the name too, such as the Palestine Electric Corporation and the Palestine Salt Company. Zionists founded the Palestine Land Development Company, the Palestine Foundation Fund and the Palestine Zionist Executive. International commissions formed reinforcing the idea, such as the 1937 Palestine Royal Commission. People institutionalized Palestine.[235]

Meanwhile, more people started to make a living writing about Palestine. The British paid Arabs to translate *The Official Gazette of the Government of Palestine* into Arabic every month. They paid other Arab officials to write reports on the state of education in Palestine. The Anglophone Arabic speaking Persian of the Bahai faith, Husayn Ruhi, was employed as general inspector at the Ministry of Education in the Government of Palestine. The British treated him to land, air and sea tours so he could write his 1923 textbook, *The Geography of Palestine*. The British hired Sabri Sharif 'Abd al-Hadi to teach natural sciences at a secondary school in Nablus. He published *A Natural Geography of Syria and Palestine* in Arabic in the same year. They commissioned Khalil Totah and 'Umar al-Salih al-Barghuthi to write a *History of Palestine* in 1923. They commissioned Khalil Totah and Habib Khuri to write *A Geography of Palestine* in

---

[234] Published by Da'irat al-Masaha in 1934. The map is held at the Israeli National Library.
[235] See Arnon Degani, "They Were Prepared: The Palestinian Arab Scout Movement 1920 – 1948," *British Journal of Middle Eastern Studies* (41)(2) (2014): 200-218; Issam Khalidi, "Body and Ideology Early Athletics in Palestine (1900 - 1948)," *Jerusalem Quarterly* 27 (2006): 44-58; see also El-Eini, *Mandated Landscape*.

1923 as well. Wasfi ʻAnabtawi and Saʻid al-Sabbagh also wrote a number of textbooks for the primary and secondary schools, including such books as the *Ancient History of Syria and Palestine.*[236]

---

[236] On Ruhi's aerial tour of the southern desert, see Husayn Ruhi, *al-Mukhtasar fi Jughrafiyat Filastin* (Jerusalem: L.J.S. Printing Press, 1923), 13. Ruhi's British sponsorship shines in his book, for example, in that he included Jewish and Arab narratives. See Hilary Falb Kalisman, "The Little Persian Agent in Palestine: Husayn Ruhi, British Intelligence, and World War I," *Jerusalem Quaretly* (66) (2016): 65-74; then see Sabri Sharif ʻAbd al-Hadi, *Jughrafiyat Suriya wa-Filastin al-Tabʻiyya* (Cairo: al-Maktaba al-Ahliyya, 1923), title page; then see al-Barghuthi and Totah, *Tarikh Filastin*; on its use in British schools, see Abdul Latif Tibawi, *Arab Education in Mandatory Palestine: A Study of Three Decades of British Administration* (London: Luzac & Co., 1956), 198; Khalil Totah and Habib Khuri, *Jughrafiyat Filastin* (Jerusalem: Matbaʻat Bayt al-Maqdis, 1923); for its use in the schools, see ibid., "Muqaddima," before page 1; then see Saʻid al-Sabbagh, *al-Madaniyyat al-Qadima wa Tarikh Suriya wa Filastin* (2nd edition) (Jaffa and Haifa: al-Maktaba al-ʻAsriyya, 1944); see also Rafiq Tamimi and Saʻid al-Sabbagh, *Hawd al-Bahr al-Mutawassit: Wa Fihi Fusul Matula ʻan Filastin wa Sharqi al-Urdun wa-Saʼir al-Bilad Suriya* (Beirut: Maktaba al-Kashshaf, n.d.).

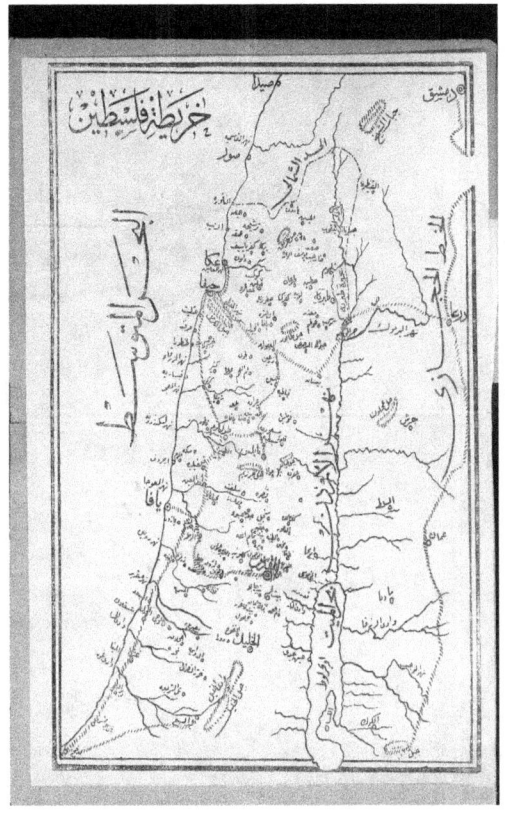

Figure 16. "Map of Palestine."[237]

Kids also studied history and geography with similar maps of Palestine. Some of these maps appeared on the back pages of textbooks, such as in figure 16 and 17.

---

[237] Cited in Khalil Totah and Habib Khuri, *Jughrafiyat Filastin* (Jerusalem: Matba'at Bayt al-Maqdis, 1923), before page 1.

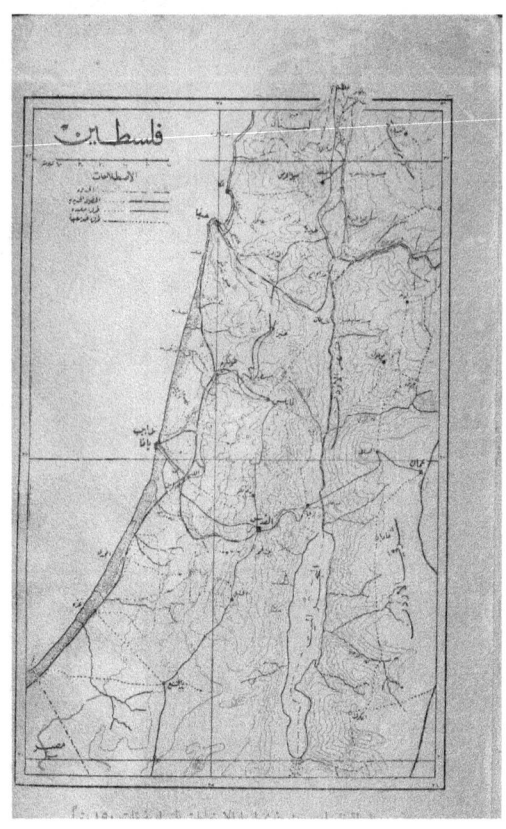

Figure 17. Map of "Palestine."[238]

The British wanted their subjects to believe that Palestine was a natural part of the world order. In 1925, they created the Committee for Palestinian Higher Education which established rules and regulations for students in the British school system. The committee wrote exams on topics such as "the history of Palestine," "the geography of Palestine" and "the archeology of Palestine." No government in the Middle East had ever paid multiple people to write books of history and geography exclusively about Palestine, much less mandated exams on Palestine's

---

[238] Cited in Wasfi 'Anabtawi and Sa'id Sabbagh, *Filastin wa-l-Bilad al-'Arabiyya wa-Sa'ir al-Buldan al-Sharq al-'Adna wa-Hawd al-Bahr al-Mutawassit* (Jaffa: Maktabat al-Tahir Ikhwan, 1946), back cover.

archeology, geography and history. Tens of thousands of kids had to prove they knew about Palestine.[239]

Meanwhile, the number of Arabs enrolled in school increased from 20% in 1922 to 50% in 1947. Among boys, the figure swelled from 17% in 1911 to 85% percent in the late 1940s. The number of public secondary schools expanded from 6 in the mid-1930s to 20 in the late 1940s, and from 2 to 8 institutions of advanced learning. More students read about the history and geography of Palestine and more saw maps of Palestine. Palestine seemed like a normal and natural part of the world to large segments of the teenage population by the 1930s and 1940s.[240]

Stories. Meanwhile, stories about Palestine proliferated. Newspaper publishers in Jerusalem, Jaffa and Haifa expanded their circulation figures from 1-2 thousand in the 1930s to 5-10 thousand by the 1940s. Authors wrote more and more books about Palestine as well: 23 in the 1920s, 45 in the 1930s, and 49 in the 1940s (see appendix 1). Newspapers covered politics, society and economics in Palestine while books dealt with Palestine's geography, history, anthropology and archeology. The proliferation of printed texts dealing with Palestine was made possible by the rapid expansion of new career paths: medicine, journalism, civil service, law, entrepreneurship, finance, politics and publishing.[241]

---

[239] The one exception was the military handbook, *Filistin Risalesi*, commissioned by the Ottomans in 1915. On the matriculation exams, see n.a. *Shahadat al-Madrasa al-Thanawiyya al-Filastiniyya* (Jerusalem: Majlis al-Ta'lim al-'Ali al-Filastini, 1925-1941); for more on the school curriculum, see Tibawi, *Arab Education in Mandatory Palestine*, 77-101

[240] On school enrollment, see Khalidi, *Palestinian Identity*, 173-4; on the expansion of the schools, see Adnan Abu-Ghazaleh "Arab Cultural Nationalism in Palestine during the British Mandate," *Journal of Palestine Studies* 1(3) (1972): 37-63; Roderic D. Matthews and Matta Akrwai, *Education in Arab Countries of the Near East* (Washington D.C.: American Council on Education, 1949), 236.

[241] In 1933, *al-'Arab* (Jerusalem) printed 1,500 copies daily. In 1935, *al-Jami'a al-Islamiyya* (Jaffa) printed 1,200 copies daily while *Filastin* printed 2,000 copies daily. One source claimed that in 1936, *al-Difa'* printed 10,000 copies daily. Circulation expanded even further in the 1940s, where the most popular papers, *Filastin* and *al-Difa'*,

Some stories dealt with the ethnic origins of the people of Palestine. John S. Salah, a Harvard-educated New York based writer claimed in 1919 that Palestine's inhabitants were a mix of Canaanite, Aramite, Hebrew, Assyrian, Persian, Greek, Roman, Crusader and Arab races. This theory bothered some because it implied Jewish blood was circulating among the Palestinians. Najib Sadaqa had an explanation for this, claiming that the Arab Palestinians formed out of the Philistines and others to populate the area only *after* its Jewish presence in antiquity. He believed in a perfect separation of bodily fluids between the ancient Jews and other ancient peoples. Palestinian blood was therefore untainted by Jewish blood, in his mind.[242]

This idea didn't sit well with others, though, because it meant that Jews settled the land first, not something to brag about in the heyday of fascism. The Catholic bishop of Haifa, Grigorios al-Hajjar, had a solution to this problem. "The Palestinian Arabs were the descendants of the original residents of Palestine who settled the land thousands of years ago *before* the Jews," he suggested. He insisted that Palestinians were both Arab and the first settlers of the land.[243]

But this theory must have seemed shallow to Wadi' Talhuq, who realized that the Arab conquerors in the 7th century were obviously not the first people to settle the land. In 1945, he asked "who were the original inhabitants of Palestine?" All the ancient civilizations to thrive in

---

printed some 6-7 thousand copies daily. See Ayalon, *Reading Palestine*, 62-5; on the 1930s, see Matthews, *Confronting an Empire*, 143; Sarah Ozacky-Lazar and Mustafa Kabha, "The Haganah by Arab and Palestinian Historiography and Media" *Israel Studies* 7(3)(2002): 58, n.17; on the 1940s, see Avraham Sela', "Khevra ve-Mosadot be-Kraz 'Aravay Filastin be-Tkufat Ha-Mandat," pp.291-347 in *Kalkala ve-Khevra be-Yemay Ha-Mandat, 1918-1948* (Beersheba: Hotsa'at ha-sefarim shel Universitat Ben-Guryon ba-Negev, 2003), 304.

[242] First, see Salah, *Filastin wa-Tajdid*, 19; then see Najib Sadaqa, *Qadiyyat Filastin* (Beirut: Dar al-Kutub, 1946), 6.

[243] On Grigorios (Gariguriyus) al-Hajjar, see Britanya al-Udhma, *al-Shahadat al-Siyasiyya amam al-Lajna al-Milkiyya al-Britaniyya* (Damascus: Matba'at al-Sha'b, 1937), 53 and al-Nafir, *Majmu'a Shahadat 'Arab Filastin amam al-Lajna al-Milkiyya al-Britaniyya* (Haifa: al-Nafir, 1936?), 31.

the Fertile Crescent were conquerors, not natives, and most of them came from the desert, he claimed. This meant, in his mind, that the Fertile Crescent had no original inhabitants, only foreign invaders. And if the foreigners usually invaded from the desert, then they were usually Arabs, and so the original inhabitants of the land were Arabs, and therefore the Palestinians. He saw human populations like branches on trees, the Palestinian branch older than all other branches. Talhuq was a magician of ideas. The Palestinians, like most peoples, developed compelling stories about their own origins.[244]

Stories also dealt with the political conflict over Palestine, at that time called the "Palestine Issue." Writers covered the Arab political movements of the late Ottoman period, the diplomatic politics of World War I, i.e. the Balfour Declaration, Sykes-Picot Agreement, Hussayn-McMahorn Correspondence, King-Crane Commission and Palestinian and Syrian National Congresses. Stories about Palestine dealt with the terms of the Mandate itself, which, as so many writers reminded us, violated the democratic will of its Arab Palestinian Christian and Muslim majority. These stories covered the political history of the Government of Palestine, jumping from flash point to flash point: the 1920 disturbances, the 1929 Western Wall riots and, of course, the Great Revolt from 1936-1939.[245]

---

[244] Wadi' Talhuq, *Filastin al-'Arabiyya: Fi Madiha wa Hadiruha wa-Mustaqbaluha* (Beirut: Majallat al-'Alman, 1945), 64-5. Weldon Matthews [*Confronting an Empire*, 54] traced similar ideas in the 1920s and 1930s in the writings of al-Khatib to the American scholar Henry Breasted's *Ancient Times*, where he traced the sources of the civilizations of antiquity to migration out of Arabia.

[245] See, for instance, Muhammad al-Tawil, *Kitab al-Haqa'iq al-Majhula: Idhtirabat Filastin al-Akhira* (Jerusalem: Matba'at al-Mulul, 1930); n.a., *Rihla Bayn al-Jibal fi Ma'aqil al-Tha'irin* (Jafa: al-Matba'a al-Jami'a al-Islamiyya, 1936); Rashid al-Hajj Ibrahim, *al-Qadiyya al-Filastiniyya Amam al-Wafd al-Britani al-'Iraqi* (Haifa: Matba'a al-Nafir, 1936); Hasan Siddiqi al-Dajjani, *Tafsil Dhulamat Filastin: Haqa'iq, Arqam, Watha'iq Hamma* (n.p.: al-Matba'a al-Tijariyya, 1936); Ghayrath Pitrus, Suriya al-Jadida, *Filastin, Shahadat al-Isti'mar al-Sahyuni* (San Paulo: Dar al-Tiba'a wa-l-Nashr al-'Arabiyya, 1940); Muhammad Rif'at, *Qadiyyat Filastin* (Cairo: Dar al-Ma'arif, 1947); Nuri al-Sa'id, *Istiqlal al-'Arab wa-Wihdatuhum Mudhakkira fi al-Qadiyya al-'Arabiyya* (Baghdad: Matba'at al-Hukuma, 1943); Sadaqa, *Qadiyyat Filastin*; Muhammad Jamil Bayhum, *Filastin: Andalus al-Sharq* (Beirut: Matabi' Sadir, 1946); Muhammad 'Ali Tahir, *Awraq Majmu'a: Kitab Ahmar 'an Fadha'i' al-Ingiliz fi Filastin wa Ghadr al-Yahud wa-Sabr al-'Arab* (Cairo: Maktabat al-Isti'lamat al-Filastini al-'Arabi, 1948); al-Hay'a al-

Writers exaggerated Palestine's glory. They claimed that cities such as Jaffa and Nablus were the bride of Palestine; that Ramallah and Safed were two of Palestine's most beautiful resort towns, with their high elevation, excellent climate, clean air and fresh water; that Palestine's lands were rich and fertile; that Palestine's hot springs were some of the best in the world; that Palestine was the stage of the prophets and heroes, the sister of the gardens of paradise; the bedrock of hope and fulfillment; that Palestine was beloved by millions of people; that it was the lord of lands and the pride of worshippers.[246]

Arabs were also romanticizing Palestine's history. "No country in the world has a history as important as our country, Palestine," read a 1934 *History of Palestine*. "Many Westerners have taken interest in studying its history and have become more intimate with Palestine their own countries." They study its history, archeology, topography and geography, but, "it is us, the Palestinians, who should love Palestine," the text continued. "This land is our land, the cradle of our ancestors, and it is our people who should study its history."[247]

'Arabiyya al-'Ulya, *Qadiyyat Filastin al-'Arabiyya* (Cairo: Matba'at al-Sa'ada, 1948?); Wadi' Talhuq, *Filastin al-'Arabiyya: Fi Madiha wa Hadiruha wa-Mustaqbaluha* (Beirut: Majallat al-'Alman, 1945); 'Asabat al-Taharrur al-Watani bi-Filastin, *Tariq Filastin ila al-Huriyya* (Jerusalem: 'Asabat al-Taharrur al-Watani, 1947); Jabir Shibli, *Asra' am Ta'awwun fi Filastin?* (Jerusalem: Sharikat Matba'a al-Umma, 1940).

[246] On Nablus's beauty, see As'ad Mansur, *Tarikh al-Nasira* (Cairo: Matba'at al-Hilal, 1924), 191; on Ramallah, see *Filastin* 14 August 1912; Rafiq al-Tamimi, Wasfi 'Anabtawi and Sa'id al-Sabbagh, *Hawd al-Bahr al-Mutawassit wa-Gharbi Uruba* (Jerusalem: Matba'at Bayt al-Maqdis, 1945), 27; on Safed, see Wasfi 'Anabtawi and Sa'id al-Sabbagh, *Jughrafiyat al-Sharq al-Adna, wa-Sa'ir al-Buldan Hawd al-Bahr al-Mutawassit wa-Gharbi Uruba* (Jaffa: Sharikat al-Tiba'a al-Yaffiyya, 1942), 52-53; on Palestine's fertile lands, see *Bashir Filastin* 22 November 1908, cited in Yehoshua, *Tarikh al-Sihafa*, 64-5; on its hot springs, see Salah, *Filastin wa-Tajdid*, 98; from the stage of prophets to the pride of worshippers, see a 1920 anonymous op-ed (perhaps written by 'Arif al-'Arif) in the newspaper *Suriya al-Janubiyya*, cited in Khalidi, *Palestinian Identity*, 169.

[247] The book was dedicated to the "Palestinian student so he could study the history of his own land." The introduction is initialed by a certain 'aleph,' 'sin,' 'lam.' See Maktabat Bayt al-Maqdis, *Tarikh Filastin min Aqdam al-Azmana ila Ayyamina hadhihi* (Jerusalem: Maktabat Bayt al-Maqdis, 1934), 5-6.

The growing importance of the state in people's lives from the 1920s onwards meant that the term Palestinian became more and more useful. Dozens of writers used the term Palestinian to discuss regional politics, especially similarities and differences between and among Palestinians, Syrians and Egyptians. People formerly part of a single central government in Istanbul now found themselves scattered across a half dozen some states. Arabic speakers in Palestine, Lebanon, Syria, Iraq and Transjordan were now subject to different laws, they carried different passports and faced different political challenges: Zionism, sectarianism, imperialism, "divide and conquer" and more. As a result, the term Palestinian became a much more useful descriptor from the 1920s onwards than it had been during the Ottoman period.[248]

As the Mandate progressed, the conflict between Jews and Arabs descended into riots, violence, bloodshed and war. Violence usually has an affect on our identities. And there was plenty of violence over Palestine. Blood had already been spilled between Jews and Arabs over the fate of Palestine as early as the 1890s, but the first large scale outbreak of violence was in 1920. Things got even worse in 1929 during the Western Wall riots, and then even worse from 1936-1939, when Arabs engaged in open revolt, and then even worse during the 1948 War—known as the

---

[248] n.a., *Jihad Filastin: al-Thawra al-Filastiniyya fi Mukhtalif Marahiluha* (Damascus: n.p., 1936), 16, 21, 24, 34, 57, 61; Ahmad Samih al-Khalidi, *Ahl al-'Ilm bayn Misr wa Filastin* (Jerusalem: al-Matba'a al-'Asriyya, 1946), 4, 7, 17, 19-26, 29-30, 32-4, 36, 39-40; *Mir'at al-Sharq* 9 June 1920; *Filastin* 3 September 1921; *Filastin* 2 May 1922; *al-Karmil* 11 October 1922, cited in Hammad Husayn (ed.), *Majmu'at Watha'iq hawl Tarikh Filastin* (Jenin: al-Markaz al-Filastini lil-Thaqafa wa-l-I'lam, 2003), 35; Mahmud al-Charkis, *al-Dalil al-Musawwar lil-Bilad al-'Arabiyya* (Damascus: Matba'at Babil Ikhwan, 1930), 7; Amin Rihani, *Muluk al-'Arab: Rihla Bayn Bilad al-'Arab* (Beirut: al-Matba'a al-'Ilmiyya li-Yusif Sadir, 1924), II, 294; al-Sa'id, *Istiqlal al-'Arab*, 73; al-Hay'a al-'Arabiyya al-'Ulya li-Filastin, *Qadiyyat Filastin al-'Arabiyya*, 7; Kunstantin (a.k.a. Constantine) Thuyudri, *Bayn Misr wa-Filastin* (Matba'at Bayt al-Maqdis, 1928), before page 1; Mamlakat Misr, *al-'Alaqat al-Tijariyya bayn Misr wa-Filastin* (Cairo: al-Matba'a al-Amiriyya, 1936), 30; Tahir, *Awraq Majmu'a*, 271; Jamal Husayni, cited in Sadaqa, *Qadiyyat Filastin* (Beirut: Dar al-Kutub, 1946), nun; Fayiz Sayigh, *Mashru' Suriya al-Kubra* (Beirut: Matba'at al-Nijma, 1946), 23; 'Irfat Mahmud Hijazi, *Suriya al-Kubra* (Dayr Mar Marqus lil-Siryan, 1947/8?), 27; Yusuf Majalli, *Filastin wa-l-Mazhar al-Jughrafi li-Mushkilatuha* (Cairo: Maktabat al-Anjilu al-Misriyya, 1948?), 84; Musa al-'Alami, *'Ibrat Filastin* (Beirut: n.p., 1949), 5; 'Arif al-'Arif, *Tarikh al-Quds* (Cairo: Dar al-Ma'arif, 1951), 128; Imil Ghuri, *al-Mu'amara al-Kubra: Ightilal Filastin wa-Mahq al-'Arab* (Cairo: Dar al-Nil al-Tiba'a, 1955), 157.

War of Independence by Jews and the Catastrophe by the Arabs. By that war's end, some two-thirds of the country's Arab inhabitants fled their homes or were expelled by gunpoint. For those who became refugees in Jordan, Egypt, Syria or Lebanon, Palestine had become more important than it ever had it.

* * *

Conclusion. Europeans and Americans entered the lands of Sham from the mid-19th century onwards as consular agents, missionaries, archeologists and travelers, and popularized the term Palestine as well as stories about it and maps of it. Tourists and pilgrims wandered around with their Palestine guidebooks, archeologists conducted surveys of Palestine's topography and Russians hosted public lectures celebrating their presence in Syria and Palestine. American, French, German, British and Russian missionary schools taught tens of thousands of kids about Palestine in class too. Increasingly, it became impossible to talk about politics or current events without reference to Palestine—the archeologists uncovering its ancient past, the consular agents publishing reports about its economy, tourists flocking to its holy sites or the Zionists hoping to transform it into a national home for the Jews. To use a word *other* than Palestine to describe things would have obfuscated the reality being discussed. Palestine was a fiction, but it became impossible to live without it.

More and more people in the modern world could pursue activities other than farm work thanks to agriculultural surpluses. This included bureaucrats, lawyers, educators, diplomats, archeologists, writers, journalists, publishers and mapmakers. Publishers could print thousands of newspapers and magazines cheaply. More people could read, which drove up demand, increased supply and decreased the price of printed texts. Newspapers were distributed to villages, towns and cities thanks to new technologies. All of these things happened everywhere in the world—Europe before the Middle East—but the effects were similar in both places: the growth in the number of people whose effect on the world was to make places like Palestine seem real.

In 1898, Palestine's Arabic speakers started using the term Palestinian. The term gained popularity first among graduates of Russian Seminary in Nazareth, then a wider circle of journalists in the 1900s and early 1910s. During these two decades, even people in smaller towns read or heard about Palestinians, but the term was still new and still not in widespread use. By the 1920s and 1930s, though, once the Government of Palestine had laid its foundation, once the effects of Zionism were widely understood and literacy rates and school attendance rose, Palestine rose dramatically in importance for everyone. A Palestinian identity was embraced. Some people picked up arms and died for Palestine. Many have since and still do today.

CONCLUSION

Too many close encounters with death have made Jews anxious of being wiped off the map. Some Jews might be surprised to learn that Palestinians have the same fear of being wiped off the map. They have faced too many close encounters with humiliation, discrimination, war, occupation and siege—a siege that starts with their very identities as Palestinians.

Such fears are reinforced when the Israeli military tries to ban people from using the word Palestine, or when Israeli heads of state declare there is no such thing as a Palestinian, or when pilots are fired for announcing touchdown in Palestine, or when a room full of powerful American lobbyists roar with applause upon hearing that "Palestine has not existed since 1948." Imagine if a room full of Washington insiders roared with applause at the thought that Europe was emptied of its Jews after World War II.

If Palestine is a fiction in our mind, not in reality, why do we believe in it? That question led us to the Pleistocene, in chapter two, because that's when we first came to believe in words, ideas or concepts like Palestine. We mastered the concept of a symbol. We learned to name objects in the world, including abstract objects like places. Natural and sexual selection led us to communicate with infinite complexity by relating symbols to one another with grammar, morphology and syntax. We made maps of Palestine and told stories about it. We also made Palestine beautiful, giving it meaning and purpose. This led us to identify with it, and even believe it was worth dying for. This was the first part of the story we told in chapter two.

Although identities based on places like Palestine have been around for tens of thousands of years, they came to dominate once sedentary life spread after the Agricultural Revolution. Agriculture led to surpluses, which inspired conquest and the rise of states. States were groups of people who agreed internally on a chain of command, and claimed a monopoly on the use of force within an area. States conquered and controlled territories, and needed to name the territories they conquered and controlled to effectively conquer and control them. Places like Palestine flourished as a result. Places like Palestine also proved useful for defense, tax collection, conscription and more conquest. Usually, place names chosen by the state became canonical without resistance. Occasionally, states used coercion to enforce them. States also built cities, which fused into regions in our minds. This is the second part of the story we told in chapter two.

In chapter three, we picked up where Palestine first entered the historical record a little more than three thousand years ago. The Philstines were settled peoples who domesticated plants and animals. The surrounding societies were also agricultural peoples. It was common around the world for settled peoples to see themselves as connected to the places they inhabited, and their neighbors as connected to their places of inhabitance. That's the setting for the first instance of the term Palestine and the Philistines in history. The Egyptians, Assyrians and Hebrews all figured out ways of recording information, and all wrote about Palestine and the Philistines. The term was adopted in the lingua franca of the time—Aramaic—and entered Greek, Latin, Arabic and English and most other modern languages. Why that term survived, while Edom, Moab and Ammon did not, seems random. But the general trend of history is not random: people settled down. States named places. We inherited them.

The agricultural surplus meant that we could collectively feed more people, leading to human population growth, cities and the diversification of life pursuits, today known as the workforce. This allowed some people to do things other than farm labor. But, as we showed in chapter three, the number of people who could pursue such activities was limited until recently. Sure, some Arabs could find work as imams, copyists or Qur'an teachers, some of whom wrote an occasional ode or poem about Palestine's sanctity. Other folks put the word Palestine on parchment, map, stone, coin or paper. But for most of history, there were no lawyers, mapmakers, artists, writers, historians or geographers who specialized on Palestine. Few libraries had any books on Palestine in the Middle East. There were no institutions, corporations and organizations dealing with Palestine either. Coffee shops, banks, scouting troops, law institutes, medical associations and newspapers—the kinds of places that would later institutionalize Palestine—didn't exist for most of history. There was no money involved in doing things that made Palestine seem real or important. The result was that few people thought Palestine was important. Since it was not that important, few people identified with it.

In chapter four, we explained that all of this changed in the past century. The number of people in the Middle East who could earn a living because of their Palestine expertise rose dramatically. New classes of people, especially teachers, bureaucrats, mapmakers, inspectors and journalists, came into existence. They taught history and geography. They sent written notes home to parents about the school's activities "in Syria and Palestine." Tourists wondered the streets, meadows and mountains of the Middle East with their "Palestine" guidebooks, because travel became cheaper, faster and more comfortable. People started to write odes, poems and balads about

Palestine. They started to call one another Palestinian. Pretty soon, they were willing to give their life defending it as well.

I am a historian, not a futurist. But if the theory proposed is correct, it should have some predictive power. If sedentary life led us to identify with regions, then it should continue to do so in the future. Although sedentary life dominates today, a new trend is taking hold—increasing mobility. The global refugee count is quickly rising. Airfare and travel are becoming more affordable, making many populations more mobile. And while the future of borders, walls and barriers between states is hard to predict, within states it's easy to predict: we are more mobile today than ever before. What can be said is that if borders open up in the future, identities like "the Palestinians" will weaken.

States are pushing things in the other direction. Palestine is nominally a state according to how I've been using the term state. It does have a chain of command, and orders are passed through that chain of command, I presume. The state does control a certain area, even though it's ultimately subject to Israel's control. The state itself uses the term Palestine to refer to the area under its control. It also uses the term to refer to more than just the area under its chastised and subordinated rule. So it's hard to imagine a world where people stop calling it Palestine. Who is going to convince politicians in Ramallah, as well as activists in Bil'in, hipsters in Jaffa and American college students in Berkeley to abandon the word Palestine, and start calling it something else? Precisely because it has so much political significance—Palestine seems unlikely to go away anytime soon. That means that identities based on it are also unlikely to disappear.

The third factor that contributed to the rise of a Palestinian identity—and which makes Palestine seem very real today—is the diversification of the workforce. Initially, teachers, bureaucrats, inspectors and journalists enjoyed careers making Palestine seem real to people. But the breadth and depth of career options having to do with Palestine expanded rapidly after World War II. People could make a living as graduate students, post-docs, lecturers and university professors because of their expertise on Palestine's economy, demography, history, sociology, ecology, political stability and many more on its political instability. People could find jobs at think tanks and NGOs as investigators, reporting officers, project managers, program associates and consultants, with an expertise on Palestine. A dissertation was even allowed that focused merely on the word, Palestine. This also means a "Palestinian" identity is here to stay.

So, in sum, where is a Palestinian identity headed in the future? The decline of sedentary life and the rise of mobile populations could eventually deal a major blow to identities like the Palestinians. But since Palestine has so much political vertigo, it's hard to see it becoming less important to people. There are just too many ways Palestine has become institutionalized. There are millions of people around the globe who call themselves Palestinians. These things seem difficult to undo, certainly not without political will. At the very last, there is so much "Palestine" content online and in print—it will impossible to erase Palestine from history. No surprise a Palestinian identity has never been stronger than it is today. And that means more people are prepared to die for Palestine today than at any previous time in human history.

www.ingramcontent.com/pod-product-compliance
Lightning Source LLC
Chambersburg PA
CBHW072335300426
44109CB00042B/1496